Ramon Llull
Doctrina Pueril

Ramon Llull
Doctrina Pueril

A Primer for the Medieval World

Introduction by Joan Santanach
Translation and notes by John Dagenais

BARCINO·TAMESIS

BARCELONA/WOODBRIDGE 2019

First published 2019
by Tamesis (Serie B: TEXTOS, 61)
in association with Editorial Barcino

ISBN 978 1 85566 309 1
COPYRIGHT DEPOSIT: B 4352-2019

Tamesis is an imprint of Boydell & Brewer Ltd
PO Box 9, Woodbridge, Suffolk IP12 3DF, UK
and of Boydell & Brewer Inc.
668 Mt Hope Avenue, Rochester, NY 14620, USA
www.boydellandbrewer.com

Editorial Barcino, S. A.
Via Augusta 252-260, 5è
08017 Barcelona, Spain
www.editorialbarcino.cat

Printed by Fotoletra
Passeig de Sant Joan, 198
08037 Barcelona, Spain

Cover illustration:
The Tapestry of Creation
Detail, 11th Century
© Museum of the Cathedral of Girona, 2019

Contents

On the Composition, Content and Readers of the *Doctrina Pueril*

1. On Books and Apparitions

Ramon Llull (ca. 1232-1316) is one of the most unique and complex figures of the European Middle Ages.[1] Born in Majorca to a family of Catalan colonists just three years after the Christian conquest of the island, he led what was apparently a rather normal life until he was around 30 years old. Sometime during these first 30 years, he had become a member of the court of Prince James (son of James I, the Conqueror), the future King of Majorca.[2] He probably performed administrative duties there. We also know that he married a woman of his own social class with whom he had at least two children. And, as he himself recounts, probably exaggerating, he dedicated himself entirely to enjoying worldly pleasures.

But when he was 30 years old, one night as he was writing a love song to a lady—who was not, we should understand, his wife—he received an unexpected visit. At least, this is the story he tells in a biography that he dictated many years later. According to the biography, the crucified Christ appeared to him as he was writing the love song. This same apparition repeated itself on four subsequent nights until Llull, at last, decided to reflect more seriously on its meaning. The result of this reflection was a radical change in Llull's life, a redirection of it toward service to Jesus Christ. For a Christian born in a territory where the Islamic element, which had been dominant for more than 300 years, was still quite present, this meant dedicating his efforts and resources to the conversion of Muslims (as well as of believers of other non-Christian religions), without neglecting, of course, efforts to reform the Christian community itself.

---

1. For an up-to-date analysis of the person and works of Llull, see Badia, Santanach & Soler 2016, Fidora & Rubio 2008, Llull 1993a.

2. James I (1208-1276), known as "The Conqueror," was Count-King of Catalonia-Aragon. He completed his conquest of the island of Majorca, then under Muslim rule, on December 31, 1229.

After his "conversion to penance," as Llull defined this life change, his interests were radically transformed. He abandoned his family, worldly literature and his responsibilities at court and dedicated himself to study and contemplation. In time, he also began to travel in search of support for his projects, visiting European royal courts, the papal Curia in Rome and other centers of power, among which we should make special mention of the University of Paris, where he spent long periods disseminating his ideas and combating certain philosophical opinions coming out of that university that he considered to be in error. He also undertook several missions to North Africa in order to dispute with Muslim sages there. And, of course, he dedicated himself to writing. More than 200 books by Ramon Llull have survived, written in diverse genres and on a broad array of medieval disciplines.

Llull tells the story of his conversion in several works, but he provides the most detailed account of it in the biography that he dictated near the end of his life, known as the *Vita coetanea* (*Contemporary Life*) or the *Vida de mestre Ramon* (*Life of Master Ramon*).[3] Whether it is found in this version or in other, more concise, versions, it is evident that a conversion scene that includes divine apparitions is not readily acceptable at face value for modern scholars, nor for the majority of modern readers. One must keep in mind, however, that Llull was a layperson who wrote on theological, philosophical and scientific topics without having gone through a course of formal study and without having been ordained in the Church. In Llull's day, this meant that he was an outsider to official culture, dominated at that time by the university and the clergy. Given these circumstances, and although his texts show that he had acquired, albeit in self-taught form, deep and current knowledge of the disciplines just mentioned, in the eyes of his contemporaries he did not have the necessary qualifications to speak about these topics, nor, as a consequence, did he possess sufficient authority.[4] Llull had to seek his authority elsewhere. And there was nothing better than to assert that his conversion was due to an

---

3. For the original Latin text of the *Vita coetanea*, see Llull 1980 and Llull 2010, which includes an English translation. The story of Llull's conversion is also presented in works such as *Desconhort* (*Disconsolation*; 1295) or the *Cant de Ramon* (*Song of Ramon*; 1300), both originally written in Catalan and in verse. For English versions of these texts, see Vega 2003: 208-228.

4. For Llull's philosophical and theological knowledge, see Ruiz Simon 1999.

inspiration received from the most authoritative of all possible sources, that is, from God himself. As we will see, Llull made use of this strategy in other contexts, not solely in relation to his conversion and the five apparitions of the crucified Christ.

During the nine years immediately following his conversion to penance, which must have taken place around 1263, Llull focused his efforts on preparing himself for the immense task that he wished to undertake. We know very little about these years, although there is no doubt that he used them to acquire those specialized bits of knowledge that his training as a courtier had not afforded him and also to learn Arabic, a language to serve him in disputes with Muslims. Everything seems to indicate that toward the end of this period he also began to write his first works. Among these, one should not fail to mention the *Llibre de contemplació* (*Book of Contemplation*), a vast work that contains the seeds of almost all the ideas Llull will develop in later writings. As Llull explains in the colophon to the book, he wrote it first in Arabic and later translated it into his own language, Catalan, and, still later, he had it translated into Latin. The vastness of the work and the number of topics discussed in it mean, however, that the work is not particularly well suited to the missionary objectives that its author had set for himself. Llull realized this early on: if he wanted to convert non-Christians, he had to find a different formula, one that was more agile and direct. Faced with this realization, he decided to go away to meditate on Mount Randa, near the City of Majorca (today, Palma). In this setting, what Llull describes as a second divine intervention occurred, an experience by which he came to know a method of disputation that would, without fail, lead infidels to accept the superiority of the Christian faith. Whether through divine illumination or by brilliant intuition, on Randa, Ramon Llull conceived his Art.

Until that time, religious disputations had been based chiefly on the interpretation of sacred texts, so that, even in those cases in which religions shared some sources, it was very difficult to arrive at any sort of agreement. In the end, each religion would end up trotting out its own authorities and exegetes. Llull's proposal, on the other hand, did without *auctoritates* and had the discussion take specific concepts accepted by all sides as its starting point: basically, a conception of the cosmos inherited from classical Greece and the idea of a Divinity composed of various attributes. Starting from this base common to

the Mediterranean region's three major monotheistic religions, one
debated, using logical arguments of some complexity, the necessary
truth of the articles of the Christian faith, with a special emphasis on
the two defining dogmas of Christianity: the Trinity and the Incarnation. To facilitate the production of these arguments and their affir-
mation or disproof, Llull created a series of mechanisms for
combining concepts—to which he gave the name *figures*. These are,
perhaps, the most easily recognizable aspect of his Art.[5]

Llull's discovery of the Art informed all of his subsequent writings,
not only because, over the years, he continued diligently drafting new
versions of his system, seeking to simplify it and make it more intuitive and understandable, but also, because the Art was based on a
specific conception of Creation and of the Creator, he applied it in
turn to the understanding of the created world. This was also a means
for validating it and demonstrating the Art's efficacy. It is for this
reason that Llull prepared adaptations of his Art to many contemporary disciplines: medicine, philosophy, theology, law, logic, astronomy, etc. And reflections of the Art can be found in works by Llull that
are not strictly related to it.

Llull's religious concerns—to which he had discovered such a
brilliant and unique response—should be situated within the much
larger context of spiritual questioning that affected broad sectors of
lay society at that time. Across the 12th century, religious movements
more or less radical in nature had arisen throughout Europe. These
movements defended a direct experience of religious faith, without
the mediation of the clergy, which was often seen as excessively tied
to earthly interests. Some of these reform movements had a notable
influence in the territories of the Crown of Aragon, including the
Kingdom of Majorca, which, despite various periods of independ-
ence, always maintained close ties with Peninsular kingdoms. Not
even the Catalan royal family remained unaffected by this influence,
and it supported and protected not only Ramon Llull but also other
notable representatives of these movements.[6] Frequently mentioned,
for example, is the role played by the famous Arnau de Villanova,
physician to kings and popes, professor at Montpellier, intimate of

---

5. For the Art, its components, and its functioning, see Bonner 2007.
6. For Llull's spiritual context, see Soler 1998 and 1999, which includes abundant
bibliography.

several monarchs and, at the same time, closely linked to certain spiritual groups and to the Beguines. Despite the originality of his proposal—or perhaps precisely because of its originality—, Llull, unlike Arnau or other individuals with still more radical positions, always avoided engaging the more polemical aspects of these movements, in a clear attempt not to distance himself from doctrinal orthodoxy. A rather different matter, of course, is the use that some of these groups made of Lullian texts after Master Ramon's death, uses that, especially beginning in the final third of the 14th-century, aroused the suspicions of the Inquisition.

Before all this took place, however, and when Llull had written just a few books, Prince James of Majorca decided to summon Llull to his court in order to have his works examined. Prince James was at that time in Montpellier, a city that was part of the territories left to him in his father's will. The results of the examination must have convinced the future king, since he provided the means to realize one of the projects that his subject had presented to him: the foundation, in 1276, of a language school at the monastery of Miramar on the northwest coast of Majorca dedicated to the training of missionaries.

In the following years, Llull sojourned many times in the southern French city, which became, in fact, a sort of base of operations from which he organized many of his strategies, activities and journeys. There were good reasons for this choice, for at the time Montpellier was home to one of Europe's most important universities, with a respected and influential school of medicine, and it was located much closer to the centers of European power than was Majorca. Montpellier was also, together with Perpignan, one of the official places of residence of Llull's protector, the then King James II of Majorca, especially during the lengthy period when he could not set foot on Majorcan soil as a result of conflicts with his older brother, Peter II, King of Catalonia-Aragon.[7]

7. The Kingdom of Majorca was formed when James I of Catalonia-Aragon divided his lands between his two sons Peter and James in his will. James was given the Balearic Islands as well as some territories in what is now continental France, including Montpellier. As James II of Majorca, he involved himself in the conflict between the Angevines and the Catalano-Aragonese monarchy, which had come about as a result of the Sicilian Vespers (1282). He chose to side with the French against his older brother Peter and allowed the French army, under the command of Philip the Bold, to cross

2. THE EDUCATION OF THE LAITY

Shortly after writing the first version of his Art, the *Ars compendiosa inveniendi veritatem* (*The Compendious Art of Finding Truth*; ca. 1274), but before the founding of Miramar, Llull composed the *Doctrina pueril*, a book very different in complexity from the *Ars compendiosa*. The works differed in terms of their content and of the intellectual demands they placed upon readers. One should note, in this connection, that it is something of a constant in Llull's *oeuvre* that, besides theological, philosophical, or scientific works intended for a moderately educated public capable of adequately appreciating his ideas, there are others addressed to readers with significant educational deficiencies. The *Doctrina pueril*, written between 1274 and 1276, belongs to this second group of texts, in which Llull sought above all to educate those sectors of society that had difficulty in accessing specific types of knowledge: that is, both general knowledge and, above all, knowledge having to do with people's basic religious and catechetical education.

With the *Doctrina pueril*, as with other works of this period like the *Llibre de l'orde de cavalleria* (*The Book of the Order of Knighthood*), the *Llibre contra Anticrist* (*Book Against the Antichrist*), or even one of his best known works, the novel *Blaquerna*,[8] Llull connects to the tradition of medieval authors who worked hard to provide their contemporaries with the minimal bases of doctrinal knowledge, which included tools that would enable them to identify and define themselves as Christians. The Church itself was aware of the deficiencies present in a good portion of the European population with regard to

his lands in the Roussillon in their attempt to depose Peter. After the unexpected defeat of the French in 1285, James himself was deposed of his Balearic territories, which were temporarily reintegrated into the Crown of Aragon. He had to take refuge in his continental territories, which he still controlled. He did not recover the Kingdom of Majorca until 1298. During these years Llull made only one brief visit to his native island.

8. For the *Llibre de l'orde de cavalleria*, translated into English from a French version and published in the year 1484 by William Caxton, see Llull 1988, and the new English versions Llull 2013b and Llull 2015 (which includes an edition of Caxton's text). For the *Llibre contra Anticrist*, Perarnau 1990: 55-158 and Llull 1996: 119-160. For *Blaquerna*, Llull 2009. There is an English translation of the complete novel in Llull 1926 (re-edited in Llull 1987) and, with the title of *Romance of Evast and Blaquerna*, in Llull 2016, and of the *Llibre d'amic e amat* (*Book of the Lover and the Beloved*), which is part of the fifth book of *Blaquerna*, in Llull 1993a: 173-237 and 1995.

this last goal, as is evidenced by certain decisions issuing from Church councils in which, among other questions related to the basic education of the faithful, there is a tendency to set forth in detail what materials should be taught in catechism. With regard to the need felt to have materials of this type available—and in dates close to the composition of the *Doctrina pueril*—, it is without doubt quite significant that in the year 1274, at the second Council of Lyons, there was a call for the composition of a brief work that could make it easier for priests to educate their ignorant parishioners.[9] That such a call was deemed necessary, on the other hand, does not speak much in favor of the confidence that the ecclesiastical hierarchy had in the quality of the training of its own priests.

Whether or not it was in response to specific conciliar directives, the fact is that during the 1270s a variety of treatises were written with the purpose of decreasing the educational deficiencies of the Christian population. A good number of these works were brief and rather simple. They generally included the Ten Commandments, the Credo, various prayers, and lists of virtues and vices. These works are often difficult to date because of their brevity and lack of distinctive features.[10] There are also, however, works of greater complexity, such as the sermons that St Thomas Aquinas gave in Naples during Lent in the year 1273, which sought to clarify certain aspects of Christian teachings for the faithful: the Our Father and Ave Maria prayers, and the Apostles' Creed. After the death of the Dominican saint, these sermons were collected in four opuscules, which, together with a previously written fifth treatise on the Articles of Faith and the Sacraments, came to constitute the so-called "Catechism of Thomas."[11]

---

9. See Mansi 1961: xxiv, col. 131. For the catechetical context in which the *Doctrina pueril* was written, see, among others, La Rosa 1991 and Neuhauser 1993.

10. See, among others, Brayer 1968.

11. The four brief works created from the Neapolitan homilies are the *De duobus praeceptis caritatis et decem legis praeceptis* (*On the Two Precepts of Charity and the Precepts of the Ten Commandments*), the *Expositio orationis dominicae* (*Explanation of the Lord's Prayer*), the *Expositio De Ave Maria* (*Explanation of the Ave Maria*) and the *In Symbolum apostolorum scilicet "Credo in Deum" expositio* (*Explanation of the Apostles' Creed, that is, the "I Believe in God"*). The fifth is the *De articulis fidei et Ecclesiae sacramentis* (*On the Articles of Faith and the Sacraments of the Church*), written between the years 1261 and 1269 at the request of Leonardo dei Conti di Segni, Archbishop of Palermo. See Thomas Aquinas 1927: 349-460.

The widely known *Somme le roi* (*Summa for the King*) by Laurent of Orleans (like Aquinas, a Dominican) is closer to Llull's *Doctrina pueril*, both in terms of the context in which it was created and with regard to some of the lay sectors that became interested in it. This book, written around 1279 or 1280 at the request of King Philip of France, the same king who just a few years later would be frustrated in his attempt to invade the Crown of Aragon (see n. 7), is composed of six parts that treat basic doctrines of the Church: the Ten Commandments, the Twelve Articles of Faith, the Capital Sins, the Virtues, the Our Father, and the Gifts of the Holy Spirit.[12] This text circulated widely in Occitania and Catalonia and was translated into the languages of those regions. Numerous fragments from the first of these translations, the Occitan version, were also included in two distinct miscellaneous compilations, both of them composed with a clear spiritual orientation that links them to lay sectors of high religious sensibility. The fact that another text included in these compilations was the *Doctrina pueril*, of which there was also an Occitan version, should come as no surprise, and it indicates the extent to which we are dealing with two texts that enjoyed a parallel circulation.[13]

Furthermore, it is indicative of these books' target readership and their interests that a significant number of them were written in vernacular languages rather than in Latin, Europe's prestige language at the time and the language in which learned and scholarly materials were customarily disseminated. Nor should it surprise us that certain works containing *exempla* and moral materials originally written in Latin were translated early on into the vernacular languages spoken by these non-university readers. This is the case, for example, of the *Legenda aurea* (*The Golden Legend*) or the *Legenda sanctorum* (*Legends of the Saints*) by Jacobus de Voragine (died 1298), which was translated into many languages, including Occitan and Catalan. The work of Voragine, widely known throughout the Middle Ages, is an extensive collection of saints' lives and was included in one of the Occitan com-

---

12. For the content of the *Somme le roi*, see Langlois 1928: xi-xii and 123-198.

13. For the reworkings (*remaniements*) in Occitan, see Boser 1895, Dando 1964 and Llull 1997: 30-36. For the Catalan translations of the *Somme le roi*, Wittlin 1983. This work was translated into Middle English at least twice as *The Ayenbite of Inwit* and *The Book of Vices and Virtues*.

pilations cited in the previous paragraph.[14] Indeed, the lives of the saints constituted one of the favorite literary genres of the very lay public that Laurent of Orleans, Jacobus de Voragine, and Llull, too, wished to instruct. It is not accidental that a work like *Blaquerna* is, at least in part, a re-elaboration of hagiographic models that were no doubt recognized and appreciated by its readers.

The wide circulation of these works, addressed to readers who frequently lacked significant knowledge of languages other than their own, was possible only if they were translated, at a minimum, into other Romance languages. Given his close relationship with the city of Montpellier, in the heart of Languedoc, Llull must have thought it natural for his works to be translated into Occitan. It is even likely that he encouraged these translations. That he took an Occitan version of *Blaquerna* and, quite probably, of the *Doctrina pueril* along with him on his first trip to Rome and to Paris (1287-1289) seems to support this idea. These Occitan translations, in turn, were clearly used during Llull's stay in Paris in these years as a starting point for the French translations of these two titles and, in the case of *Blaquerna*, also for the Latin version of the *Llibre d'amic e amat* (*Book of the Lover and the Beloved*), the famous mystical opuscule that closes the novel. Many years later, in 1313, after Llull's strategy for the dissemination of his work had changed in various ways, Llull oversaw a Latin translation of the *Doctrina pueril*, for which the Occitan version, which had been the basis for the French tradition of the *Doctrina*, was again used.[15]

In addition to its chiefly catechetical content, Llull's text includes chapters of encyclopedic and not strictly theological orientation that are also aimed at readers with little education. The breadth with which questions of basic religious instruction are treated, together with the presence of chapters on a wide array of topics, no doubt helped in the broad dissemination the work received. We can also attribute this success to the text's clarity of exposition and to the sim-

---

14. For the Occitan version of the *Legenda aurea* used in the compilation mentioned, see Tausend 1995; for the Catalan translation, see Voragine 1977.

15. The *Doctrina pueril* was the object of further early translations (we have two additional Latin translations and one Spanish one), although they are dated after Llull's death. See, on the Latin versions, Llull 2005 and Santanach 2011. For the role that Llull had in the initial dissemination of his work, see Santanach 2005; for strategies for the dissemination of his work, especially in relation to the Occitan translation of his books, Badia, Santanach and Soler 2009a, as also 2009b and 2010.

ple language in which it is written. All of this together helped in providing an unlettered public with knowledge they could only have access to with difficulty by other means, and it shows how well Llull was capable of adapting the expression and content of some of the chapters in which he did not avoid questions of significant complexity for the readers possessing very little previous instruction that he envisioned for his book.

The information that we have about the people who owned the work, which comes from inventories of possessions, wills, and other documents, suggests that, indeed, a significant sector of the readers of the *Doctrina pueril* were laypeople with little or no university training. These sources tell us that the readers were primarily merchants, city-dwellers, and artisans, although there were also some jurists and nobles and even the occasional clergyman. The social spectrum of owners of copies of the treatise coincides, broadly, with the portrait that the inquisitor Nicholas Eymerich gave of Llull's followers in the final quarter of the 14th century. Eymerich, who devoted great efforts to fighting the heterodoxies and doctrinal errors he asserted Llull's works contained, described Lullists, who refused to accept the inquisitorial condemnations, in rather contemptuous terms:

> Could your folly be any greater, for you, who are not geometers, not arithmeticians, not grammarians, not logicians, not mathematicians, not metaphysicians, not natural philosophers, not surgeons, not canonists, not jurists, not astronomers, not theologians, not philosophers, not musicians, not emperors, not marquises, not kings, not nobles, not potentates, not knights, not barons, not military cadets, not dukes, not princes, but are, rather, uneducated people, common people, merchants, artisans, tailors, cobblers, fullers, ditch-diggers, peasants, carpenters, blacksmiths, silversmiths, sellers of paints and wool-workers, refuse to believe the Masters in Theology, the canonists, the jurists, your ordinary priests, the cardinals (the true north of the church and of the world), or even our most Holy Lord Pope, Vicar of Christ in the mystery of faith?[16]

---

16. «Nonne est vestra summa insipientia quod vos, cum non sitis geometrici, non arithmetici, non grammatici, non logici, non mathematici, non metaphysici, non physici, non cirurgici, non canoniste, non legiste, non astrologi, non theologi, non philosophi, non musici, non imperatores, non marchiones, non reges, non nobiles, non potentes, non milites, non barones, non tirones, non duces, non princepes, *sed potius sitis homines vulgares, homines communes, homines siquidem mercatores, cerdones, sartores, sutores, fullones, fossones, agricultores, fabri lignarii, fabri ferrarii, argentari, pigmentarii et la-*

It goes without saying that the point of view evident here is a bi-
ased one and that, as has already been pointed out, manual laborers
without philosophical or theological training were by no means the
only people who took an interest in Lullian texts. But the Inquisitor's
goal was to emphasize the lack of formal education, and therefore of
critical faculties, among Llull's followers.

The physical characteristics that we find in the numerous surviving manuscripts of the *Doctrina pueril*—numerous for the period in
question—also suggest a reader who was city-dwelling and reasonably
well off, though not exactly rich. Among the twenty-odd medieval
manuscripts that have come down to us—especially those in Catalan,
but also those in the other languages we have mentioned—, we find
that most are rather small volumes, with paper rather than parch-
ment leaves, and generally with very little decoration, sometimes almost without any at all. The choice of the materials used in the
manuscript and the number of decorative elements to be included
were features that directly influenced the product's final price. The
surviving manuscript witnesses of the *Doctrina pueril* suggest, then,
that its readers could permit themselves the expense of a copyist to
transcribe the text but that they were only in rare cases interested in
contracting a miniaturist to decorate it—or else, that they could not
afford to do so. There are a few exceptions to this general pattern,
such as the luxurious manuscript that contains the French version of
the work. This manuscript is written on remarkably delicate parch-
ment and contains numerous illuminations and profusely illustrated
capitals with no sparing of gold. It should be noted, however, that this
manuscript, certainly commissioned by a French noble toward the
end of the 13th century (and which is now in the Bibliothèque Na-
tionale in Paris) contains, in stark contrast to the showiness of its
decoration, an extremely defective version of the text.[17]

---

narii, nolitis credere theologie magistris, canonistis, legistis, prelatis vestris ordinariis,
Cardenalibus, mundi et Ecclesie cardinibus, qui nimmo nec sanctissimo domino nos-
tro pape Christi vicario in fidei mysterio?». See the *Dialogus contra lullistas* in De Puig
2000a: 168-169. In the same work Eymerich mentions the *Doctrina pueril* explicitly
(2000a: 224). It is worth recalling, of course, that one of the Lullian works in which
Eymerich stated there were heretical propositions—four of them—was the *Doctrina
pueril*, which was a customary reading for certain radical spiritual groups against whom
the inquisitor often directed his accusations; see Madre 1973.

17. For the readers, owners, and surviving manuscripts of the *Doctrina pueril*, both
medieval and post-medieval, see Llull 2005, which includes references to additional

Aside from this last case, which is not particularly representative, the information about readers and owners and the high number of surviving medieval witnesses (which represent only a fraction of those that must have been in circulation) demonstrate the broad reception of the work in the old Crown of Aragon—as also, although to a lesser extent, in Occitania and in the lands of the *langue d'oïl*.[18] This was not the only Lullian text that attracted the attention of these lay groups, however. Books such as the *Llibre de contemplació*, the more narrative *Llibre de meravelles* (*Book of Wonders*), the *Proverbis de Ramon* (*Proverbs by Ramon*) and the *Arbre de ciència* (*Tree of Knowledge*), which also combine encyclopedic content with doctrinal materials, are commonly found in inventories of the period.[19]

So it seems likely that during the 14th and 15th centuries Llull had become a point of reference and authority in the Crown of Aragon—and not just in Majorca—, and one far less controversial than the periodic persecutions by the Inquisition might lead us to believe. It also seems likely that these works were among the resources to which people who aspired (however informally) to a level of knowledge roughly similar to that of university students might have recourse, even if it was outside the classroom. In the end, these Lullian texts (as would also happen a bit later with the works of the Franciscan Francesc Eiximenis) made learned scholastic content, appropriately adapted to new uses, available to laypeople.[20] Within this group of texts, the *Doctrina pueril* would be located at the foundation of the educational process.

In the overall production of the Majorcan author, the *Doctrina pueril* and the other vernacular-language books just mentioned tended to follow lines of transmission quite different from those of treatises directly related to the Art, which were of more clearly philosophical and theological orientation and were intended for a

---

sources. For the French manuscript, see also Soler 2010: 206-207. For full descriptions of surviving witnesses of the work, see Llull 2005: LIV-LXX, and for the principal manuscripts used in preparing the edition used for this translation, see the list in the Bibliography.

18. For documented readers of the work, see Llull 2005: XLV-XLVI, with references to the corresponding bibliography.

19. There is an English translation of the *Llibre de meravelles* in *SW* II, pp. 647-1105. An English translation of the *Arbre de ciència* is Llull n.d.a.

20. On Eiximenis (1330-1409), who was from Girona, and who wrote most of his works in Valencia, and an English language anthology of his works, see Eiximenis 2008.

highly-educated readership. These latter works circulated primarily in Latin, whether they were based on translations from Catalan or, as was more often the case, were written directly in the learned language. They enjoyed a broad circulation throughout Europe until the 18th century. Indeed, groups of Llull's followers were by no means limited to the Crown of Aragon, and numerous Lullist centers arose throughout the continent, starting with Portugal and Castile, and, in the modern period, spreading as far away as Eastern Europe, including Russia. There was also, of course, an extremely significant and early presence of Lullism in France, Germany, and Italy.[21] Such was the case for texts relating to the Art. In contrast, the *Doctrina pueril* and other works intended for the education of laypeople, as we have noted, circulated principally through the lands of the Western Mediterranean, that is to say, in the arc stretching from the Iberian Peninsula to the Italian territories. Obviously, North Africa remained outside this arc. For this area, Llull was preparing another sort of text: one specifically designed to be used in religious disputation.

3. Tradition and Lullism in the *Doctrina Pueril*

The broad circulation that the *Doctrina pueril* enjoyed until well into the 15th century was due not only to the topics that Llull included there, which coincided fully with the cultural and, above all, religious interests of broad sectors of medieval lay society, but also to the particular way in which Llull treated them. Llull was clearly aware that he was addressing a rather specific type of reader for whom he had to make access to the contents of the book easier both with regard to the language and style in which it is written as well as with regard to the level of difficulty, deliberately limited, with which even the most complex questions are treated in the book. Llull sought to ensure that the reader could understand and correctly assimilate the knowledge he put at the reader's disposal in the *Doctrina pueril.* It is with this purpose in mind that he developed a variety of strategies.

---

21. For an overall view of Lullism, Carreras Artau 1939-1943 is still indispensable. For the beginnings of Lullism in France, see Hillgarth 1971; for Italian Lullism, see Batllori 2004.

Among these strategies, the first was the choice of the language in which he wrote the book. He chose not to write it in Latin, despite the fact that much of the work deals with theological topics, but in Catalan. As the book's prologue recommends, the reader's first contact with the topics of study must occur in his native language. This statement, contrary to the way in which it has sometimes been interpreted, does not contradict Llull's clear promotion of the need for learning Latin in this same prologue or his more general insistence on the importance of studying the learned language.[22] It is evident that approaching certain types of knowledge in one's own language facilitates comprehension, above all when one takes into account the limited training—or the complete lack of training—that Llull ascribes to the reader of the *Doctrina pueril.*

Ramon Llull, thus, writes the *Doctrina pueril* in his readers' vernacular so that they can have access to its contents, and, for the same reason, he will have it translated into other Romance languages. He also writes it "as simply as he can," as he states in the prologue. That is, he writes in a simple, carefully structured language, far from the terminological and syntactic complexities that we find in many other works by Llull that are intended for a more highly educated audience accustomed to reading far less accessible philosophical and theological treatises. To write a book "plainly"—and "briefly," as he also indicates—refers to the treatment of the work's subject matter and to the manner in which the topics included there are developed. It refers not only to the language used but also to the selection of contents and the manner in which they are presented: topics are presented in summary form and in as simplified and straightforward a manner as possible. This commitment to simplicity does not mean that the text contains no complex passages, although Llull makes an effort to avoid them, and sometimes explicitly states this intention (see, for example, Ch. 77.1). In the end, the goal of the text is for the reader to be able to "enter more easily and more quickly into the knowledge through which he can know how to know and love and serve his glorious God" (Prologue).

---

22. The proposal in favor of the universalization of Latin that Llull made in Ch. 94 of *Blaquerna* is especially well known. See Llull 2009: 414-415 and Llull 2016: 407-410. In the *Doctrina pueril* he again defends the usefulness and the benefits of studying the Latin language: at the beginning of Ch. 73, "On Grammar, Logic and Rhetoric."

As for the typical reader for whom Llull wrote the *Doctrina pueril*, his treatment of the topic of faith and its relation to reason is quite revealing, chiefly because of the absence of the possibility of approaching the Articles of Faith through reason. This characteristic, which would in no way be remarkable in other medieval authors is, in a work by the inventor of the Art, without doubt extremely significant. In the initial chapters, the fourteen Articles of Faith are enumerated and defined in detail, but in no case does Llull attempt to demonstrate their necessity by means of reason or logical arguments. In fact, already at the beginning of the book, the necessity of believing in them by faith is stressed. As we read in the first paragraph of Ch. 1, "the Articles consist in believing and loving true and marvelous things about God." The book's reader, then, must try to approach the truths and marvels of God by means of the will—one of whose functions is, precisely, to love (*amar*)—, and not by means of the intellect, which would involve getting reason involved in the process. Llull explains a few chapters later, in his discussion of the Article of Faith regarding the conception of Jesus: "by our fragility and by the sovereign work of the Highest we are all obligated to believe those things we cannot understand concerning the coming of the Son of God" (Ch. 6.8). It is necessary, then, to supplement the deficiencies in human understanding—without doubt more prevalent in an untrained intellect—with faith, and to help prevent these intellects, little accustomed to arguments on complex themes related to Church dogma, from reaching erroneous conclusions. Faith, not reason, is the principal path that one must follow in these cases.

The pre-eminence granted to the act of believing and the bracketing off of the act of understanding help to define the type of reader Llull sought to reach in the *Doctrina pueril*. Clearly, he had in mind readers who would have had difficulty taking on a demonstration of the Articles based on "necessary reasons." Rather, one had to offer them alternative means of access to the Articles. Thus, if it is not possible to communicate "meanings to the human understanding through necessary reasons that the fourteen Articles are true truth," as the *Llibre de contemplació* indicates, it will rather be necessary that "they follow another technique by which they can contemplate the fourteen Articles, that is, that they contemplate them with the will and with the memory, for faith is formed by these two virtues.... Therefore, since it is so, by means of faith one can love the Articles, and, by loving the Articles, one can love the Articles' laws, which love is of very great merit."[23] In the face of an approach that gives priority to contemplation "by means of faith," it is evident that the Art will necessarily be affected in some form. And so it is that in the *Doctrina pueril* the Art is largely absent and is not explicitly mentioned even in those passages that include some of its features. Any reader minimally familiar with Llull's system, however, cannot fail to note that the detailed explanations of the combinations of elements (Ch. 94) or the discussion of the powers of the soul (Ch. 85) correspond, respectively, to the functions of the Elemental Figure and Figure S of the Art. Or that the list of divine dignities in Ch. 1.55 and Ch, 84.5 corresponds to the one found in Figure A of the *Ars compendiosa inveniendi veritatem,* the central work of the period when the *Doctrina pueril* was written. In the same vein, one must mention the lengthy treatment of the opposition between vices and virtues—fourteen chapters in all—, a topic related to Figure V of the Art.

Regarding this last point, it is important to note that we are dealing here with two sets of concepts that are absolutely obligatory in any medieval work that, like the *Doctrina pueril,* seeks to provide the reader with the foundations of the Christian faith together with recommendations regarding the behavior necessary for avoiding eternal damnation. If the necessity of including these two septenaries in such a work is obvious, given its goals, what is not quite so expected is that Llull, who based his hopes for the conversion of infidels and the reform of Christian society on the Art, makes no reference whatsoever to the corresponding figure of the Art. This absence can only be explained if we conclude that such an omission was deliberate.

The bracketing off of the components of the Art is consistent with the silence one notes in the text regarding other characteristically Lullian themes, which give way here to elements quite foreign to Llull's teachings and, indeed, to his general practices in writing. A good example of this approach is the long list at the end of Ch. 77 of Aristotelian (and some pseudo-Aristotelian) works on the science of philosophy, including brief summaries of each work's contents. In stark contrast to the usual practice of medieval authors, Llull almost never argued from authority or even cited other authors in his works.

---

23. See Ch. 288, 14 and 15 of the *Llibre de contemplació* in *OE* 2.892. The italics in this citation, as in the rest of the citations in this section, are mine.

And so it is quite exceptional that Llull should have included this list of titles: this is something that occurs nowhere else in his writings. And it is not just the list. In the same chapter, right before the list of Aristotelian works, Llull offers a synthesis of the principles of natural philosophy that is completely in line with the Aristotelian and scholastic presuppositions generally accepted in his period. Absent here, too, are other, more typically Lullian approaches that he does, in fact, develop in works aimed at a more highly educated reading public that would already be familiar with the doctrines that circulated among the European schools of philosophy and theology. This approach must correspond, once again, to a deliberate decision by Llull, who, in this work, opts to present the reader with brief syntheses of diverse aspects of reality in accord with a set of ideas and doctrines taken as givens by the majority of writers and not based on the philosophical system and worldview that he was elaborating on his own at the same time. In some ways, in the *Doctrina pueril*, Llull suppresses his own system and doctrines in favor of the very tradition that he had taken as their starting point. And, in so doing, he offers us a truly unique synthesis of the religious and ideological foundations of Western Europe in the low Middle Ages.

Llull's determination to link the *Doctrina pueril* to a tradition broader than the strictly Lullian one is also evident in the didactic formulations of the text. In it, Llull presents a series of concepts that refer to the Christian catechetical tradition and he does so, as we have said, by setting aside all overt references to his own system. We must understand in the same sense the formula that Llull uses to address the reader, calling him, "dear son" without further specification. The literary convention that presents a wise voice that interpellates a second person who is in need of teaching goes back to biblical and proverbial literature and has taken many forms through the centuries, whether it was that of the teacher instructing his disciple or the father educating his son. This point was made in 1521 by the Lullist Joan Bonllavi in what is quite probably the first critical note on the *Doctrina pueril*. As we read in the *Epístola proemial* (*Introductory Letter*) that opens Bonllavi's edition of *Blaquerna*, "in the book *Doctrina pueril*" the author "speaks with his son in the manner of Solomon in the Book of Proverbs." Concerning this literary model, he had earlier remarked that "in Proverbs, by teaching the young child through the use of proverbs, he seeks to make him experienced and attentive to things related to God and so he frequently speaks as if he were speaking to a child in order to move and to inspire him with love." Addressing the reader as "son," then, was, above all, a technique to make the doctrine contained in the work more effective.

The discovery of Llull's will, dated 1313, which mentions the names of his children Domingo and Magdalena, called into question Bonllavi's interpretation of the use of the expression "dear son" as a means of addressing the reader.[24] Knowing the name of a male child of Llull gave rise to the temptation to identify "Domingo" with the *Doctrina pueril*'s anonymous "dear son," and this interpretation eventually became the dominant one. Thus, the text became for critics a sort of living will, or a pedagogical surrogate, that Llull left for his son Domingo when he left his family in order to follow his missionary calling. This interpretation affected not only the *Doctrina pueril* but also the other books in which Llull used the formula of a father speaking to his son: the *Llibre d'intenció* (*The Book of Intention*), which in all likelihood was written in the decade of the 1280s, and the *Arbre de filosofia desiderat* (*The Desired Philosophy Tree*), dated somewhat later, in 1294.[25] We are dealing, then, with three books written over a span of almost 20 years. This is a rather long time for the education of one specific child, and even more so if we consider that we do not know the date of Domingo's birth (though it can probably be dated to shortly after 1257, the year of Llull's marriage to Blanca Picany). In any case, regardless of Llull's biographical circumstances, the didactic framework of a father teaching his son acquires its full meaning within the pedagogical and catechetical tradition in which this scheme originated and it is in this context that the *Doctrina pueril* must have been understood by its numerous medieval readers, as the words of Joan Bonllavi attest.

4. CATECHISM AND ENCYCLOPEDIA

The *Doctrina pueril* contains more than just the elements of a basic religious education, although this subject matter occupies the great-

---

24. For Llull's will, see ROL 18.261-263 and Hillgarth 2001: 87-88.
25. See Llull 2013a. For an English translation (and working software version) of the *Arbre de filosofia desiderat*, see Llull n.d.b.

er part of the work. Following the sixty-seven chapters on strictly cat-echetical matters, the book fills out the one hundred chapters that provide its structure with a second part that includes contents of an encyclopedic nature and which, thus, serves to broaden the work's scope significantly. Nevertheless, in these final sections, religious top-ics not developed in previous chapters are by no means excluded.

The division of the book into two parts is signaled implicitly in the Prologue in which, after the customary invocation of the Divinity and the defense of the vernacular language as the primary means of ac-cess to knowledge, Llull announces that the education of children must begin with the catechism. That is, before anything else, they must know the Articles of the Catholic faith, the Ten Command-ments, the Seven Sacraments of the Church "and the other chapters that follow" (Prologue). Only when these topics have been assimilat-ed correctly can the educational process of the student-reader move forward and can one present him with the opposition between "the glory of Paradise and the infernal punishments," which will involve, then, a further reflection on "the other chapters contained in this book" (Prologue). For it is only when the reader knows the enemies that he must confront—the vices—and has the weapons necessary to confront them—principally, the virtues—, that it will make sense to show him the consequences of giving priority to one or the other of these sets in his life. In line with this approach, it is quite significant that the chapters "On Hell" (Ch. 99) and "On Paradise" (Ch. 100) are situated at the very end of the book. In this way, the reader will be able to understand quite clearly that, at the end of his life, depending on how well he has assimilated the content of the previous ninety-eight chapters, he will have to face his eternal destiny in one or the other of the two places discussed in the final two chapters.

Looking beyond contents, one observes no significant differences between the chapters of the two parts, either regarding the tone or the depth of the discussion of the material or the structure of the text. An indication of this stylistic consistency is that the internal or-ganization of the book's one hundred chapters remains quite con-stant throughout the work, with each chapter's opening paragraph containing a definition of the chapter's theme or purpose and with the body of each chapter presenting an ordered exposition of the topic. The chapters also include a final reference to the Divinity—with the mention of "God" or of one of the persons of the Trinity—, which, with very few exceptions, appears as the last word of the last paragraph of each chapter.[26]

The catechetical part of the *Doctrina pueril* and, thus, the book itself, opens with two extensive sections dedicated to two basic aspects of Christian doctrine: the fourteen Articles of Faith and the Ten Commandments, which are essential and required knowledge for any Christian who wishes to consider himself as such and who aspires to conduct his life in accordance with the ordinations of divine law.[27] Each of these two sections is made up of several chapters, twelve in the case of the Articles of Faith (Chs. 1-12; the three articles referring to the Trinity are collected in a single chapter, Ch. 2) and ten for the Ten Commandments (Chs. 13-22). Following this is the book's first septenary, the one concerning Sacraments, clearly fundamental for the believer who hopes to enter, remain, and die in the bosom of the Church and who, of course, seeks to act in accordance with its norms and morality.

After the three series just mentioned, there are five more that relate to the catechetical context: the Gifts of the Holy Spirit, the Beatitudes, the Joys of Our Lady, and the septenaries of the virtues and the vices, which close the first part of the book. Except for the Joys of Our Lady (Chs. 45-51), which had very little previous catechetical tradition, the remaining four series constitute the most common topics found in texts dedicated to the basic teachings of the Faith, although their origins must be sought elsewhere, since they have to do with concepts coming from the mystical tradition. Their origins can be related, then, at least as objects of theological speculation, to specific texts that describe in detail the soul's efforts to overcome its earthly limitations and conflicts and to lift itself toward the Divinity. One could attempt to describe this process, which is ineffable by nature— as mystical poetry teaches us—by presenting an interplay of parallelisms and oppositions among the diverse series of components. Basic, in this regard, is the contribution of Hugh of St Victor (1096-1141), who, in his influential *De quinque septenis* (*On the Five Sevens*), established a series of relations among the septenaries alluded to in the

---

26. The only exception would be Ch. 45, the first in the series dedicated to the Joys of Mary, which ends precisely with the mention of "Our Lady."

27. For a detailed commentary on the catechetical contents of the *Doctrina pueril*, see Santanach 2002.

title in order to describe the process of freeing the rational soul from its subjection to the Seven Vices. According to Hugh, once the soul comes to understand its subjected condition, it must strive to rid itself of its sins, opposing them with the petitions of the Paternoster and placing its hope in the Seven Gifts of the Holy Spirit. The granting of these Gifts, in turn, makes possible the development of the virtues that will confront the sins. Each of the Seven Gifts of the Holy Spirit empowers the virtue most appropriate to confronting the corresponding vice, enabling each virtue to combat its corresponding vice with greater efficacy. In the end, the triumph of the seven virtues makes possible the attainment of the seven Beatitudes or Blessings, one for each virtue.

But beyond this mystical application, these concepts also proved to be useful didactically, since, at the most basic level, the septenary of the vices constituted a list of behaviors to be avoided. It should come as no surprise, then, that the list of sins was modified and adapted at will, depending on the historical and social reality to which it was to be applied, a phenomenon that made this list the most unstable of all the septenaries.[28] In the same way that the vices signaled behaviors to be rejected, the other septenaries gave form, or at least a name, to specific tools designed to resist the influence of acts that were considered pernicious.

The circulation in catechetical form of these series of concepts, still linked to the relations among them established by Hugh of St Victor during the final quarter of the thirteenth century, may be seen, for example, in the previously mentioned *Somme le roi* by Laurent of Orleans, which, indeed, was often known by the title *Liber de vitiis et virtutibus* (*Book on Vices and Virtues*). In the final portion of this manual for moral education, following discussions of the septenaries of the vices, the virtues, the petitions of the Paternoster, and the Gifts of the Holy Spirit, the confessor to the king of France puts into play various correspondences, Victorine in origin, among the components of septenaries.[29]

Four of Hugh's five septenaries are included in the *Doctrina pueril*, although the specific components of these septenaries do not completely coincide. Only the petitions of the Paternoster are left out, al-

---

28. For the history of the septenary of the vices, see Casagrande & Vecchio 2000.
29. See Langlois 1928: 134.

though the prayer itself is, of course, included (Ch. 8.3). As for the other four septenaries, Llull adopts the functions traditionally associated with each septenary, although he makes these functions explicit only in a very few passages and practically does away with the systematic correlations that Hugh had established among their components. In effect, the relationships set out in the *Doctrina pueril* among groups of concepts only rarely make reference to oppositions or complementarities regarding specific components. Rather they show these oppositions and complementarities among entire groups or between the components of one septenary and a specific component of another series. We find an example of this in the chapters dedicated to the Gifts (30-36) and the Beatitudes (37-44). In Ch. 33.3, in which the role played by the Gift of Fortitude is described (not to be confused with the created virtue of Fortitude) we read that "the strengthening of faith, hope, charity, justice, and the other virtues comes from the strength of the Holy Spirit, without which no man can combat or overcome the vices, which are contrary to the virtues just mentioned."

The *Doctrina pueril* has little more to say about the support that each Gift gives to the virtues in the fight against the vices, at least in individual form. Nor is much said about the Beatitudes or about the states that the soul that has conquered the vices and has persevered in the exercise of the virtues with the help of the Gifts will enjoy. We find only two such comments. For example, in speaking about the first of the Beatitudes, on Reigning, the *Doctrina pueril* comments: "The kingdom of this world is the virtues through which you will possess the heavenly reign. Therefore, if you want to have heavenly beatitude, hold the fullness of God in your heart in this world" (Ch. 37.7). It is only stated in very general terms that, in order to achieve this heavenly beatitude, you must have exercised virtues in this world, not that its attainment is the direct result of the defeat of one specific vice by one specific virtue, thanks to the intervention of the most appropriate Gift of the Holy Spirit. We find a similar passage in the definition of the Beatitude of Fullness, in which it is stated that this is "the heavenly beatitude that satisfies the longing for justice, desiring works of hope, charity and the other virtues" (Ch. 40.1). The performance of acts of virtue, again in generic form despite the specific mention of the desire for justice, fosters the attainment of the Beatitude of Fulfillment. This tendency to put broad groups of concepts into play does not exclude that, exceptionally, some concrete links between individual elements may be found in the text, such as the definition of the Beatitude of Patience, where it is stated that "Patience is restrained desire brought about through wrath converted into charity" (Ch. 43.1). The struggle of the virtue of Charity against the sin of Wrath has a long tradition, and Llull relies on his readers' familiarity with this tradition here.

The sections on the Gifts of the Holy Spirit and the Beatitudes both come from biblical texts: the first from Isaiah 11:2-3, and the second from the Sermon on the Mount, included in the Gospel of Matthew 5:3-10. These are organized, as we have seen, in sevens.[30] The septenary of the virtues (Chs. 52-59) is composed of the three theological and the four cardinal virtues. Thanks to this septenary, the Christian will be able to resist vices and worldly temptations. As Llull writes in Ch. 57.5 in a passage on the virtue of fortitude, "remembering and understanding and loving God and His power and the other virtues that pertain to God, and remembering and understanding and loving faith, hope, charity, justice, prudence, temperance and the other virtues that are appropriate to man reinforce the strengths and powers of the soul." That is, keeping the virtues everpresent by using the powers of the soul—remembering them with memory, understanding them with understanding and loving them with the will—helps to strengthen the soul and, thus, enables Christians to defend themselves against the assaults of the vices with greater guarantees of success.

Following the chapters dedicated to each of the virtues, the series closes, significantly, with an eighth section—on salvation—in which Llull insists that the exercise of virtue does not in itself guarantee Christians entry into Paradise since "there is no man, for all the good that he may do, who deserves salvation, but God grants salvation to those who have virtue and saintliness against vices and evil deeds" (Ch. 59.3). The granting of this reward lies exclusively in the hands of God. It is a grace that God alone grants to men, given that in no case whatsoever can men's merits be equal to the gift of eternal salvation. It is hardly surprising, then, that the chapter closes with a reference to free

---

30. Hugh of St Victor had also extracted the list of Beatitudes from the same Gospel passage although, in order to maintain the systematic correlations with the rest of the series of concepts, he had reduced the eight Beatitudes of the Gospel to seven, considering the last one to be a synthesis of the remaining ones.

will and a warning to readers not to rely on any merits that they may believe they possess, since they may, quite literally, get burned. They must put all of their hopes in "the gifts of God" (Ch. 59.8).

Ramon Llull adopted the series of vices that we find in his early works from the widely circulated *Summa virtutum ac vitiorum* (*Summa on the Virtues and Vices*; 1236-1249?) written by the Dominican William Peraldus.[31] We find the same series in the *Doctrina pueril*. In the chapters that Llull dedicates to the septenaries of the Deadly Sins (Chs. 60-67), the emphasis is, above all (and it could hardly be otherwise), on the necessity of exercising virtues in order to avoid them. The oppositions, again, are not established between one particular virtue and a particular vice, but more often between a group of virtues and the specific vice that is the subject of a given chapter. This does not exclude, however, the possibility that there may be an ideal virtue for resisting a specific temptation, or that a specific virtue, if attacked by a specific vice, might open the door for the rest of the vices if it is defeated, as we find in another doctrinal text, which Llull also addressed to an unnamed "dear son," the *Llibre d'intenció*, which is in many ways quite close to the *Doctrina pueril*: "whenever you are tempted by sloth, have recourse to the intention by which hope, charity, etc. are within you. And see with which virtue the devil tempts you most strongly toward sloth and reinforce that virtue with the other virtues."[32] Differently from the Victorine tradition, in which it was clearly established which virtue was ideal to confront each specific vice, Llull recommends strengthening the virtue that is wavering using the remaining virtues of the septenary. In the *Doctrina pueril*, Llull is not a proponent of narrow solutions, which, in his readers, little accustomed to such subtleties, would doubtless only serve as an impediment to the effectiveness of the process of curing the soul affected by the vices.

Parallel with Ch. 59, "On Salvation," which comes at the end of the series of the virtues as a synthesis and admonition to the reader to strive to make himself worthy of celestial glory, there is also a chapter that closes the septenary of the vices: Ch. 67, "On Damnation." This final part of the text's catechetical section has a close and complemen-

---

31. See Dominguez 1987: xxxiii. For Peraldus, Dondaine 1948 is still essential.

32. See Ch. V, 12, 2 in Llull 2013a: 165. The citation also shows that Llull understood well the possibilities of the interplay between vices and virtues as a means of representing the tension between the human tendency toward sin and the moral structure that works against it.

tary relationship with the chapter that closes the septenary of the virtues. For example, Llull insists here, again, that, were it not for the
grace of God, all humanity would find itself cast into eternal damnation. It is essential, then, that people learn to use their free will correctly.

The order of the various groupings of concepts in the *Doctrina
pueril* that allowed Llull to structure the process of the ascent of the
soul from vices to Beatitudes is worthy of special note, above all because it does not coincide with the order that the Victorine tradition
had sanctioned. In the *Doctrina pueril*, the Gifts of the Holy Spirit and
the Beatitudes come first, followed by the Joys of Our Lady, which are
not a part of the process just described. Next, we find the septenary
of the virtues and, lastly, that of the vices, despite the fact that it was
precisely the individual's subjection to the vices that would have trig-
gered the action of the remaining groups of concepts. Ramon Llull,
aware of his readers' limited training, opted deliberately for a new
type of organization.

He shifted the subtleties that the theological and speculative tradition had developed around this question, especially those regarding
the systematic correspondences between specific components of the
septenaries, to a secondary plane and he emphasized their most practical and useful aspects for his readers—the exercise of the virtues
and the avoidance of the vices—by placing them in a prominent position: at the close of the catechetical portion of the book. These are
two septenaries that were especially significant in the works of other
contemporary authors involved in the basic instruction of the faithful, which again explains why a text like the *Somme le roi* was also
known by the title *Liber de vitiis et virtutibus*.[33] In the *Doctrina pueril*, the
importance attributed to the virtues and vices is highlighted by
the inclusion of a chapter at the end of each series that describes the
consequences that the predominance of one or the other of these
two septenaries can have for Christians in their passage through this
vale of tears. We do not find summary chapters like these at the end
of any of the book's other series.

---

33. The technique of situating the virtues and vices in a prominent place can be
seen in other works by Llull, such as the *Art de contemplació* (*Art of Contemplation*) included in the fifth book of *Blaquerna*, the final two chapters of which deal with the
virtues and vices respectively. These are Chs. 113 and 114 of the novel, which come
immediately before the work's final chapter (Llull 2009: 569-576).

With the catechetical sections completed, the book's contents become more diverse, although this does not mean that one cannot glimpse the organizing principles behind them. In effect, one can encounter several groupings of chapters based on similarities of content. The first of these series is centered on the religious situation in the Mediterranean world of that day (Chs. 68-72), with sections dedicated in turn to each of the three great monotheistic religions, to Natural Law, and to Gentiles—among whom Llull includes, not without a certain malice, since he recognizes that they are Christians, the Greek Orthodox. Llull's discussion of religions different from his own, contrary to what one might expect from the author of the congenial *Llibre del gentil e dels tres savis* (*Book of the Gentile and the Three Wise Men*), written shortly after the *Doctrina pueril,* is absolutely contemptuous.[34] This is true above all with regard to Islam, but it is also true in the case of Judaism. This simplistic approach must have to do, again, with the intended audience of the catechetical treatise and the need to avoid the possibility that a less combative approach, like the one we find in the *Llibre del gentil,* might lead his reader to errors because of the polite interfaith conduct it portrays. The dialogue of the three wise men is a text intended for more educated readers, who are able to follow its arguments and arrive on their own at the correct solution, which is nothing other than that Christianity is the only true religion, while the other two are in error. One must arrive at this conclusion using reason, and we have already witnessed the scant confidence that Llull shows in the logical capacity of the readers of the *Doctrina pueril.* The underlying ideology is the same, but the strategies have been adapted appropriately to their audience.[35]

Following the pages on religious faiths, there is a seven-chapter section on the principal academic subjects of the Middle Ages (Chs. 73-79). This section is preceded by the epigraph "On the Seven Arts," which, strictly speaking, does not refer to the entire section—and even less to all of the remaining chapters of the *Doctrina pueril*—, but only to the section's first two chapters (73-74), dedicated to the arts of the trivium and the quadrivium, the propaedeutic for the study of

---

34. For the critical text of the *Llibre del Gentil,* see Llull 1993b, and, for the English translation, *SWI,* 91-304 or the abbreviated version in Llull 1993a.

35. For interpretations of the *Gentil* and the literary strategies that Llull uses there, in addition to the introduction by Anthony Bonner in Llull 1993b, see Badia 1993 and Santanach 2008a. Bonner 2008 and Santanach 2008b are also useful.

more advanced materials. The rest of the disciplines discussed in this section (theology, law, philosophy, and medicine) are appropriately identified as "sciences," since they represent the four basic subjects of the medieval university. The exception is this section's final chapter, "On the Mechanical Arts"—that is, on the manual trades—, which were not a topic of study in higher education, but which serve to enrich the broad portrait of medieval lifeways that Llull sketches in these chapters on the medieval fields of study, as also in those chapters immediately following.

After this, Llull dedicates three brief chapters to describing the role and function of princes, the clergy and the various forms of the monastic life. He also includes a fourth chapter, reflecting on a topic that was especially dear to him: the conversion of infidels (Chs. 80-83). Concerning these chapters, one should add that a collateral branch of the work's manuscript tradition includes, just after the commentary on the figure of the prince, a section on the order of knighthood and the obligations—and the privileges—of its members. This chapter, which has come down to us in Latin and French versions (but not in Catalan) has sometimes been considered apocryphal.[36] It is worthwhile to remember, however, that both the Latin version that transmits the chapter and the French translations were created during Llull's life. In this sense, the chapter's style and contents, especially in the Latin version, as the French text is very poor, are in no way out of keeping with the rest of the *Doctrina pueril*. If Llull was behind the redaction of this chapter, as seems likely, it would imply that he added it after he had already considered the *Doctrina pueril* complete, with its prologue and precisely one hundred chapters, and when copies were already in circulation, since the section on knighthood has only been transmitted by one branch that, despite its antiquity, is of rather secondary importance in the textual tradition.[37]

In any case, the possibility that Llull decided to return to the *Doctrina pueril* at some point in order to incorporate a new chapter in it is in no way in contradiction with what we know concerning his strategies for circulating his works and the ways we know that he adapted them to

---

36. This text is translated below from the Latin version following the chapter on princes.

37. For this chapter and the hypotheses of its authenticity, see Santanach 2005, as well as Llull 2005: xliv and 287-294.

new uses and different circumstances. This strategy of Llull's was at times so marked that in some cases one can recognize a clear relation between his texts' composition and their circulation. It is worth noting, in this sense, that everything seems to indicate that Llull was the true author of another chapter, often considered spurious, that was added to the *Art de contemplació* (*Art of Contemplation*) that is part of Book 5 of *Blaquerna*. Llull presumably added it not too long after the redaction of the chapter on knighthood in the *Doctrina pueril* and when *Blaquerna* was already considered finished, and copies had begun to circulate, with the result that the chapter in question has been transmitted as a part of the oldest tradition of the work, but not by all traditions.[38]

The section on topics related to the different social strata is situated at the beginning of the last twenty chapters of the *Doctrina pueril*, chapters in which Llull included all those matters he deemed useful for his readers' basic education but which he had not been able to find a place for in any of the previous sections. The organizational structure of these last chapters, then, is less clear, although this does not prevent us from detecting certain lines of thematic coherence there, whether it be within the group of chapters or in relation to the preceding chapters. A clear example of this is Ch. 84, "On Prayer," in which several previously defined catechetical concepts are put into practice. The next chapter, which discusses the soul and its powers or faculties, can be related, on the one hand, to the previous chapter since both deal with the necessity of learning to use the understanding, the will, and the memory correctly in prayer (and thus to avoid, for example, that they become disordered, as discussed in Ch. 84.17). On the other hand, this chapter begins a brief, more physiologically oriented series with chapters dedicated to the human body, to life, and to physical death (Chs. 86-88), to which one must also relate Ch. 92, on rational movement and the passions of the soul, and Ch. 94, on the four elements that make up everything that exists beneath the sphere of the moon. According to Galenic medicine, these four elements find their physiological expression in the four humors of the human body and in the four complexions.

---

38. See the reflections by Salvador Galmés on this chapter, which the scholar considered apocryphal, in Llull 1914: 461 and, with regard to the text, pages 499-506. For a different understanding of the issue: Llull 2009: 67-70, and 688-697. The same has been proposed recently with respect to a passage in the *Llibre d'intenció*, see Llull 2013a: 77.

Following these chapters, and just before the final ones, there are several chapters covering a variety of topics related to moral and religious matters that develop previously mentioned topics, such as hypocrisy and vainglory (Ch. 89), temptation (Ch. 90), predestination and free will (Ch. 95). There is also a pair of chapters on social education: Ch. 91 discusses how to raise and educate a child during its first years of life (an unusual topic not only for a catechetical work but for any non-medical text), while Ch. 93 offers general observations on good habits.

Chs. 96 and 97, on the coming of the Antichrist and on the seven ages of history respectively, deal with the evolution of this world from its origins until its future necessary end, in accordance with the Christian theological concept of historical time. The chapter on the seven ages, again, makes evident how much Llull conceived the *Doctrina pueril* as an introductory text to medieval knowledge. To this end, in this work Llull brought together aspects of knowledge that he never used in his own doctrinal or evangelical strategies. History—the historical dimension of humanity—was one of the topics to which he dedicated very little attention in later works.[39] This is not the case, however, with the figure of the Antichrist, which should be related to the biblical prophecy of his coming and to the battle he will wage against the Church before the end of the world, and for which Christians will have to prepare themselves adequately. It is not at all surprising, then, that, shortly after writing the *Doctrina pueril*, Llull should write a work explicitly dedicated to this very question: the *Llibre contra Anticrist* (*Book against the Antichrist*).[40]

The final chapters emphasize, once again, the soul's fate in the other world, a theme seen previously in the conclusions found at the ends of the series on the virtues and vices that close the catechetical part of the work. In this case, the eschatological theme is preceded by Ch. 98, "On Angels," including the fallen ones and the evil influence they have on humans. In this way, the battle between angels and demons for the souls of mortals paves the way for the work's two final chapters on Hell and on the glory of Paradise (Chs. 99 and 100).

The placement of these two final sections at the very end of the second part of the *Doctrina pueril* establishes a parallelism that looks

---

39. See Badia 2009: 19-20.
40. For the *Llibre contra Anticrist*, see n. 8.

back to the corresponding chapters that synthesize the results produced by the prominence of the septenaries of the virtues and vices
(Chs. 59 and 68), where Llull speaks about the reasons and behaviors
that can lead to Heaven or Hell as described in the two final chapters.
The overall effect of these two chapters is to reinforce the structural
and intentional unity of the *Doctrina pueril*, which, by emphasizing the
afterlife at book's very end, seeks to create a greater, and thus more
effective, impact on the readers' imaginations and to remind them
that their passage through this world will inevitably condition the
eternal destiny of their soul. It is surely with this same desire to pen-
etrate the mind of the reader that every chapter of the work ends with
an explicit mention of God.

Years later, Llull used the same strategy in his *Llibre de meravelles*,
where he dedicates the two final books to Paradise and Hell after eight
books about God and diverse aspects of creation. It is not by chance
that the most extensive of these books and the one immediately prior
to the last two, is the eighth, on Man, of eminently moral content.[41] In
the *Doctrina pueril*, too, the most extensive section refers to the moral
and catechetical education of the reader and makes explicit the consequences of an imperfect assimilation of this education, for, beyond
teaching the reader, the text's chief purpose is to set out the reader's
path through this world, although the reader may not fully compre-
hend the reasons for some of the behaviors that are demanded. Hence
the scant room left in the book for doubt and the emphasis on the
importance of keeping the afterlife ever in mind. Readers must be
made keenly aware that their otherworldly fate depends on the choices
they make in this world. Therefore, it must be made absolutely clear to
readers, without any possibility for confusion, what the correct choices
are. In the end, their eternal salvation depends upon it.

5. THE TEXT OF THE *DOCTRINA PUERIL*

The *Doctrina pueril* has been transmitted in a rather large number of
manuscripts, in Catalan and in other languages, as well as in some
older printed editions. In all, between the complete and fragmentary

---

41. For the structure of the *Llibre de meravelles*, see Gayà 1980: 66-67, and Llull
2011: 27-30.

witnesses of the text, we have sixteen Catalan manuscripts copied between the 14th and the 18th centuries, plus a 1736 edition in modernized language. To the Catalan witnesses, we can add four Occitan manuscripts, a French manuscript and two French-language incunables, three discrete Latin translations (two of which are medieval and the third of which is from the 18th century), and, finally, a fragmentary 18th-century manuscript and a 1742 Spanish-language printed edition.[42] This extensive textual tradition is evidence of the interest that the work aroused until well into the 18th century and also explains why the work has three distinct critical editions to date.

The critical edition of the *Doctrina pueril* that appeared in 2005 as volume 7 of the Nova Edició de les Obres de Ramon Llull, prepared by the author of this introduction, took as its base text the manuscript used in the 1906 edition that is presently found in the Biblioteca de Catalunya in Barcelona: Ms. 3187 (14th century=Ms. *B* in the list that follows). In places where the text of *B* is illegible, I have used Ms. *M* (17th century), a reasonably faithful copy of *B*. In the case of the three and a half chapters missing from *B* due to a loss of folios at the end, I use the medieval Ms. *A* (14th-15th century). The 2005 edition also took into account the totality of the surviving textual tradition of the work, including the various medieval translations. The present translation is based on the text of the 2005 edition.[43]

Joan Santanach
Centre de Documentació Ramon Llull
Universitat de Barcelona

(Translated by John Dagenais)

---

42. For the early tradition of the *Doctrina pueril*, in both manuscript and print, see Santanach 2005: LIV-LXX.

43. The letters designating each manuscript are the same as those used in Llull 2005. For more detailed descriptions of all the manuscripts of the *Doctrina pueril*, see Llull 2005 and http://orbita.bib.ub.es/llull/, which includes additional bibliography. The translation of the chapter on knights is based on the Latin version found in *L³* as transcribed in Llull 2005 edition, pp. 287-89 (see list of manuscripts). These are the texts used in the respective translations of these sections.

Translator's Preface

I first read Ramon Llull's *Doctrina pueril* more than four decades ago when I was just beginning my study of the European Middle Ages. For me, it was a fascinating introduction to the medieval world, and I thought at the time that it would be an excellent introductory text for students like me who were just beginning their exploration of the medieval European world and world view. The book can be thought of as a sort of "Everything You Need to Know in the Middle Ages." It offers a remarkably concise and coherent understanding of medieval Christian world view, encyclopedic in scope, but aimed at adolescents and, as Joan Santanach argues in the Introduction to this translation, at laypeople of all ages who possessed only the rudiments of an education. I am very gratified, then, to have had the opportunity to prepare this English version of the *Doctrina* for Barcino/Tamesis.

In the 100 brief chapters of the *Doctrina pueril,* Llull covers his world: the basic tenets of the Catholic faith, the other major faiths known to him (pagan, Judaism, Islam), the liberal arts, medicine, law, natural philosophy, mechanical arts, the soul, history, the social order (with some mordant observations on doctors, lawyers, astrologers and social climbers in general), death, angels, Hell and Heaven. The *Doctrina pueril* shows how one extremely thoughtful medieval person, living on the Mediterranean frontier between the Christian and the Islamic worlds, understood his universe and the place and purpose of his own human life in that universe. Such a view, at once comprehensive in its goals and highly individual in its point of view, is quite rare for the Middle Ages.

Although it is true that the *Doctrina pueril* deliberately avoids many of the complexities of Llull's highly idiosyncratic Art, including its geometrical figures and the intricacies of its combinatory system, this does not mean that it is a simple book. It is clear that Llull sought here to train his "son" in the basic processes of thought that underlie his system, to establish habits of the mind that would facilitate the understanding of the Art when the time to learn it arrived.

The *Doctrina pueril* is best understood as a dynamic mixture of "facts" and "thought experiments" designed to enable its readers, gradually, to internalize many of the intellectual processes that are essential to the Art. For the reader of this translation who wishes to venture a bit further into these processes, I highly recommend reviewing the various "conditions" found in Llull's *The Book of the Gentile and the Three Wise Men*, written in 1274-1276?, that is, at around the same time, perhaps slightly after, the *Doctrina pueril*.[1] In the *Book of the Gentile and the Three Wise Men*, the three sages—a Jew, a Christian and a Muslim—agree to accept the validity of a set of ten conditions and two "meta-conditions" as they begin their debate of the truths of their respective religions. These conditions are to guide their discussion. Most of these same conditions are constantly invoked, implicitly and explicitly, throughout the *Doctrina pueril*, though the term "condition" itself appears but rarely. So, in addition to offering his "son" the basic facts of the human world and the divine order in which it exists, in the *Doctrina pueril* Llull reveals a lively intellectual world in which these elements interact through hierarchies of value (greater, lesser, equal), beginning, middle and end, contrarieties and concordances, conditions and impossibilities, likenesses, dissimilarities and equalities, that govern these actions and the "first intention"—to serve, love and know God—that sets them all in motion.

I have sought to present a readable translation for the general reader, but one that does not gloss over the characteristic and meaningful syntactic and linguistic difficulties (and awkwardnesses) of the text. I have sought not to archaize unnecessarily, but at moments in which Llull echoes biblical language or the language of sermons, I have allowed some older syntax and vocabulary to creep in. In both the translation and notes, in the spirit of Llull's own goals for the text, I have placed the emphasis on presenting the medieval Christian understanding of the created universe, as viewed by Llull, rather than on Llull himself or on his difficult Art. There are excellent materials available in English for those who wish to pursue a deeper

---

1. *SW* 1.114-115. One of Llull's earliest and most enthusiastic students, the French physician Thomas le Myésier, writes that "in these conditions...lies the entire virtue of all of Ramon's Arts" (cited Bonner 2007: p. 67, n. 88). On the conditions, see Bonner 2007: pp. 67-68 and accompanying notes. Llull defined "conditions" in another place as "the mixing of principles, with some conditioned by others according to their definitions and properties" (cited in Bonner 2007: p. 67 and 130-134).

knowledge of Llull and his Art (Bonner [especially 2007], Fidora & Rubio, Johnston, Pring-Mill, Yates; Badia, Santanach & Soler). A very good place to begin the study of Llull is Joan Santanach's Introduction to this translation.

A few notes on the translation: The Catalan term "virtut" can have several meanings for Llull. The *divine* "virtues" (or "uncreated virtues") are, in the *Doctrina pueril*, the following: goodness, greatness, eternity, power, wisdom, love, virtue, truth, glory, perfection, justice, generosity, mercy, humility, lordship, patience (bonesa, granesa, eternitat, poder, saviesa, amor, virtut, veritat, glòria, perfecció, justícia, llarguesa, misericòrdia, humilitat, senyoria, paciència). The number of these virtues varies across Llull's career. At times, they are also referred to as "dignities" or "properties." But the term "virtut" appears in many other contexts in the *Doctrina pueril*: as the "virtues," that is, medicinal properties, of plants, for example, or the powers of the human soul, as well as in its more familiar sense as the opposite of human "vice." I have translated it variously as "virtue," "power," "property" (as in physical properties), but when the term "virtue" appears in the translation, it should be understood often to embrace several of these meanings.

Another characteristic of Llull's text that functions within its economy of concordance and contrariety is his use of what we may call the "adversative 'and'." Two opposing conditions are simply given equal value or force but are joined by the conjunction "and," leaving the reader to discover the opposition implicit in the juxtaposition. To take some examples from the *Doctrina pueril* itself, in Ch. 61, "On Lust," commenting on the vice of lust in old men, Llull says: "their body is no longer up to lustful activities and, in their will, they continue to lust." Yes, these are two simultaneous conditions in lustful old men, but for Llull, the opposition, and the irony of the situation (more than irony, really, for it involves a deadly sin), depends on our seeing the opposition between the desires of the will and the capacities of the body, a meaning perhaps fully realized only if we mentally substitute "but" for "and" in the sentence above. Thus, in the *Doctrina pueril*, it is sometimes up to the reader to determine whether a given "and" means "and" or if it is better understood as "but." Here's another example, from the opening lines of Ch. 62, "On Avarice": "Avarice is to hoard things that are more than you need for yourself and are necessities for the poor." Here, too, a rather flat definition acquires new relief if we understand that the point is "but are necessities for the poor." These are relatively simple cases, but there are others throughout the *Doctrina pueril* when understanding that an "and" governs an opposition is crucial to the correct understanding of Llull's text and of the moral world he presents. This, too, is a part of Llull's program in the *Doctrina pueril*. As in his Art and in his thought in general, Llull sets up a set of conditions whose relative values and interrelations it is up to us to determine. This means that we need to understand the *Doctrina pueril* as, yes, a textbook or a reference book, but also as a *workbook* containing sets of exercises the reader must complete. Such an understanding is entirely in keeping with the goals Llull announces in his preface and, indeed, in the very title of his book as we might translate it literally: "The Education of Children."

Perhaps more striking for modern readers will be the absence of "and" in places where we might expect, even demand, it. This usage is clear evidence of the ways in which Llull's Art and his desire to expose his inexperienced readers to its rudimentary moves underlie the *Doctrina pueril*. In normal discourse, in both English and Catalan, it is usual to place an "and" before the last item of a list. But in the *Doctrina pueril*, the vast majority of Llull's lists lack this final "and." It is a sometimes confusing—almost always distracting—feature of the text, and I have not sought to "correct" this in the translation because it is an essential characteristic of Llull's program here.

Why should this be? Here again, I think, Llull is setting a list of conditions or "virtues," at equal value and weight. He wishes to avoid even the suggestion of hierarchical distinctions among them: the "first things first" mentality. He is writing prose and therefore must work within the linear world of language, but he wishes to suppress, as much as possible, that linearity and any sense that last is least. This is our clue to what these lists, in many cases, are: they are "figures." That is, they are, in fact, the linear prose version of the famous geometrical "figures" of Llull's Art in which the properties of circles, for example, allow Llull to list a set of "virtues" or "vices" as elements of equal value (though this value may be positive or negative), outside any linear or hierarchical economy. It will help to understand this feature of the text, then, if we view the lists not as linear lists in human language but as symbols placed around the circumference of a circle with no beginning or end that might suggest priority or superiority. We can, in fact, find Llull's solution to the problem of the linearity of language in the first work in which he uses geometrical figures and, especially, in his Figure A, first found in the *Ars Compendiosa Inveniendi Veritatem* (1271), which, in fact, shows the 18 "uncreated virtues" on the circumference of a circle (Bonner 2007: after p. 92).[2]

As a final tip to the reader who seeks to understand Llull's world and his thought, I recommend reading first Ch. 85, "On the Soul," and an examination of Figure 2, illustrating the structure of the rational soul. Here the psychological system that underlies so much of the *Doctrina pueril* is set out most clearly and completely. Essential is Llull's belief, usually said to be of Augustinian origin, that the human soul possesses three powers (or "virtues"): memory, understanding and will. The interplay of these three powers informs much of the *Doctrina pueril.* In particular, it is important to understand that the power of will acts through "love" (or hate). Thus, when Llull speaks of "loving" or "desiring" or "hating" (and, on occasion, when he speaks of the heart metaphorically) he is speaking quite specifically of acts of the will as one of the powers of the human soul.

In other cases, it may seem that Llull's language is unnecessarily repetitive, as when he says that "the memory remembers" or "the understanding understands." But these, too, are features of Llull's language that I have not tried to "clean up": these verbal similarities between powers and actions are signs, proofs, of the design of Creation. They are essential aspects of Llull's world view and, thus, of his language.

The foregoing is intended simply as a set of basic guidelines for readers of this translation; it is in no way an attempt at a full-fledged introduction to Llull's Art or its invocation at the "elementary" level in the *Doctrina pueril.* If one comes away from reading this text with the rudiments of a feel for the constant directed movement of the intellect in Llull's thought, this translation will have achieved its own

---

2. Also concerning "and": Llull's original text, like most medieval texts, exhibits a high level of "parataxis," the joining of phrases with a simple coordinating conjunctions such as "and" that often seem to us to add little to the meaning of the text. I have not sought to eliminate such usage ruthlessly, but I have also not sought slavishly to preserve it. The resulting text has a somewhat higher usage of "and" for this purpose than the average modern English text and a rather lower degree of such usage than Llull's original text.

final intention. I invite the reader, then, to enter into the play of
Llull's thought through the very door that he envisioned for his
"son": his *Doctrina pueril.*

For the uniform titles and dating of works I have used the information from the online resources of LlullDB, the "Base de Dades
Ramon Llull" (http://orbita.bib.ub.edu/llull/), except that I have
regularized the medieval orthography: "Libre" to the modern form
"Llibre."

In some cases, in the notes, I point the reader interested in learning more about the "encyclopedic" ideas in Llull's text to general
sources in English on such things as medieval medicine or Canon
Law, but the notes make no claim to bibliographic exhaustivity. In
many ways, the notes reflect in a very personal way the directions that
reading the *Doctrina pueril* forty years ago sent me in as I began my
study of the European Middle Ages.

Some early Latin and French versions of the *Doctrina pueril* add an
entire chapter on "Knighthood," perhaps at the direction of Llull
himself or at the request of some knightly patron who felt Llull had
neglected the noble class in favor of religious orders (see the Introduction). I have included a translation of that chapter, using the
Latin version, in the place in which it is found in the Latin and French
versions: between Ch. 80, "On Princes" and Ch. 81, "On Clerics."

This translation has benefited at every stage from its base text: the
critical edition of the *Doctrina pueril* prepared by Professor Joan Santanach i Suñol for the project of the Nova Edició de les Obres de
Ramon Llull. Beyond this, it has benefited from the affection Professor Santanach and I share for this text, and from afternoons I spent
discussing finer points of meaning with him. Without his knowledge
and insights, not to mention his editorial labors, this translation
could not exist. It has been a pleasure to work with him.

My thanks also go to Pamela Beattie, Scottie Hale Buehler, Tom
Burman, Brian Catlos, Elizabeth Comuzzi, Mark Filarowicz, Mark D.
Johnston, William D. Paden, Ryan Szpiech, and Jadranka Vrsalovic
Carevic, who helped me to resolve many important points in the
translation and notes along the way. Especially, I would like to thank
Marcel Ortín, the reader of this manuscript for Barcino/Tamesis. His
meticulous reading helped me resolve numerous questions in the
translation and the notes. Paul Cella read the translations of both the
Introduction and the text itself with a careful eye for detail and sug-

gested many improvements. This translation was supported by the Committee on Research of the UCLA Academic Senate, and the UCLA Center for 17th and 18th Century Studies. I express my thanks to them, as well as to the Fundació Carulla, here.

I also take this opportunity to express my gratitude to Anthony Bonner for his kindness and support over the years. Until one has actually tried to translate Llull from medieval Catalan into modern English one cannot fully appreciate the ground-breaking achievement of his translations of Llull's works in the 1980s. I have often turned to these translations for their elegant solutions to the problem of translating Llull's often idiosyncratic diction into readable, enjoyably readable, English. Needless to say, any errors of interpretation or infelicities of language that remain are mine.

My most important thanks go to my father Ralph W. Dagenais who, at age 92, read every word of the translation-in-progress and offered many useful corrections and suggestions for its improvement, as he has done with almost every important thing I have written throughout my career. For me, it was a special privilege to have had the help of my own father in preparing this compendium of a father's advice to his "dear son." I dedicate this translation, then, to my dear father.

John Dagenais
University of California, Los Angeles

FIGURES

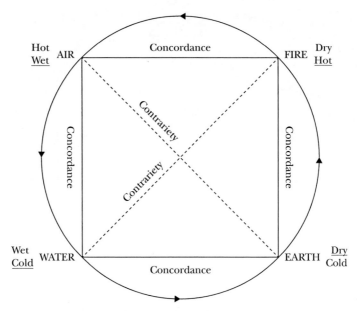

Figure 1. The Four Elements. The "proper" qualities of each element are underlined; the "appropriated" qualities are not. See especially Chs. 77 and 94 and n. 215. Figure design after R. Pring-Mill.

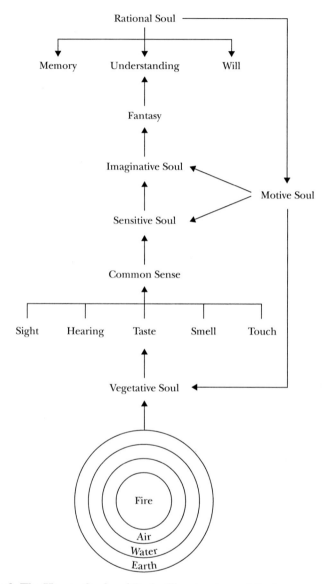

Figure 2. The Human Soul and Body. The structure of the human soul and body as described in Chs. 85-86. The arrangement of the circles of the elements within the human body is that described by Llull in Ch. 86.10, in which he notes that while within the circle of the sublunar world (see Fig. 3) fire is the outermost element and earth the innermost, this order is reversed in the human body.

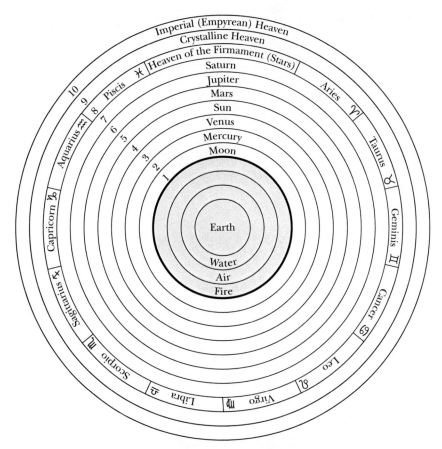

Figure 3. The Heavens: The Lullian Universe. The circles of the heavens, the planets and the sublunar world as described in Ch. 98.

Doctrina Pueril

Honored God, our glorious Lord, with your grace and blessing we begin this book, which concerns the foundations of childhood education.

PROLOGUE

[1] God wants us to make haste and strive to serve Him, for life is short and death draws nearer each day. For that reason, we should hate to waste our time. In the beginning, you should teach your son those things that are general in the world so that he can learn how to move his understanding from general things down to specific things. And in the beginning, you should have your son spell out his lessons in the vernacular language so that he can understand what he is reading.[1] Next, he should be set to construing the text in this very book,

---

1. In the prologue, Llull sets out an entire program for becoming a literate person in the medieval West, from basic literacy in the vernacular to the rudiments of the learned language: Latin. First, the student of the *Doctrina pueril* (hereafter, *DP*) should sound out the vernacular text, letter by letter, syllable by syllable, word by word. Once the student has sounded out a full word in the vernacular, he will recognize it and will learn to read it, and, eventually, to understand the text. Once the student has mastered the text in the vernacular, and once the *DP* has been translated into Latin, the student will "construe" (a term familiar to generations of students of Latin, meaning "to translate the Latin text out loud" or, more abstractly, "to analyse or trace the grammatical construction of a sentence," *OED*) the text in that language, learning its grammar at the same time that his knowledge of the content of the text is reinforced through repetition in the learned tongue. Llull envisions the *DP*, then, as a multilayered pedagogical tool. The student can use it to learn to read in both the vernacular and Latin, move on to mastering its contents and, ultimately, to absorbing some of the basic thought processes underlying Llull's *Art* along the way. Some of these ideas are repeated in Ch. 73. See also Chs. 83, 85, 91 and 100, where Llull recommends "further readings" for students of the *DP*, as well as Ch. 77, where he seems to recommend much of the Aristotelian corpus for study. In Ch. 2.5 of the *Romance of Evast and Blaquerna* (hereafter *Blaquerna*), Evast, Blaquerna's father, sets him to studying "as explained in the *Doctrina pueril*" at age eight (*Blaquerna*, cited by chapter and paragraph; for Catalan ed.: Llull 2009; English trans.: Llull 2016). In Ch. 34.6 of *Blaquerna*, an abbess recommends both

which should be translated into Latin, for in that way he will learn Latin more quickly.

[2] And so, since this is true, with this desire, a poor, sinful man, despised among the peoples, blameworthy, miserable, unworthy of having his name inscribed in this book, writes this book and others— as briefly and as simply as he can—for his dear son, so that he can enter more easily and more quickly into the knowledge through which he can know how to know and love and serve his glorious God.[2]

[3] In the beginning, you should teach your son the Fourteen Articles of the holy Catholic faith and the Ten Commandments our Lord God gave to Moses in the desert and the Seven Sacraments of the holy Church and the other chapters that follow.

[4] You should show your son how to contemplate the glory of Paradise and the punishments of Hell and the other chapters contained in this book, for by such reflections the child accustoms itself to love and fear God and is open to good instruction.[3]

---

the catechetical portions, in particular, and "many other parts" of the *DP* to a nun in her convent.

2. With "since this is true," Llull is referring back to the first ideas of the preceding paragraph that life is short and that, therefore, we should not waste our time.

3. Llull refers here to the final two chapters of the book, where he suggests a variety of ways to "contemplate" first Hell and then Heaven. The Catalan word for "instruction" here is "nodriments." Llull defines "nodriment" in Ch. 91.1 as "to accustom another person to habitual behaviors that bring him closer to natural conduct." "Nodriment" is obviously a keyword in a book on childhood education and I translate it variously in this text as "nurture," "education," "instruction," "upbringing," "breeding" (as in "good breeding"), "habits," "advice," according to the context.

ON THE FOURTEEN ARTICLES[4]

1. ONE GOD

[1] Son, you should know that the Articles consist in believing and loving true and marvelous things about God. [2] The first Article is to believe in one God, who is the beginning of all beginnings and the beneficent Lord of all that is. [3] You must believe that there is one God alone, in whom there is no defect. Rather, he is the perfection of all perfections. [4] This God is invisible to your corporeal eyes and visible to the eyes of your soul. He is worthy of all praise and honor. [5] In God are goodness and greatness, eternity, power, wisdom and love, virtue, truth, glory and perfection, justice, generosity, mercy, humility, lordship, patience. There are many virtues like these in God, and each one of these virtues [separately] and all of them together are one God alone.[5]

[6] You must believe and love these things. You were created and came into this world for this purpose: so that you might believe in one God alone and adore and love and fear Him. And if you do not do this, the punishments of Hell—where you will suffer unending torments—are beckoning to you.

---

4. In this heading, Llull follows an understanding of the Articles of Faith as being fourteen in number, as presented, for example, by Llull's contemporary Thomas Aquinas in his *Summa Theologiae* II^a-II^{ae} q. 1 a. 8. The Articles of Faith reflect the most basic statement of Church doctrine and the first elements of the catechism: the Apostle's Creed.

5. These are the sixteen "uncreated virtues," which Llull will refer to in later works as "dignities." The fact that there are sixteen (4^2) such virtues in Llull's system at this time is one of the reasons, along with its heavy reliance on arguments based on the four elements, that this phase is known as the "quaternary phase" of Llull's Art (see n. 212). "Senyoria," which I translate as "lordship," is also referred to as "dominion" (cf. Rubio 2008: 254-257; Bonner 2007: 31-33). Note that here, as often throughout the *DP*, there is no "and" before the last item in the "list" (see Translator's Preface). Indeed this is not precisely a "list" at all, but rather the presentation of individual "virtues" equal in force and value.

[7] God must be loved, for He is all good. God is great, for everything that exists ends in Him. God is everlasting because He has no beginning and no end. God must be feared, for all power is in Him and He knows all things.[6]

[8] Son, love God so that He loves you and makes you pleasing to the people. [9] The power that you have in seeing, hearing, smelling, tasting, touching, you have entirely from God. [10] Love truth so that divine truth does not know you to be a liar.

[11] Despise the glory of this world—which lasts so briefly—so that you can possess the glory that has no end. [12] Satiate your soul with God's perfection, for nothing else can fulfill it.

[13] Son, love justice because, if you do not, justice will condemn you to suffer eternal flames. [14] Do not be stingy with what God has given you, for He can give you more and take more away from you than anyone else. [15] Have mercy if you wish to be forgiven. [16] Humble yourself before God, who lifts up the humble and casts down the proud.

[17] Do not be ashamed to honor, serve and obey God, for He is an honored lord. Love patience so that you do not fall under the wrath of God.

[18] Son, if you believe in one God, you must do all these things and many others like them if you wish to be pleasing to God.

2. ON THE TRINITY

[1] You must believe, dear son, in the Holy Trinity of our Lord God, who is one God existing in three persons, that is, Father and Son and Holy Spirit. To believe in one God is the first article. To believe in God the Father is the second article. To believe in God the Son is the third article. To believe in God the Holy Spirit is the fourth.

[2] God the Father engenders God the Son from himself, and from God the Father and God the Son proceeds God the Holy Spirit, and the Father and Son and Holy Spirit are one God alone. [3] Infi-

---

6. In this and the following paragraphs, Llull's language echoes the biblical book of Proverbs, a style he takes up again toward the end of the book in Ch. 93.

nitely, eternal and with complete perfection, God the Father engenders God the Son, and God the Holy Spirit proceeds from God the Father and God the Son.[7] [4] The Father is one person and the Son another and the Holy Spirit is another and together these three persons are one power, one wisdom, one love.

[5] Son, what I am telling you about God's Holy Trinity and His unity is true and even better than I can tell you. If you believe this with the light of faith in this world, you will understand it with the light of an understanding illuminated by divine intelligence in the other world.

[6] Do you know, son, why you cannot understand and are obligated to believe what you do not understand about the Holy Trinity? Because God's unity and Trinity are greater than your understanding and because I am not explaining them to you in a way that you can understand.[8]

[7] Do not disbelieve everything that you cannot understand, for if you do that you are seeking to make your own understanding greater than all things. And do you know why I speak so subtly to you? So that your understanding becomes accustomed to rising up in understanding and your will in loving God.

[8] Do not look down on this book, son, because it is told so simply, for it is not written for an exalted understanding. Rather, it is written so that the intellects of children can be lifted up to understand this world and God.[9]

---

7. Llull repeats the statement that the Holy Spirit proceeds from both God the Father and God the Son. This is a key issue for him, and the fact that Greek Christians believe that the Holy Spirit proceeds from the God the Father alone is significant enough for him that he includes Greek Christians among the "Gentiles" in Ch. 72.4-6.

8. Explaining the doctrine of the Holy Trinity convincingly to Jews, Muslims and gentiles is one of the principal goals of Llull's *Art* and we glimpse in this passage both one of its motivations—the need to explain, and prove, the truth of complex concepts in reasonably accessible ways—and a recognition of the limitations of the simpler approach he has adopted in the *DP*. For Llull's more sophisticated explanations of the Trinity from this period, see *The Book of the Gentile and the Three Wise Men* [hereafter *Gentile*], Book 3, 2-4 in *SW* 1.193-217.

9. In this second chapter of the *DP*, Llull continues some of his explanation of the goals and methods of the book from the prologue: it is designed to "lift up" simple intellects toward the dual understanding of the world about them and of God.

3. ON CREATION

[1] The Creator is the Maker who made the world from nothing. Now, in the beginning, God created Heaven and earth, and the first day was Sunday, the day on which He created the angels.[10] On that day, the demons fell from heaven because they wanted to be equal to the Highest and God confirmed the angels in the state in which they could not sin.[11]

[2] On Monday, God created Heaven, where the angels stand before God. [3] On Tuesday, God created the sea and the land and the plants and the trees and their seeds. [4] On Wednesday, God created the sun and the moon and the stars to illuminate the sea and the land. [5] On Thursday, God created the birds and the beasts. [6] On Friday, God created man, who was named Adam. And when Adam had fallen asleep, God took a rib from him, with which He created woman, that is, Eve. And we are all descended from Adam and Eve.

[7] On that same day, God put Adam and Eve in the earthly paradise and made Adam lord of all the beasts and all the plants and all the birds and of all that the earth produces and sustains.

[8] On the seventh day, God rested in order to demonstrate that He had given the world everything that it needed. And for that reason, the seventh day was created to be a holy day and a day for praising and honoring and contemplating God, in order to demonstrate that the same day of the week on which the world began would be the day to complete the fulfillment of our redemption.[12]

[9] Son, if you want to attain salvation, you must believe that God is the Creator of everything that exists, and that everything that exists would return to nothing if God did not sustain it, and that without God everything that is would not exist.

---

10. In addition to discussing God's creation of the universe as an Article of Faith, Llull uses this opportunity to tell his "son" the story of God's creation of the world as found in Genesis. This chapter, then, is a continuation of the project outlined at the close of the preceding chapter: to help the learner understand "this world and God."

11. Cf. Chs. 64.4 and 98.

12. We should understand that two different ideas are being discussed here: 1) that the seventh day, Saturday, should be the day of rest and worship (for the Jews) and 2) that this Jewish day of rest on Saturday "demonstrates" ("signifies" by analogy) that on "the same day of the week on which the world began," that is, Sunday, there would come the day in which Christ redeemed humankind. In Ch. 15.2-3, Llull explains the ideas in this paragraph in clearer detail.

[10] Behold, son, what great things God has created, such as the sky and the sea and the land, and behold how many diverse creatures He has made, and see how beautiful and how useful the things of Creation are. Therefore, if there is so much good in Creation, open the eyes of your soul and see how great and noble and good is the Creator who has created all things.

[11] All the kings who exist and all the men of this world could not create a single flower or beast, nor could they create anything at all, nor could they forbid the sun its movement or the rain its fall.

[12] God has given greater abundance to those things that are most necessary to man, such as earth, air and water and fire and salt and iron and wheat and the other things like these.

[13] God created wings for the birds so that they can fly, and He gave them feathers to be their clothing, and He created hooves for the beasts to be their shoes, and for the trees, He created leaves so that their fruits can ripen, and for the fishes, He created the sea so that they can swim. And for each created thing, God created those properties that are necessary to it.

[14] God created the horse for man to ride and the hawk for hunting and sheep for eating and their wool for wearing and the fire for heating and the ox for plowing, and God created all the other creatures to serve man.

[15] When you are at the table, son, and you have the foods that you are about to eat in front of you, remember how many created things you see, which God has created, and understand that God has had all the things that you are eating brought to you from different places.

[16] God created your eyes so that with them you see Him in the created things that represent Him to the eyes of your thought.[13] God created your memory so that with it you remember Him, and God created your heart to be the chamber where you keep Him and love Him, and God created your hands so that you can do good works, and He created your feet so that you can travel His ways, and He created your mouth so that you can praise Him and bless Him.

---

13. Here Llull refers to the idea that God has written the "Book of Nature," which can be read along with God's other book, the Bible, as humankind seeks to understand God and his creation. The physical world is perceived by our physical eyes which then represent, not just the objects they see, but also God himself "to the eyes of our thought," that is, to our intellectual and spiritual understanding of the world. See also Chs. 34, 68 and 75.

[17] I could not tell you, son, all the things that God has created, nor would I know how to explain the dominion that He has given you over them, nor could you understand how great is the debt that you have incurred for the great benefit you have received from your Creator.

[18] Remember how God could have made you a stone or wood or a beast if He had wished, and understand how He might have made you deformed or a Jew or a Saracen or a demon or some other thing for which it would be better not to be than to be.[14]

[19] You should consider, dear son, and think about all these things so that while you are in this world you do works by which you may be pleasing to the saints in glory and to your God.

4. ON RE-CREATION[15]

[1] Re-creation is to recover what our Lord God had lost in His people, and re-creation is to take away the devil's power, which he held over us.

[2] The entire human lineage, son, fell into sin and error because of our first father Adam and our first mother Eve, who were disobedient to God, the Lord of Glory. And for that reason, it was necessary for sin to be overcome and conquered by the One who is more contrary to sin than is any other thing.

[3] When God—may He be blessed!—had created Adam and Eve and had placed them in the earthly paradise, He made the commandment that Adam could eat all the fruits except one, for if he ate of that fruit he would surely die. The devil, in the form of a serpent,

---

14. This is the first reference in the *DP* to members of the major non-Christian religions of the western Mediterranean in Llull's day: Jews and Muslims ("Saracens"). These peoples were Llull's neighbors and were an integral part of the cultural landscape that Llull is presenting to his "son." They are also a major focus of Llull's own life mission of converting "infidels," as is seen throughout the *DP*. Here, he rather strikingly groups members of these religions with demons and deformed persons.

15. The term "re-creation," that is, "to create anew," vividly represents Llull's understanding of the nature of Christ's redemption of humankind. This expression was also known in English. *OED*, s.v. "re-creation" gives the following example from around 1410 (I have modernized orthography and usage): "God's Son had more travail in recreation and redemption of mankind than he had in making all this world."

came to our mother Eve and counseled her to find a way to make Adam eat of the fruit that God had forbidden him. And because Adam ate of that fruit and was disobedient to our Lord God, the death and suffering that you see today came down upon us and discord was created between God and the human lineage.

[4] If Adam had not sinned and broken God's commandment, no man would die or be hungry or thirsty or hot or cold or sick or afflicted. But because of original sin, you must know, son, we all fell under the wrath of God, and Adam and Eve were cast out of paradise on the very same day that they had been placed there.

[5] All people who died went to the eternal fire until it pleased the Sovereign Father that His Son, by the grace of the Holy Spirit, should take flesh in Our Lady Saint Mary. Thus, the Son of God, through His great mercy, came to a virgin maiden called Our Lady Saint Mary, who was of the lineage of David.

[6] The Son of God was incarnated in and born from that maiden—who was a virgin—without her being corrupted and without her losing her virginity. And from this maiden, God and man were born together, that is our Lord Jesus Christ, in whom there are two natures, that is, divine nature and human nature. These two natures are one single person.

[7] This Jesus Christ came into the world to re-create the world and to lift up the human lineage, which had fallen and which was now lifted up by virtue of the joining of divine nature and human nature and by the suffering and Passion that He endured out of love for us.

[8] Son, you must believe in this Lord Jesus Christ I am telling you about, for if you do not, you will not be re-created nor will the sin be taken from you, the sin that was given to you by our first father—the sin in which the Jews and Saracens and other infidels remain because they do not believe in the coming or in the Passion of our Lord God Jesus Christ.

[9] If sinning and being disobedient to God are such bad things, son, that through one sin alone we all fell under the wrath of God, and if, in order to erase that sin, the Son of God wished to be incarnated, and if, in the humanity that He took on, He had to suffer anguish and pain and a cruel death, then guard yourself, son, from sin, because, in sinning, man is disobedient to the Highest, and God is man's enemy when he sins. And by disobedience and sin, sinners go

to the eternal fire to suffer grievous torments and to lose the eternal glory of our Lord God.

5. ON GLORY

[1] Glory, son, is continual and frequent bliss without end in praising the One who gives glory, which glory is given by our Lord God, who, glorying in glory, gives glory to the saints in glory. Therefore, son, if you wish to attain glory, it is necessary for you to believe that God is the glorifier of the blessed in Paradise and that they are glorified in His glory and that God glorifies them in His very glory.[16]

[2] Just as fire heats itself with its own heat, the divine King of Glory gives glory with His own glory to the angels and to saints who are in glory.

[3] If, in this world, God gives your body the blessing of worldly, corruptible things that are not glory and do not have glory, how much more, son, the King of Glory, who is glory, can give glory in Paradise to those who love Him.

[4] Know, son, that the glory of Paradise is to see God and to love God and to praise God, and that each of the saints in Paradise is glorified in the glory of the other.

---

16. This paragraph and this chapter, in general, are prime examples of Llull's rhetorical world, with the repetition of the same root word "glòria" in a variety of nominal and verbal forms. This practice may appear unnecessarily repetitive to modern readers, but, for Llull, these different word forms reflect a necessary and essential "participation" of the forms of language with thought and with universal reality. As Mark D. Johnston puts it, "the easiest way to grasp this perspective is to imagine that it regards the existence of all things, their understanding by the human mind, and their representation in words as somehow homologous" (1996: 34-35). It is also important to understand the rhetorical underpinnings of such passages according to Llull's rhetorical ideas. Put simply, if the thing a word refers to is beautiful, then the word itself is, of necessity, beautiful. As Llull explains in his *Llibre de contemplació* [see n. 304 for this text], Ch. 359, the beauty of a word comes not from its sounds, as we might expect, but from the place in a hierarchy of values of the thing to which it refers: "it is more beautiful to name an apostle than a cardinal and a cardinal than a bishop and a bishop or religious than a cleric...and it is more beautiful to name good than evil...and health than illness...and peace than war..." (trans. by Mark D. Johnston in Llull 1996: 40). According to this principle, then, this passage on "glory," in which one of the most supremely beautiful things in the universe (and one of God's "virtues"), "glory," is named repeatedly, can be understood to be exceedingly beautiful. The full synthesis of Llull's ideas on rhetoric is found in his *Rhetorica nova* of 1301 (Llull 1994).

[5] Do not believe, son, that in glory man eats or drinks or lies with women, for all these things have defects and foulness and belong to this world, which is dirty and corruptible and full of flaws.[17]

[6] Do you see, son, the dead body of the just man, which rots in the earth when he is buried? That body will rise up on Judgment Day and will be more resplendent than the sun, and it will never die. And it will have more glory than all the glory that is in the men of this world together.

[7] If, son, you despise the glory of this world so that you can have the glory of the other, you will have glory that will last as long as God's glory. And so, remember and understand that by despising scant glory, which lasts but a brief time, you can enjoy a glory that will last as long as the glory of the Highest.

[8] Ah, son! And how great a malediction is upon those who lose heavenly glory without end for a bit of worldly bliss and go to eternal torment to be subjected to infinite sufferings!

[9] If, son, you enter into glory, wherever you are, you will have glory and you will find glory. And do you know why? Because the Glorifier and the Lord of Glory is in all the places of glory.

[10] Those who are in glory love as greatly as they understand and understand as greatly as they love, and they possess all the things that they love and understand. Thus, if you cannot possess all the delights you understand in this world, son, take care not to lose for your will the glory that your understanding cannot understand.[18]

---

17. This is a direct reference to what Christians understood to be the Muslim view of paradise, which included earthly delights such as exquisite foods, wine and women for the faithful (*EI2*, s.v. "Djanna"). See also the description of "Paradise and Hell" that Llull places in the mouth of the Muslim sage in the *Gentile*, Book 4.12 (*SW* 1.288-293). That Llull took the time to deny the validity of such ideas here, in the midst of a chapter on "Glory," suggests that he perceived the attractiveness of the Muslim idea of paradise to offer a particular danger to his untutored Christian readers living in close proximity to Muslims. It is important to bear in mind what Vose (2009) called the "fluidity of religious identity" in the Crown of Aragon at this time. The Dominican "friars' primary aim was the protection and nurturing of the faithful rather than conversion of unbelievers" (7). Although Llull certainly had as his primary aim in life the conversion of unbelievers, concern about the "protection and nurturing of the faithful" seems, clearly, to have been also his concern in these "nodriments" addressed to his "son."

18. This passage, based on the interactions of two of the three "powers" of the human soul—understanding and will—, illustrates well how Llull uses a series of semantic correspondences to construct arguments about, in this case, "glory." "Love" is understood here, as throughout the *DP*, as the act of the will, the movement of the will *toward* something. So we might paraphrase this passage: "you understand that many delights

[11] If, son, you would not sell your hand for a penny or your head for two, take care not to exchange heavenly glory for the glory of this world. And if you would despise the glory of the other world for the glory of this world, stick your finger in the fire and gauge whether you would be able to endure the infernal flame forever, as the damned endure, for you will have to endure that fire if you despise the glory of our Lord God.

6. ON THE CONCEPTION

[1] You must believe, son, in the conception of our Lord God Jesus Christ, that is, in the Son of God's uniting of Himself with human nature, which was joined with divine nature by the grace of the Holy Spirit in the womb of Our Lady Saint Mary, glorious Virgin.

[2] In the beginning, when it pleased our Lord God to humble himself in order to re-create his people, He sent the angel Saint Gabriel to Our Lady Saint Mary. The glorious angel brought salutations to Our Lady Saint Mary from our Lord God and said to her "Ave Maria, gratia plena, Dominus tecum, benedicta tu in mulieribus, et benedictus fructus uentris tui; Spiritus Sanctus superueniet in te et uirtus Altissimi obumbrabit tibi."[19]

(that is, things that draw the will toward them) exist in this world, but that does not mean that you are capable of possessing all of them. Thus your desire (will) and your understanding are in different quantities in this world. Since, in the next world, the soul's powers of understanding and willing/loving are equal and reciprocal (one understands everything that one loves and vice versa), if you reject possession glory in the next world because your understanding fails to understand it, that means that you would lose the possibility of possessing glory because you would neither understand it nor (as a consequence) 'will' it. Your understanding would be deficient, and so your will/love would also be deficient since it would be in the same quantity, in glory, as your understanding." Hence, the necessity of faith (believing things about the next world and about God that one cannot understand in this world), as Llull states in the first paragraph of the chapter. This is a theme that appears in many guises throughout the *DP*: the need to hold the doubts raised by our limited understanding in check so that faith can allow us to see truths we do not understand. See Chs. 6, 25, 58, 75, 84. The most important exposition of this idea appears in Ch. 52.

19. "Hail Mary, full of grace, the Lord is with thee: blessed art thou among women and blessed is the fruit of thy womb. The Holy Ghost shall come upon thee, and the power of the Most High shall overshadow thee." As is the case with the Lord's Prayer (Ch. 8) and the "Adoramus te" prayer (Ch. 84), Llull gives the text of the prayer in Latin, not Catalan. The Hail Mary prayer (cf. CCC 2676-2677) as found in today's cat-

[3] Speak these salutations to the glorious Virgin often, son, for the greatest pleasure and the greatest honor you can grant her is to greet her with the same greeting that the angel Saint Gabriel brought her from our Lord God. And as soon as the Virgin Mary acceded to the words that Saint Gabriel spoke on behalf of Our Lord, she conceived true God and true man, and she was overshadowed by the Holy Spirit.

[4] All three divine persons participated in that conception, but the person of the Son alone was incarnated in order to demonstrate the diversity that is among the Father and the Son and the Holy Spirit.

[5] The Son of God is He who is a single person with humanity. This humanity was taken from the precious, pure flesh and the sanctified blood of Our Lady Saint Mary.

[6] At the same instant, son, the soul and body of Jesus Christ joined with divine nature. And his soul and his body entered together into the womb of Our Lady. And in the very moment that they entered, the body of Jesus Christ had all its members and all its form. Christ instantly possessed the same wisdom and power and virtue at the moment when He was joined with the Son of God that he would have when He had grown and reached adulthood.

[7] Do not marvel, son, at the words I have just written for you about the conception of the Son of God, for it was a miraculous act, carried out above the laws of nature by divine power, which can do all things.

[8] You are obligated, son, to believe these things I tell you about the conception of the Son of God and you must hold your understanding captive so that you may be lifted up by the light of faith, for just as we are all obligated by nature to die, so, by our fragility and by the sovereign work of the Highest, we are all obligated to believe those things we cannot understand concerning the coming of the Son of God.[20]

---

echism was not fixed in its present form in Llull's day. Llull combines elements of the prayer as it was known in his time with passages taken from Luke 1:28, 35 and 42.

20. With the idea of "holding your understanding captive," Llull means that we should not let our inability to understand the nature of Christ's conception lead our intellect to doubt the truth of it. By holding back any intellectual doubts we may have about the possibility of a virgin conception and Christ's dual nature, we give faith (and the "light" that comes from it) an opportunity to believe even those things we do not

[9] The coming of the Son of God, Jesus Christ, was announced in advance by the holy prophets and the holy fathers, to whom it was revealed by divine inspiration.

[10] Open the eyes of your mind, son, and behold the great honor that the Son of God has granted to all the human lineage in that He wished to take on our nature and He wanted to be in a single person with it.

[11] Remember the goodness, greatness, eternity, power, wisdom, love and the other virtues of our Lord God and see how marvelously and clearly they are manifested in the conception and Incarnation of the Son of God.[21]

[12] Since the sovereign heavenly Son has honored you so greatly by taking on a human nature like yours, dear son, I advise and I beg and I command you, as forcefully as I can, to put all your effort into knowing, loving, honoring, praising, serving our Lord God Jesus Christ so that your words and your life and your works may be pleasing to the God of Glory.

[13] Therefore, if you wish to be honored, honor the Son of God, who has honored you so greatly. And if you wish to love, love Jesus Christ, who has loved you so much. And if you have troubles and sorrow, take consolation in Him who, for your sake, has joined humanity to Deity.

7. ON THE NATIVITY

[1] In the ninth month after the Son of God was incarnated, He wished to be born of Our Lady Saint Mary, from whom he was born, God and man, without pain and without corruption of Our Lady Saint Mary.

---

understand. This theme recurs throughout the *DP* (see n. 18) and is one of its most basic principles: that the understanding (to which Llull seeks to teach many things in this book) ultimately can take us only so far without faith and that, in fact, it may at times be necessary to suppress our rational understanding of the world so that we can see more clearly by the light of faith.

21. Here Llull refers to the "uncreated virtues" once again (see n. 5) but lists only six of them specifically, referring to the others as a group. This practice of providing only an abbreviated list of the uncreated virtues is the one he will follow from here on out in the *DP*, except for Ch. 84, where he recommends adoring each of the uncreated virtues in turn as a framework for prayer and mentions them by name.

[2] Know, son, that Our Lady Saint Mary was a woman poor in worldly riches, but she was rich in virtues and was born of a distinguished lineage. And for that reason, when it pleased the Son of God to be born, He was born in a poor place, that is, in a manger where the beasts fed.

[3] If the sons of kings and of great barons are born in palaces and in chambers and in cloths of gold and silk, the Savior of the world was born in a stable and in the straw that the beasts were eating.

[4] Ah, son! How short were the cloths in which the Son of God was wrapped and how few they were, and by how few persons was He served and attended! But all men who are born are born in blame and in sin, and the Son of God was born to erase and to destroy blame and sin.

[5] When you see, son, some beautiful young woman, poorly dressed, and the sight of her signifies honesty to you, and she carries her beautiful son, also poorly dressed, in her arms, then think about the Nativity of the Son of God who, in the arms of Our Lady Saint Mary, was poorly clothed.[22]

[6] Just like any other small infant, the Son of God allowed Our Lady to care for Him, and His body grew slowly despite the fact that His power and His virtue were in actuality greater than any other power and any other virtue in Creation.

[7] Consider, son, how sweet was the regard between Jesus Christ and Our Lady, who knew Him to be her son and the Lord of all the world, and Jesus Christ, who knew His mother to be the best and the noblest and the most beautiful woman that ever was or ever will be.

[8] Dear son, you were born and came into this world to honor and serve the Son of God, whom I am telling you about, for which reason I admonish you to love Him and to desire to see Him. For if you do not love Him or serve Him, you will act against the very thing for which you have come into this world, and you will be a slave and

---

22. Here Llull proposes that something as incidental as the chance sighting in the street of a poorly dressed, beautiful young woman can "signify" both a moral quality, here, honesty, and offer an opportunity to contemplate the birth of Christ to a poor woman like the one we see. Llull's world, as was the medieval world in general, was full of meanings that went beyond the physical realities of the world and "signified" at both a moral (here, "honesty") and spiritual level ("the Nativity of God's Son"), if one learned to "read" them. This is one of the primary skills Llull seeks to teach his "son" in the *DP*. See Bonner 2007: 261-266.

a captive of eternal suffering, to which you will be condemned by the righteous sentence of our Lord God.

8. ON THE PASSION[23]

[1] The holy Passion of our Lord God Jesus Christ should be recounted to you with love and tears, for that Passion was the heaviest burden of death and pain that ever was and ever could be.

[2] At the time when our Lord Jesus Christ was thirty years old and was preaching to the people of Israel and performing many miracles, it came to pass that the Jews plotted His death. And Judas Iscariot, who was one of the twelve Apostles, sold the Son of God, our Lord Jesus Christ, to the Jews for thirty pieces of silver. And the Son of God, who is the Lord of all that is, allowed Himself to be sold and delivered to death and to suffering in order to deliver His people from the power of the devil.

[3] As the Passion of Jesus Christ drew near, on the day He was to die, Jesus Christ spent the night in prayer, and He revealed His Passion to the Apostles and to those who were with Him, and He asked them to remain in prayer and to say these words: "Pater noster qui es in celis, sanctificetur nomen tuum; adueniat regnum tuum; fiat uoluntas tua sicut in celo et in terra; panem nostrum cotidianum da nobis hodie, et dimitte nobis debita nostra sicut et nos dimittimus debitoribus nostris, et ne nos inducas in temptationem, sed libera nos a malo."[24]

[4] On that night, while Jesus Christ was worshipping as a man and bowing to the holy Deity in order to demonstrate that He was a man, Judas came with a great multitude of armed Jews who took and

---

23. The word "Passion" refers, of course, to the events of surrounding Christ's crucifixion, but also contains the root meaning of the term "passió": "suffering." Unless Llull is referring to the specific event of Christ's Passion, and, in order to avoid confusion with the modern English meaning of "passion" as an overwhelming, often sexual, emotion, I use the word "suffering" here and elsewhere in the translation for "passió."

24. This is the second of the prayers Llull gives in Latin in the text, the Lord's Prayer: "Our Father who art in heaven, hallowed be thy name. Thy kingdom come. Thy will be done on earth, as it is in heaven. Give us this day our daily bread, and forgive us our trespasses, as we forgive those who trespass against us, and lead us not into temptation, but deliver us from evil" (*CCC* 2759).

bound our Lord God Jesus Christ and took Him away to be crucified and killed.

[5] Behold, son, how great was the humility of Jesus Christ, for He, who was and is the Lord of all the world, let Himself be bound by the Jews. See and understand how deeply in His heart He loved the salvation of His people, who were to be saved by His death.

[6] The Apostles and all those who were with Him, all of them, abandoned Him and all of them fled, except for Saint Peter, who alone followed Him. Nevertheless, Peter denied Him three times that night and said that he did not know Him.

[7] Know, son, that the Jews stripped the Savior of all the world and spit in His face and blindfolded Him and beat Him and slapped Him and then they asked Him to say who had beaten Him.[25] They insulted and mocked Him in every way they could, and He had come to save them and to wrest them from the power of the devil.

[8] Until the dawn, they beat and mocked the Son of God without ceasing, and in the morning they handed Him over to Pilate, who was the Procurator of the lord of Rome, and he had Him whipped so violently that His body's so precious skin was all broken and torn and blood ran down His entire body.

[9] When they had whipped Him, they made Him carry the cross to the place where they would crucify Him and nailed Him to it, and then they raised the cross and He hung on the cross so that all could see Him.

[10] They gave Him salt and bile and soot and vinegar to drink and they crowned His head with a crown of thorns so that the spines pierced His head. With a lance, they stabbed Him in the side so hard that they split His heart down the middle.

[11] The Son of God endured that suffering and pain for the love that would save His people and He died so that you could have the law fulfilled by which you can have glory. For if the Son of God had wanted it so, neither the Jews nor all the men nor all the demons that exist could have tortured Him or killed Him, for He is the Lord who holds power over all of them. But because His death was necessary in order for Him to save His people, He agreed to let men torture Him and kill Him.

---

25. Luke 22:64.

[12] Know, Son, that one drop of the blood of Jesus Christ would be sufficient to redeem all mankind, but, because of the great love that He has for us, He wanted all His blood to be spilled for us, for just like a bottle that is so completely shattered that no wine can remain in it, so the body of Jesus Christ was pierced and wounded in so many places that no blood at all remained in it.

[13] Dear son, if you wish to live in glory, weep for the death of your Lord Jesus Christ, and if you cannot weep, you do not love Him as much as your own mother loves you, for she would weep if someone killed you and tortured you before her very eyes.

[14] Son, not only was Jesus Christ mocked on the day that He hung dead on the cross, but He is also scorned and blasphemed and mocked in this time in which we now live, for many are the men who do not weep or die for Him, nor are they thankful to Him for the suffering that He endured for the love of them.[26] And many are the infidels who do not believe in Him and who take His name in vain and who believe that He was a false and deceitful man.

[15] Son, look at the cross and see how it represents to you the Passion of Jesus Christ, who is there with His arms stretched out and who hopes that, just as He died for the love of saving us, in the same way, we will not fear to die to honor Him.

[16] You must die, son, whether you want to or not. Therefore, since you have to die, seek to die to honor the Lord who created you and gives you everything that you possess, and who can give you eternal fire, and who wants to give you glory without end, and who wished to die for love of you.

[17] Do you know why you do not want to die for Jesus Christ? Because death frightens you and because you love being in this world more than being in the other one. Now, if you were Jesus Christ, you would not have wanted to die nor would you have died, since it is a fact that Jesus Christ would not have died had He not wanted to.

[18] How can it be that the Lord wished to die for his vassal but the vassal does not want to die for his Lord? And why do the knights of this world die in battle to honor their lord? And why do people

---

26. With the idea of the "many men who do not die for Him," in this and the following paragraphs, Llull introduces one of the principal themes of the *DP*, and, indeed, of his life-long endeavors: the duty of Christians to be willing, rather, eager to die as martyrs for their faith, especially in the course of efforts to convert those who do not believe in Christianity.

fear death, which is the gateway to the life where all the saints in glory are?

[19] Can you tell me, son, which death is better and sweeter: to die of love or to die of illness? Wouldn't you like to love so much that you desired and knew how and dared to die? And if you do not die out of love, will you know how to desire it?[27]

[20] Know, son, that natural death bears no fruit or reward, nor does the person who does not love know how to die, nor does the person who does not dare to die find himself in a state of salvation.

[21] Remember, son, how many men die trying to accumulate money and to possess the vainglory of this world, and see how many die for love of the Savior, the Lord of all the world, who died out of love for us.

[22] Dear son, since I have many other things to tell you, we must leave this topic, about which many holy and devout words could be spoken pleasingly to our Lord God.

9. He Descended into Hell

[1] In the time of the prophets and of the Holy Fathers, before the Son of God was incarnated and crucified, all the prophets and saints who believed in the coming of the Son of God went to Hell due to original sin. Now, when it pleased the Son of God to be incarnated and born, Saint John the Baptist went as the Son of God's messenger to the saints, who were tormented with infernal punishment, and he revealed the coming of the Son of God to them, by which the saints were made happy and were consoled.[28]

[2] Know and believe, dear son, that when the soul of our Lord Jesus Christ departed from His body, which was dead upon the cross, He immediately descended into Hell and went to Adam and Abra-

---

27. That is, "how will you know how to desire death?" If you are not motivated by love, how will you know how to desire, that is, love, death, which should be desired/ loved as the gateway to eternity as is explained in the following paragraph.

28. See Ch. 99 for a description of this and the other divisions of Hell according to Llull. One possible source of the idea that John the Baptist preceded Christ into Hell to announce to the souls of the righteous that Christ would come to liberate them is the apocryphal *Gospel of Nicodemus*, which is cited extensively in Voragine's *Golden Legend*, compiled at around the same time that Llull was writing the *DP* (Voragine 1993: 1, 223).

ham and the other prophets and saints and dragged them by force from the demons of their prison and took them to heavenly glory, which will have no end.

[3] When Adam saw his Lord and his Creator come to deliver him from the suffering and from the pain in which he had existed for 5,000 years, he said, "These are the hands that made and formed me, and this is the Lord who has remembered us in His glory."[29]

[4] I could not describe to you nor could you imagine, son, the great joy that Adam and the other saints felt. However, you can reflect on how you would feel great joy if someone pulled you from a pit full of fire and sulfur and serpents and darkness and raised you up into heavenly glory.

[5] If, because of one sin by Adam, the souls of the prophets— who did not consent to the sin—were in Hell so long and would have been there forever if the Son of God had not come, remember, son, how great is the justice of God, who punishes sin so strongly. And do not think, son, that the Son of God will come a second time to deliver the sinners who are in Hell.

[6] Know, son, that the Son of God stayed with the body of Jesus Christ on the cross and He descended into Hell with His soul while the body remained in the place where He was crucified. And do you know why? So that it might be signified that the Son of God is in all the places that exist, for all of Creation is not as great as is the Son of God.

10. ON THE RESURRECTION

[1] You must believe, son, that on the Friday when our Lord Jesus Christ was crucified and died to save us, Joseph of Arimathea asked Pontius Pilate for the body of Jesus Christ so that he could bury Him in a very beautiful tomb that he had had made for himself.

[2] Now, since the body of Jesus Christ was given to Joseph of Arimathea and was the greatest gift that he could receive, and since that

---

29. The phrase "Thy hands have made and formed me" is from Psalms 118/119:73, but it may have been traditional for Adam to speak similar words when greeted by Christ in the episode of the Harrowing of Hell. The Chester Mystery Cycle, for example, somewhat later than Llull, has Adam say, when greeted by Christ in Hell, "Me thou madest, Lord, of clay" (Mills 1992: 304).

so precious body was humbled by being put beneath the ground, remember, son, what I am telling you if you wish to have humility.[30]

[3] Know, son, that on the third day He rose and, in order to demonstrate the great mercy of our Lord God, He wished to appear first to Mary Magdalene, who had been a very sinful woman. Because she loved Jesus Christ with great charity and because charity is the greatest virtue that a person can possess, in order to demonstrate that charity is greatly agreeable to Him, the Son of God appeared to Mary Magdalene.

[4] While the Apostles were in a chamber and the doors were closed, our Lord Jesus Christ appeared to them to show that He had risen with a glorified body that has no impediment in going through any place. And in order to demonstrate that He was truly a man, He asked for food.[31]

[5] There is no one who could describe the great joy that was among the Apostles when they saw their risen Lord. And for that reason, when Jesus Christ had left them, Saint Thomas, who was one of the Apostles, arrived and they told him that Jesus Christ had risen. But Saint Thomas answered that he would not believe it until he had put his fingers into the wounds of Jesus Christ. And because faith and belief are pleasing to the Son of God, He brought it about that Saint Thomas had the opportunity to believe. [6] Because Saint Thomas refused to believe, our Lord Jesus Christ appeared to him, saying, "Thomas, put your fingers in my wounds and you will know since you do not want to believe." Thus, in order to show that an understanding that rises up to know the truth is pleasing to our Lord God, He allowed Saint Thomas to put his hands in His side, and Saint Thomas said, "You are my Lord and my God".[32]

[7] Dear son, the Resurrection of our Lord Jesus Christ represented and signified our own resurrection, which will happen on Judgment Day when we will be resuscitated and judged by the Son of God.

---

30. Here, and in the following paragraphs, Llull uses his narration of the events of Christ's Resurrection to point out examples for reflection on human moral virtues such as humility and charity, as well as on God's uncreated virtue of mercy. The chapter is also full of "demonstrations" of Christ's divinity and humanity, of the truth of the Resurrection ("Doubting" Thomas) and of the way in which Christ's resurrection "represents and signifies" our own resurrection on Judgment Day.

31. Cf. John 20:19; Luke 24:33-45.

32. John 20:26.

11. ON THE ASCENSION[33]

[1] Understand, dear son, these words I say to you and believe in them: know that forty days after our Lord Jesus Christ was resurrected, He rose to heaven to sit at the right hand of God the Father. Now, since this world is a place of corruption and defilement and since the holy glorious body of the Son of God is glorified, son, it would not be fitting for such a glorious body to remain here below in this world among us, who have a mortal and corruptible body.

[2] The Ascension of the Son of God signifies the assumption and ascent that your body will make to heaven, son, on Judgment Day if you are the servant and lover and praiser of the Son of God in this world. For, just as the Son of God came into this world to assume our nature and ascended to heaven with it, so all the bodies of those who are—and of those who will have been—His servants in this world and who believe in His Incarnation and who weep to honor His honors will rise into heaven. But if by chance you are a sinful man, son, and are displeasing to our Lord God in this world, and you do not believe in the Articles of the holy Catholic faith, you should know for certain that on Judgment Day your body will descend into Hell and you will remain there with the demons in eternal fire.

[3] Behold, son, how birds fly and rise up through the air and remember what great glory you will have if you can go through the air wherever you want. And see what great pain you will suffer if your body descends into the infernal abyss and into a dark prison and captivity, without consolation and with no escape.

[4] Just as all the angels and all the saints of glory, with a song of very great sweetness and in a great procession, went out to receive our Lord Jesus Christ to honor Him when He rose into glory, so the demons of Hell come out making terrifying faces to greet sinful men when they pass from this world into the other, in order to put them into eternal fire and to torment them.

[5] If you, son, want to ascend into such a high and excellent place as Heaven, it behooves you to begin—while you still have time—

---

33. The word "assumpció" appears in the Catalan title and text of this chapter, but the chapter refers to the event more commonly known as the Ascension. I translate it thus here, in part to avoid confusion with the "assumpció" of Our Lady, the theme of Ch. 51.

to do good works and to take care that sin does not make your body so heavy that it cannot rise into the heights through which those who, by the path of penance carried out through fasting and good works, climb to heavenly glory.

[6] Son, if you wish to ascend to where Jesus Christ is, let your thoughts and your desire ascend to Him, and let your memory descend to the vileness from which you came and the defilement in which you exist in this world, and despise this world so that you may be praised in the other.

[7] The demons fell from that place where all the saints in Paradise reside, and they are in the middle of the earth buried in sulfur and in boiling water and in fiery coals. And to that place where the devils fell will descend and will remain the sinful men who despise and disbelieve in the glory of our Lord God Jesus Christ.

12. ON JUDGMENT

[1] When the number of the saints who will be in glory equals the number of seats left vacant when the demons fell, there will be a general resurrection of the good and the bad, and all will come to hear their final sentence, from which no man can make an appeal or escape.[34]

[2] On that marvelous day, men's bodies, which are ashes and dust in the earth, will be resurrected and await the sentence to be given on Judgment Day by the Son of God. [3] Then one bone will connect with another, and each arm will recover its hand, and each limb will take its form, and each soul will recover that same body in which it lived in this world.

[4] If God created everything that exists from nothing in order to demonstrate His great power, you can reckon, son, that God will wish to bring the dead to life in order to demonstrate His great justice. Each man will come alive to receive the reward for what he has done, and each will come with his book in which will be written the good

---

34. On the various medieval ideas of what would happen to the seats among the angels left vacant by the demons who fell from Heaven, see Keck 1998: 26-27. Llull's idea is that when the number of human saints has filled the vacant seats, this will trigger the general resurrection of humankind.

and the evil that he did in this world, and each will have to render an accounting before the Son of God.

[5] On that day, you will see the Son of God, who will come in the clouds with the angels of Heaven and will show the wounds through which His blood flowed on the day of His Passion when He redeemed the human lineage. [6] That day will be very pleasing to all those who were His servants in this world and will be very horrible and terrifying for those who died in sin.

[7] Dear son, the one who will give the sentence of infinite glory or eternal suffering will be our Lord Jesus Christ, Son of Our Lady Saint Mary, who came into this world to suffer passion and death to restore the human lineage, which had been lost.

[8] That glorious, righteous judge I am telling you about will say, "Go, blessed ones, to the heavenly kingdom to have perpetual glory. And go, damned ones, to the infernal fires to have eternal torment." [9] On that same day, the saints will go to glory and the sinners to suffering. And the saints will be in glory forever and the sinners forever in pain.

[10] Ah, son, and how blessed will be those who make an accounting to the Son of God showing the wounds and the tribulations that they suffered for Him in this world! And how damned will be those who come with their hands empty on that parlous day and who have nothing with which to give an accounting to the Son of God, who will make an accounting to them with the wounds of His body, with the Passion that He suffered for love of them.

[11] On that day, sinners will hate the resurrection, but they will not be able to escape their sentence, for God is in all places and knows all things. They will not be able to hide or resist: neither pleas nor excuses—nothing—will save them.

[12] Beloved you are, son, to my soul, for I remember that I engendered you and I have hope that you will be saved. And you will be hateful to me if I see you a sinner and your sins signify to me that you are damned.[35]

---

35. Although few scholars now believe that Llull wrote this book specifically for his own son Domènec (see Introduction), it is clear, nonetheless, that the relationship between father and son comes up in special ways several times in the *DP*, ways that, as here, suggest that issues concerning the father-son relationship were a significant aspect of the conception of the book. See, for example, Chs. 53.3, 87.6, and 88.6.

[13] It would be a good thing for the man who can be certain that he will have sons who are just, lovers, servants of God, to desire children, but since most men in this world are in sin, for what reason, then, is a child to be desired and why, for his son, would any man lose the grace of God?

On the Ten Commandments

13. You Shall Have One God[36]

[1] A commandment is for you to do what is the lawful thing to be done. The first commandment is to worship, love and serve one god, for it is a fact that there is no more than one god alone.

[2] You must believe, son, that our Lord God gave the Law of the Jews on Mount Sinai, and it was a commandment that no one should worship or serve more than one god, who made and created all that exists.[37]

[3] At that time, son, the Jews were friends of our Lord God, and they believed in Him, and they were opposed to the people who believed in idols of stone, gold or silver or of other things, and each ruler made a figure in the image of a man out of wood or some other thing and they worshiped it as if it were a god.

[4] For that reason, the God of heaven and earth ordered Israel, which was the Jewish people, not to make strange gods, that is, not to make idols, and to worship the one true God alone.

[5] Know, son, that the Law of the Jews was given at the beginning and it is called the Old Law. The law which the Christians now follow is called the New Law, which was given by our Lord Jesus Christ. The New Law is the Gospels that you hear read in the holy Church.

[6] Do you know, son, why God gave the Law to the Jews? So that they would not be in the same error that the other peoples, who believed in idols, were in, and so that among their people there would be prophets to announce the coming of our Lord Jesus Christ, and so

---

36. "I am the Lord your God; you shall not have strange Gods before me." If Llull's heading for a commandment varies significantly from modern usage, I give the versions found as "A Traditional Catechetical Formula" in *CCC* (table following 2051) in the notes.

37. See Chs. 68-72 for a fuller explanation of what Llull means by the Law of the Jews and the Old and New Laws, also discussed three paragraphs below.

that Our Lady Saint Mary, in whom the Son of God would be incarnated, could be born from the Jewish people.

[7] The Old Law had to come before the New Law, just as the foundation must come before the chamber. And because the Jews do not repent for their guilt in bringing about the death of our Lord Jesus Christ, they are in error, and they think they follow the Law of Moses, which law they do not follow because they do not follow what the Old Law signifies about the New.[38]

[8] Dear son, do not hold more than one god in your heart, for those who love certain things more than the true God—who created you and who will judge you for heavenly glory or eternal torment—hold many false gods in their hearts.

[9] If there were any flaw in that God whom I command you to worship and serve and He were not sufficient for what you need, it would be lawful for me to command you to believe in that god who could offer you what you need. But because the God of Glory has all perfection in Himself, He has the plenitude to be your perfection.

[10] Do you know, son, why there are many men in this time in which we live who make gods out of idols? Because they do not have knowledge of the true God, who is in glory. And do you know why we who believe in the God of Glory do not go to preach and to show them the God of all the world? Because we are afraid of death and we fear to die while teaching about the God who gives perpetual life in His glory divine.

14. YOU SHALL NOT SWEAR FALSELY[39]

[1] The second commandment, son, is not to take the name of God in vain. Those who swear on God or on His works take his name in vain, and they lie and say things contrary to the truth.

[2] Know, son, that those people love the thing about which they are swearing falsely more than they love the God on whom they swear.

---

38. This is the idea that the Jews are unable to correctly read their own scriptures because they are "blind" to the prefigurations of the coming of Christ that are contained, "typologically," therein. See n. 165.

39. "You shall not take the name of the Lord your God in vain."

And because that is a great sin, God made the commandment that no man should swear falsely.

[3] If it is not a lawful thing, son, for you to swear "God help me" or "God bless me," how much less lawful it is for you to swear "may God not help me" or "God damn me."

[4] Remember the first commandment, son, when you want to swear an oath, for the person who lies knowingly makes a god out of the thing for which he is lying.

[5] The truthful man has no need to swear an oath and the lying man has no qualms about swearing many oaths.

[6] Dear son, truth in your mouth is much better than gold or silver laid up in a coffer by swearing false oaths. Man is given a mouth to speak the truth and a will to hate lies.

[7] Do you know, son, why a lying man swears many oaths? Because he is not believed when he swears a single oath.

[8] Son, do not swear on your head, for you would not give it for all the king's treasures. And do not swear on your soul, for you do not know, nor can you imagine, the glory and the power that you could have in it.

[9] Son, do not swear on your father or your mother, for you cannot give them as much good as you have received from them. And why do you swear on your faith when you lie, if you have no faith?

[10] Son, if you want to swear, say "it is true" or "it is certain" or "truly," for with these oaths you can have success in everything you buy or sell or affirm if you are truthful. And if you are a liar, you cannot have success through any oath.

[11] If one single drop of blood from the body of our Lord Jesus Christ is worth more than all the created things that exist, imagine, son, what a great sin it is to swear on the head of God and on the mouth or the belly or the liver of God.

15. YOU SHALL WORSHIP[40]

[1] To worship is to make a holy day on which you remember God and prayer and the deeds that you have done during the week.

---

40. "Remember to keep holy the Lord's Day."

[2] In that time, son, when God created the world in six days, He rested on the seventh day to signify that man should rest physically on the seventh day, and that—both spiritually and physically—he should show reverence and honor to our Lord God. For that reason, when He gave the Old Law to Moses, the God of Glory made the commandment that all the people of Israel should worship on Saturday so that on that day they would not work on worldly things and so that on that day they would pray to God.[41]

[3] When it pleased the Son of God to be incarnated and He had given the New Law to the Christian people, the day of worship on Saturday was moved to Sunday to signify that, as God—may He be blessed!—began to create the world on Sunday, it was fitting that the day for worship take place on Sunday, when the Son of God redeemed the human lineage by re-creation.[42]

[4] Know, son, that at the beginning when a person begins to do some act, he has the intention of bringing that act to completion. Therefore, it is appropriate, according to divine ordination, that on that day of the week on which the world was begun and created there be a celebration in which a person thanks God for the beginning of His work and for its completion.

[5] The day of worship, son, is for you go to church to obey and honor the priest in God's stead and hear the words he speaks to you about God and confess all your sins to the priest and offer him your body and your soul and give him some of the goods of this world that God has given and entrusted to you.

[6] That holy day, son, is a day of prayer and contrition and of weeping for the sins that you have committed, and on that day in particular, you should remember the vanities of this world and the glory of Paradise and the infernal punishments.

[7] Blame and error have increased in the world, son, and full are the roads by which men go to suffer infinite torments. And, for that reason, there are more banquets and sins accumulate more abundantly on holy days than on other days. On that holy day, son, which God has reserved for Himself during the week so that man can honor Him more than on the other days, on that day, son, people commit

---

41. See Chs. 69-70.
42. See Ch. 3 and n. 12.

more vanities in eating and drinking, and in speaking and in running around and in other things like these.

[8] Dear son, it is a commandment in the law that your slave and your ox also rest one day in the week so that it may be signified that, just as your slave and your ox rest on your holy day, in the celebration of this world is signified the glorious celebration in the other world in the presence of our Lord God.[43]

16. YOU SHALL HONOR YOUR FATHER AND YOUR MOTHER

[1] You must honor your father and your mother, son, for this is God's commandment, signifying that, just as you are obligated to honor your father and your mother because you came from them and they have raised you, you are obligated to honor God, who has created you and who sustains you, and from whom everything that exists has taken its beginning.

[2] Love and fear accord with honor, for dishonor is created by hate and contempt. Therefore, son, you should not hold your father or your mother in contempt. Do not hate them by loving the possessions that they possess from the goods of this world.[44] For that reason, God wants you to honor your father and your mother.

[3] You will understand, son, that God wants you to be honored, for in honoring your father and your mother, you gain honor, and

---

43. Llull's point is that slaves, who might well be of a different faith, should also be excused from work on the Christian holy day. In Llull's analogical reasoning, the "celebration" of a day of rest by non-Christians is to the Christian celebration of a holy day in this world as the Christian "celebration" in this world is to the eternal celebration in God's presence in Heaven.

Slavery was common in the Mediterranean world of the time and we know that Llull himself owned at least one slave: the "Saracen" he purchased to teach him Arabic (*Vita coetanea* [Llull 1980]: §11-§13; hereafter: *VC*; I use the translation by Bonner in Llull 2010, citing by the standard section numbers). Mummey & Reyerson (2008) find the presence in Mallorca in the later centuries of the Middle Ages of "enslaved, indentured, and freed populations of Greeks, Tartars, Circassians, Muslims, and Sardinian prisoners of war living and working in public and private spaces alongside the indigenous population of Christians and Jews" (917). Domínguez & Gayà observe that "the incidence of slavery was much higher [in Mallorca] than in other parts of the Mediterranean" (2008: 32).

44. The criticism here is of those who love their parents' possessions, which they are eager to inherit, more than they love of their parents for themselves.

in dishonoring them, you are dishonored and despised by the people.

[4] If, through your father's and your mother's labors, son, you have riches or honors, your father and your mother take pleasure in your honor. Remember, then, that you are duty-bound to do them honor.

[5] If it were a fault to honor prior things and the beginning, it would be licit, son, not to honor God. Therefore, if you do an evil deed or commit a fault against your father and your mother, know that you are dishonoring the God of Heaven.

[6] As the strength of your body in this world increases, son, the strength of your father's and your mother's bodies weakens and fails. Therefore, if helping the weak and disempowered honors the strong, son, you can have honor in honoring your father and your mother, which will be pleasing to our Lord God.

17. You Shall Not Commit Homicide

[1] Homicide is to destroy and kill men whom God wants to live. Therefore, son, so that your will is not contrary to God's will, He commands you not to commit homicide.

[2] If God does not want you to kill another person, then God does not want you to kill yourself. And if the beasts and birds—who are without reason—do not kill themselves, how much more unfitting is it, son, for you—who possess reason—to kill yourself!

[3] Dear son, one man can kill another man but he cannot give life back to the person he has killed. Therefore, if you kill a man and God asks you for the thing you have taken from that man, what will you do?

[4] Many times it happens that in killing a man one kills his soul in eternal fire because one is the occasion for the wrath and the ill will in which the person whom one kills dies, for which wrath and ill will, God kills the soul of that person in infernal fire.[45]

---

45. Since "wrath" is one of the Seven Deadly Sins, the person who dies in a state of wrath is condemned to Hell as a result; the person who kills him is the cause of the wrath in which the murdered person dies, and is, therefore, responsible for the death of his soul.

[5] Dear son, if God commands you not to kill the body, how much more does He command you not to kill a soul in sin, because it is a fact that the soul is much better than the body.

[6] A vest or a cloak gets old, but homicide does not grow old in the fear of the person who kills or in the wrath of the family of the person one has killed.[46]

[7] Dear son, do not wish to be a murderer and do not wish to kill any man, for many men who plan to kill another person die before they can commit the act, and God kills many men so that they will not kill another.[47]

[8] Dear son, do not wish to destroy or kill what God creates and sustains in life or the reason for which God incarnated Himself and died, because, if you do, you are holding God and His works in contempt.

[9] From the moment man is born, he begins to die, for each day he draws nearer to death. For that reason, son, there is no need for you to kill another person: leave death to kill the person and pardon him from death for the love of God.[48]

18. You Shall Not Commit Adultery

[1] Son, fornication is lust, which is filthiness of the body and the mind. In place of that filthiness, you should choose chastity and virginity.

[2] Dear son, do you know why God commands you not to commit adultery? So that, with obedience and cleanness of body and mind, you fight your body every day against the delights of the flesh, which are engendered in such filthy matter that it is a horrible thing for them to be named.

---

46. In other words, the murderer will always have to be looking over his shoulder since the family of the murdered person will surely seek retribution.

47. That is: people who are plotting the death of another person may die "first," "beforehand," before they can commit the murder because God takes their lives in order to prevent the crime from taking place.

48. That is, since the person you wish to kill will die in due course anyway, you can afford to "forgive" that person the death you wish to visit upon him, out of love for God.

[3] Consider, son, the cleanness that is in the flower and in the virtuous soul and think on the great filthiness that is in the act of lust, which I do not dare to name or write so that I do not name or write such ugly words.

[4] God has commanded you, son, not to commit adultery, for fornication destroys the body that God has created, and it destroys the riches that God has entrusted to man, and it destroys the understanding of the soul, which is the mirror in which God shows His virtues and His works.

[5] Lust casts loyalty and truth and God and the angel that God has given man as his guardian from his heart and puts falseness and lies and the devil into that same heart.[49]

[6] Through lust, women fall under the wrath of God and of their husbands and of their family, and through lust they make their children despised among the people.

[7] Dear son, lust makes the nations wage war and it makes men—and women—kill and wound, and it makes them destroy and burn towns and castles, and it makes bastards inherit illegally.[50]

[8] I could not tell you, son—nor would I know how to—the evils that come from lust. And because lust causes so much evil and is the occasion for so many sins, our Lord God has commanded man to be the enemy of lust and the lover of chastity, by which chastity he may be called into the glory of God.

19. You Shall Not Steal

[1] God has commanded man not to steal, for if a person possesses something that he has stolen and does not return it, he cannot be saved, and he will be condemned to be tormented by demons for as long as God shall be in Heaven.

[2] Dear son, do not steal, for the One who created you—and from whose sentence you cannot escape—does not wish it. And if you need something, do not steal it, but ask God for it: He can

---

49. For more on the guardian angel, see Ch. 98.
50. That is, if lust has led a woman to commit adultery, an illegitimate child who is the result of that adultery might be mistaken for a legitimate child and inherit his father's rank or possessions "illegally."

give it to you just as He gave it to the person from whom you wish to steal it.

[3] Do not be a lover of vainglory, son, for such people steal from God the goods and the benefits that they have received from Him by attributing them to their own achievement.

[4] If it is a bad thing, son, to steal money or cloth or other things like these, which you can return, then it is a much worse thing to steal time and reputation and other things like these, which you cannot give compensation for, or return.

[5] Because of theft, gallows are built to hang thieves, and because of their thievery, they cut off the nose and the ears of thieves and whip them through the streets. Because of theft, they torture people so that they give back the things they have stolen.

[6] Theft, son, is to steal what God has given. Theft shames you before the people and makes you despise the great generosity and mercy of our Lord God.

[7] Know, son, that God commands you not to steal so that you have hope in Him and you ask Him for things and you give to your neighbor so that God multiplies the gift for you.

[8] It is a better thing, son, to be a fearful poor person than a rich and proud thief and it is a better thing to say "no" than to steal in order to give.[51]

[9] Before you become disobedient or a thief or disagreeable to God and to the people, rather go begging from door to door for the love of our Lord God![52]

20. YOU SHALL NOT BEAR FALSE WITNESS

[1] Know, son, that to witness is to present to a judge the testimony by which he will award merit or punishment. For that reason, son, God commands man not to bear false witness, because, through false witness, those who deserve to prosper are punished and those who deserve punishment prosper.

---

51. That is, it is better to say "no" to someone who is asking you for something than to steal something in order to be able to give it to them.

52. Llull neatly embeds here, in his usual end of chapter mention of God, the common plea of those begging alms: "Per amor de Déu" ("For the love of God"); see also Chs. 35, 84, and 98.

[2] Defamation and false witness are in accord against truth, and praise and false witness are in accord against truth and justice. Therefore, for that reason, son, take care not to be a blamer or a praiser of anything in which there is false witness.[53]

[3] God wants you not to bear false witness so that you may be a witness to God's truth, in opposition to which there are many who speak ill because they are evil and many who speak ill out of weakness and fear.

[4] Dear son, desire to die giving true witness of God, who created and re-created you.[54] And if you are afraid of death, remember how God has honored the Apostles and the other martyrs in Heaven and on earth because they gave true witness of His praise and His honors.

[5] To deny the truth of your God and not to speak His praise in the places where you hear Him denied and despised is to bear false witness about your God, for the final cause for which God created you does not follow from this; rather it signifies, falsely, that God has an imperfect nobility.[55]

[6] Ah, son! It is so easy to say that one should not bear false witness, but it would be so very difficult to tell about all the people who bear false witness about God!

[7] The Son of God came among us here below to give true witness about the glorious heavenly Father. Therefore, if someone wishes to resemble Him, he must not be a slave of death, which makes man fearful to confess the truth before those who bear false witness concerning our Lord God.[56]

---

53. That is, both praise and "defamation" can be false. Llull demonstrates this possibility in *Felix, or the Book of Wonders* (hereafter, *Felix*) where he criticizes the minstrels "who praise what should be blamed and blame what should be praised." See *SW* 2.806-807. Cf. Ch. 74 and n. 200.

54. Cf. Ch. 4.

55. Llull points out that even the failure to praise God amongst the enemies of the faith is a form of false witness. Man's final cause, which should also be man's "first intention" as defined in Ch. 92, is "serving, loving, knowing" God.

56. For Llull "slaves of death" are the people who fear to die as martyrs witnessing the truth of God. Martyrs resemble the Son of God who undertook death in order to give true witness of the "glorious heavenly Father."

21. You Shall Not Covet Your Neighbor's Wife

[1] Covetousness is to desire, with sadness, someone else's goods.[57] For that reason, son, our Lord has made the commandment not to covet your neighbor's wife, for sadness in the desire of the soul blinds the eyes of the understanding.

[2] Dear son, each person is the neighbor of another person in their human nature. And because it is the express commandment that you love your neighbor as you love yourself, son, the God of Glory commands that no one covet his neighbor's wife, in which commandment is signified another commandment, that is, that you love your neighbor and yourself.[58]

[3] Coveting your neighbor's wife, son, is to despise and hate your neighbor and to despise his wife and his wife's family. And because our Lord God wants us not to despise that creature that is like us in nature and wants us to know that our own wife possesses the same thing for giving carnal delight that our neighbor's wife possesses, God commands you not to covet your neighbor's wife.

[4] Dear son, so that you can be obedient to God's commandments and are not covetous, remember the filth that you can understand, and understand what a grievous thing it would be for you if someone desired your wife and dishonored her from the order of matrimony.[59] And consider if it is worthwhile to lose God's love and glory for such great filthiness and to have torment in eternal fire.

[5] Son, if you were nobler than everything that God has given you, it would follow that you were not created. Therefore, son, since you are a creature created out of nothing and because you would return to nothing if God took His grace away from you, understand that God commands you not to be covetous in order to signify that you are a creature created by our Lord God.

---

57. The connection between envy and sadness is quite literally "proverbial" in Llull: his collection of proverbs known as the *Proverbs by Ramon* (*Proverbis de Ramon;* Ch. 217, #15) includes "all envy causes sadness" ("Tota enveja dóna tristor"; *ORL* 14.240).

58. This is one of four passages in the *DP* (out of 100 in total from Llull's works) that the 14th-century Inquisitor General of the Aragonese Inquisition, Nicolau Eymerich, found to be heretical. His condemnations of Llull were eventually overturned. See also Chs. 24.2-3, 28.3 and 54.10 for other portions of the *DP* condemned by Eymerich.

59. See Ch. 28, on the sacrament and the order of matrimony.

22. You Shall Not Covet Your Neighbor's Goods

[1] Do you know, son, why God, who is the perfection of all goods, has made the commandment not to covet your neighbor's goods? So that you can have hope in God that He will give you goods like those that He has given your neighbor.

[2] Son, do not covet your neighbor's goods, for God has given them to him and wants him to have them. For if God had wanted, He could have given those same goods to you. Thus, if you want to have what God has not wished to give you, you make your own will contrary to the will of God.

[3] Do not covet the goods of others, son, for if you had them, you do not know if you would have even a single hour in which to possess them. And if all the temporal goods in this world were yours, they could not give fulfillment to the desire of your soul.

[4] Son, the goods of this world are not desirable in themselves, rather they exist to serve God. Therefore, if you are covetous of your neighbor's goods, your desire is to serve yourself in opposition to the will of God.

[5] Do not covet your neighbor's goods, son, for he has need of them. In those goods that you want there is a flaw in that they are corruptible and are possessed through labor and suffering and fear.

[6] Through covetousness, the demons, who were covetous of God's glory, fell from heaven. Therefore, son, if you wish to climb into the glory from which the demons were cast down, it will be necessary for you to climb by means of things that are contrary to covetousness.

[7] The poverty in worldly goods that our Lord Jesus Christ and Our Lady Saint Mary and the Apostles had in this world preaches to you and teaches you not to be covetous of the goods of this world, for if our Lord Jesus Christ had wanted to have them, He could have had many and He could have given many of them to Our Lady Saint Mary, whom He loved so much, and to the Apostles and to the other saints, who suffered so much torment in this world for love of Him.

[8] The greater your riches, son, the more you will be held responsible if you do not do the good that you could do with them and the more you will be blamed and obliged to hear the cruel sentence of our Lord God.

[9] If you do not do as much good as you could with the goods that you possess, why are you covetous of the goods that you do not

have? And why does covetousness make you love your neighbor's treasure, which is not as like you as is your neighbor?[60]

[10] Consider, son, the great sins that covetous men commit, for covetousness makes them miserly, false, mendacious, treacherous and deceitful. And covetousness makes them say disparaging things to people, falsely, and it makes them despair of the mercy of God.

---

60. Here is one of Llull's arguments based on "likeness": we should most love the things most like us; therefore, we should love our neighbor, who is a human being like us, more than we love his goods, which are less like us in nature. For other arguments based on "likeness" see Chs. 46, 62, 63, 64, 80 and the supplemental chapter on knights following Ch. 80.

On the Seven Sacraments of the Holy Church

23. First, On Baptism

[1] A sacrament of the Church, son, is a granting of one's heart and is a miraculous sanctified mystery through which the path to heavenly glory is illuminated.

[2] The first sacrament of the holy Church, son, is baptism, which is a cleansing from the general blame that fell upon the human lineage by the act of original sin.

[3] You should know, son, that there are three types of baptism. The first is of water, which was signified at the time of the flood when all the world was renewed and cleansed by water.

[4] The second type of baptism is of fire, and this baptism of fire was signified in the sacrifice that the prophets and patriarchs made to God when they performed the holocaust.[61] And it was signified by the three children who were placed in the fire and did not burn, as the holy prophet Daniel recounts.[62]

[5] The third type, son, is of blood, and this baptism of blood was signified in the Old Law by circumcision and by the death of the Innocents, whom Herod slaughtered because he was hoping to kill Jesus Christ.

[6] Dear son, these three types of baptism were not fulfilled until the Son of God came and was baptized of water and of blood, and He was conceived by the fire of the Holy Spirit in the womb of the glorious Virgin, Our Lady Saint Mary.[63]

---

61. That is, burnt animal offerings, a form of sacrifice described in Genesis 8:20.

62. This is the story of Shadrach, Meshach and Abednego in the fiery furnace, told in the third book of Daniel.

63. The purpose here is to show that Christ received all three types of baptism: he was baptized of water by John the Baptist, he was baptized of blood by his Crucifixion, and his conception by the "fire" or "flame" of the Holy Spirit in the womb of the Virgin Mary constituted his baptism of fire.

[7] Son, after your birth you were taken to the church to be baptized with water sanctified by the power of words and by the intention in the heart of the priest who baptized you and in the godparents who carried you to the font and held you.

[8] At the time you were baptized, son, your godparents promised on your behalf that you would renounce the devil and affirmed that you wished to be a Christian and that you committed yourself to serve God and to follow the path of our Lord God Jesus Christ.

[9] Dear son, baptism of fire is signified by a thought in the mind that desires baptism. Therefore, because sometimes one cannot obtain water, it is necessary for there to be a baptism of desire in human thought whenever it may be required for the conversion of the infidels who are converting to the holy Catholic faith.[64]

[10] Baptism of blood is such a noble and marvelous thing that it cleanses a man from every fault and from every sin, for the blessed martyr who dies in order to love and honor the holy Catholic faith could not make his body suffer any more—nor could he give any more—than when he delivers himself to death to honor his glorious God.[65]

24. ON CONFIRMATION

[1] The sacrament of confirmation, son, is a figure of and a consenting to the baptism that you have already received. At confirmation, the bishop—who is your spiritual father—confirms you and gives you a blow on the cheek so that you remember your confirmation, and he ties a band on your head so that it may be manifest to the people that you have confirmed the holy sacrament of baptism.

[2] This sacrament of confirmation was created so that children, when they have reached the age of understanding, reaffirm what their godparents promised on their behalf on the day they were bap-

---

64. Llull shows here that "baptism of fire," "the baptism of the Holy Spirit" and "baptism of desire" mean the same thing. According to the present-day catechism of the Catholic Church (as applied to catechumens who may die before they are baptized), the baptism of fire/desire rests on the catechumens' "explicit desire to receive it [baptism], together with repentance for their sins, and charity" (*CCC* 1259). The "thought in the mind that desires baptism," refers, then, to this necessary explicit desire (the *votum* or mental vow) to receive baptism.

65. Here again, Llull promotes Christian martyrdom as the highest form of baptism: baptism of blood, resembling Christ's sacrifice on the Cross.

tized, on which day those children did not have sufficient understanding to be able to consent to the sacrament of baptism.

[3] Dear son, when you receive the sacrament of confirmation, the godparents who held you at the font and who promised for you that you would keep the sacrament of baptism are freed from their promise. And you, son, make a sacrifice of yourself to God and offer yourself to be God's servant and the defender of the holy Christian faith.

[4] The evil Christians who, out of fear of death or poverty or false belief or for some other reason, deny and do not believe in the holy Catholic faith, those Christians, son, reject and break the sacrament of baptism and all the other sacraments that are necessary in the Catholic faith. And for that reason, they cannot partake of the power of baptism, and when they die, demons take them to eternal fire.

[5] Dear son, by the virtue of this sacrament and by all the other sacraments of the holy Church, you take part in all the benefits that are created in the holy Church. Therefore, strive as much as you can to keep and preserve this sacrament and all the others, [6] for if you break the vows you make when you receive the sacrament, you make yourself a companion of the demons and sinners in Hell and you abandon the company of the angels and saints in glory.

[7] You can remember, son, how beloved and agreeable the sacraments of the holy Church were to our Lord God, for out of love of them, He sent His Son in human nature. In this nature, He was crucified and killed so that the holy Church could be established and illuminated. Therefore, if you, son, go against the sacraments of the holy Church, you can imagine what a great sin you commit and how very deeply it is displeasing to our Lord God.

25. On Sacrifice[66]

[1] Dear son, the holy sacrifice of the body of Jesus Christ is invisible grace enacted in visible form, that is, in the sacred host, which is transubstantiated into the true flesh of our Lord Jesus Christ.

---

66. The present-day name for this sacrament is "Eucharist." This sacrament can also be referred to as "the Holy Sacrifice" or "holy sacrifice of the Mass," "since it completes and surpasses all the sacrifices of the Old Covenant" (CCC 1330) or, as Llull would say, "the Old Law" (see Ch. 69).

[2] This most marvelous holy sacrifice, through which we can save ourselves, was instituted, son, on the Thursday of the Last Supper, when our Lord God Jesus Christ was eating with the Apostles and He blessed and divided the bread and the wine and He said that the bread was His flesh and the wine was His blood.

[3] Dear son, by the virtue of these words that God Jesus Christ placed in the bread and the wine, the host and the wine that you see raised at the altar become the body of Jesus Christ when the priest sings mass and says the words that Jesus Christ said on the Thursday of the Last Supper.

[4] To demonstrate, son, that the God of Glory is the Lord of nature, He performs an act that is beyond the power of nature when He makes the holy glorious body of Jesus Christ exist in the form of bread and wine.

[5] If your eyes tell you, son, that the sacred host is bread, the power and wisdom and love and the other virtues of our Lord God tell your soul that that sacred host and sacred wine are truly the very body of Jesus Christ, who, in order to save you, hung on the cross on Good Friday at Easter.

[6] Dear son, because your eyes are created things and God's virtues are the Creator, and because a creator is a nobler and truer thing than the thing created, for that reason, son, you must believe more in the testimony that God gives with His virtue than in the testimony that nature gives through your eyes and your other physical senses.

[7] Understand, son, that the eyes lie about some things, for according to corporeal vision, it seems that the sea and the earth touch the sky, and the sick person's sense of taste finds bitterness in the apple and in honey and in other foods that are sweet.[67]

[8] Dear son, God's virtue cannot lie, for there is nothing that can make it lie. But the five bodily senses often lie because certain other things that are more powerful than they are cause them to lie. Therefore, since God's virtues tell your soul by the light of faith that you must believe that the sacred host and the sacred wine are the holy body of Jesus Christ, and your corporeal senses falsely deny what God's virtues are telling you, and because the corporeal senses are

---

67. Llull explains the physiological reasons for a sick person's confused sense of taste in Ch. 78.

mendacious and God's virtues cannot lie, you are obligated to believe what God's virtues signify to you by their very virtue.[68]

[9] Do you know why God wants you to believe that the body of Jesus Christ is in the sacred host and commands you to believe this way? So that you may believe more through God's virtues than you can understand through your physical senses, for by the lifting up above the five corporeal senses that your understanding undergoes by the light of faith, it climbs higher to understand greater things through God's virtues than it can understand through the workings of nature or through the bodily senses.[69]

[10] So that God's great power and wisdom and love can be demonstrated each day and in many places in the world, God wants the sacrament at the altar to be true, for a created thing can have no better way of understanding that the power and the wisdom and God's other virtues exist in very great perfection than it does by means of the sacrifice at the altar. And so, son, you can understand that this thing must be established among the sacraments of the holy Church so that man can better understand the great virtues of our Lord God.

26. ON PENANCE

[1] Penance, son, is contrition of the heart and anguish of the soul for the sins that you have committed, which you repent and vow never to do again, and you punish your body with fasts and prayers and pilgrimages and with other things like these.[70]

---

68. An important principle of Llull's understanding of the human soul is the stark divide between its physical, corporeal powers and its spiritual capacities (see Figure 2). On the inability of the physical senses to perceive spiritual objects, see also Chs. 32 and 85.

69. Just as the physical senses are limited in their ability to perceive spiritual truths, so, too, the understanding—one of the powers of the rational soul that is, in theory, able to understand spiritual truths—is also limited and must sometimes be helped along by faith in order to achieve full understanding of God's virtues. For a list of other appearances of this important principle, see Ch. 5, n. 18.

70. Lull's "conversion to penance," as it is described in the *VC* §1, partakes very much of the idea that the sacrament of penance is also a "sacrament of conversion," a "second conversion," in fact, of a previously baptized individual (Cf. *CCC* 1423-1429). Among the types of penance that Llull lists here, we know that he went on two pilgrimages shortly after his "conversion to penance": to the shrine of Saint Mary of Rocama-

[2] It is a great sacrament and a powerful one, son, the sacrament of penance, for through penance, all the demons and all the sinners in Hell could be delivered from their never-ending torments if only they could do penance for even a single hour.

[3] Through the penance that a man does in this world, son, he escapes the infernal punishments and the fire of Purgatory. And when a man passes from this world to the other, he arrives in heavenly glory, which lasts for all time.

[4] Dear son, since penance causes all the sins that you commit to be forgiven and all the blessings of Paradise to be given, while you are in this world, son, do penance, for in the other world, the sentence is given for glory eternal or fire infernal.

[5] In that time, son, when our Lord Jesus Christ was in this world and went around with the Apostles, He gave the keys of penance to Saint Peter in the person of our holy Mother Church and He said that everything that Saint Peter bound and loosed on the earth through God's virtue would be bound and loosed in the heavens.[71]

[6] Through the power that God gave Saint Peter, son, the holy Apostolic Father, who holds the place of Saint Peter, and the priests, who stand in the place of the pope, have power to give penance. And for that reason, people go to priests for confession to receive their penance from them.

[7] The reason why God wants man to do penance is so that he may trust in the great mercy of our Lord God and so that God has a reason to pardon His sinners who submit themselves to endure the afflictions given as penance.

[8] If you wish to lessen the afflictions that are bitter to your body in penance, think of the infernal torments and of the glory of Paradise, for then the sufferings that you endure in the act of penance will seem pleasing to you.[72]

[9] To sin and to hold the holy sacrament of penance in contempt, son, is to have contempt for the glory of Paradise and for the

---

dour in southern France and to the tomb of Saint James in Santiago de Compostela in northwestern Iberia (*VC* §9). *VC* §11, says he abandoned "the grand style of life which he had previously led and put on a lowly habit of the coarsest cloth he could find" on his return to Majorca following these pilgrimages.

71. Matthew 18:18.

72. In the final two chapters of the *DP* Llull gives specific instructions on how to contemplate the punishments of Hell and the glory of Paradise.

infernal torments and for the companionship of angels and the saints in glory and our Lord God.

27. ON ORDERS

[1] Holy orders is a sacrament that is given to the officials of the holy Church, for our Mother Church, son, is such a holy thing that its officials must have holiness and ordinations through which their Mother Church may be honored.[73]

[2] It would be a great vileness and a great disorder if the officials of the holy Church were sinful men and men without order and men ignorant of the Holy Scriptures of the holy Church. For that reason, son, the bishop, when he establishes orders, orders the subdeacon to read the Epistle and the deacon to read the Gospel and the priest to sing the mass.

[3] The bishop establishes other orders, son, which the altar boys who serve the priest who sings mass receive. Now, all these people are officials of the holy Church and each of them, when he receives this sacrament, promises to be a praiser and honorer and a person committed to the exaltation and honoring of the holy Church.

[4] Know, son, that the most honored office—and the one in which there is the most virtue and holiness—is that of the priest, for the priest alone has the power that, by his words, holy bread and wine are transubstantiated into the true flesh and true blood of our Lord Jesus Christ.

[5] The priest alone, son, has the power to pardon your sins. And the priest stands in the place of Jesus Christ in this world. The Holy Apostle, who is a priest, should be the lord of all the world, and all the kings and the princes of this world ought to obey him.[74]

---

73. Holy orders involves the process of incorporation of an individual into an "order" (*ordo*) such as the "order of the priesthood" (*ordo presbyterorum*) through the process of "ordination" (*CCC* 1537-1538). In the following paragraphs, Llull explores the semantic relations among these words and ideas (these are not simply "puns" for Llull): "order," "disorder," "being without order," "establishing order." He also makes concrete references to specific types of orders existing within the Church hierarchy: the order of deacons (*ordo diaconorum*) and the order of attendants at the mass (*ordo acolytorum*), for example.

74. That is, the Pope.

[6] Remember, son, what a great thing it is to be a priest, for the kings and the other barons and all the men who exist should kiss the hand and the foot of the priest when he sings the mass.

[7] Dear son, as God gives a nobler order to the priest than to any other man, the priest is more obligated to love God and to thank God for the grace and honor that He gives him in this world.

[8] If orders, son, are more greatly honored in a priest than are all the other orders in this world in the other men who are not priests, you can remember, son, the great responsibility and the great obligation that priests have to be good so that they may be pleasing to our Lord Jesus Christ.

28. ON MATRIMONY

[1] Matrimony, son, is an ordered physical and spiritual union for the purpose of having children who will be the servants of our Lord God and who will receive the grace and blessing of God.[75]

[2] In that time when God had created the world and had placed Adam and Eve in the earthly paradise, He created the marriage of Adam and Eve. Therefore, son, you are obligated—and all those who desire to be in the order of matrimony are obligated—to have that same intention when you are in the order of matrimony with which God created matrimony in the earthly paradise.

[3] You are obligated, son, to be in either the order of matrimony or a religious order, for any other status is in discord with the final intention for which you were created.

[4] Dear son, just as God has given you eyes to see and a tongue to speak, He gives you a woman to serve you when you take her for a wife. For just as your members are instruments ordained to serve your body, your wife is an instrument ordained to serve you.

[5] When, dear son, you enter the order of marriage, you also give yourself to serve your wife, so that both of you together are the serv-

---

75. When Llull says that marriage is "ordered," he means that it, too, like the priesthood, belongs, through the sacrament of marriage, to a Christian order (see Ch. 27 and Ch. 82), in this case, what we still call today "the Order of Matrimony." The ideas of ordering, ordaining, disorder (that is, acting outside the order of matrimony) found in this chapter all stem from the idea that marriage is an *ordo* (see n. 75).

ants of God in such a way that God is loved and known and praised by
both of you.

[6] Matrimony, son, resides in the power of words and in the intention in your mind, and it is a vow and a promise that you cannot
break without the consent of your wife. For that reason, son, many
men are deceived by many bad women and are falsely bound by the
order of matrimony, from which bonds they cannot escape except in
death.[76]

[7] Be ordered, son, in keeping the order of matrimony, for without the ordered state you cannot maintain it. And order your wife as
much as you can to be your helper in keeping this order, for a bad
woman and a disordered one make men wander and stray from the
order of matrimony.

[8] Charity and fear and humility, truth, justice and the other virtues like these are helpers in keeping the order of matrimony. And
an excess of fancy clothing and made-up faces and disordered
thoughts make men break the sacrament of matrimony.

[9] The honors of a good family or wealth in possessions or money are not as powerful in preserving the order of matrimony as is a
good upbringing. Therefore, dear son, when you take a wife, do not
covet a great dowry or a beautiful appearance or status, for all these
things are not as strongly in accord with the order of matrimony as is
a good upbringing.

[10] Dear son, according to whether a man's body is big or small,
his members are in proportion to it, for men who are small have small
hands and small feet, and men who are big have bigger hands and
bigger feet than small men. This, son, signifies to you that, just as God
gives each body the members that are appropriate to it, so a man
should take an appropriate wife with regards to age and to the status
of her parents.[77]

[11] Just as in the number 5, 3 is in greater quantity than 2, son,
man is better and nobler than woman in the order of matrimony. For
that reason, son, it is fitting that the man rule over his wife so that he

---

76. For a useful brief review of some of the legal complexities of medieval marriage, see Brundage 1995: 72-75.

77. Here, again, Llull takes a physical phenomenon of God's created world and
shows that it "signifies" a truth about the moral and social world. In the following paragraph, he uses the nature of numbers to make a similar point about the relations between husband and wife.

maintains his own nobility for himself and that by his teaching and by her fear of him, his wife will be obedient to our Lord God.

29. ON UNCTION

[1] Unction, son, is the final sacrament of the Holy Roman Church. This sacrament reaffirms and confirms all the other sacraments.

[2] When a man is gravely ill, son, and symptoms indicate imminent death, he should ask for this final sacrament to signify and demonstrate that he has preserved and kept the previous sacraments.

[3] At that time, son, clerics come with the sign of Jesus Christ by which the sacraments of the holy Church are ordained, that is, the cross, which represents the holy Passion that Jesus Christ suffered to save His people. And they bring the holy chrism, with which you received the first sacrament.[78] And, saying prayers, they anoint you in the places where you have committed sins and transgressions.

[4] On that day of unction, son, you should cast all worldly things from your heart, and you should accept in your heart that the hour of death has come, and you should not have hope of living any longer in this world. And before you have come to this sacrament, you should have confessed and taken communion, and you should have made your will and should be prepared in all ways to receive death.

[5] Dear son, this final sacrament, in which you are anointed with the chrism and with oil, signifies the holy unction of the Son of God, which He received on the holy cross with His body's precious blood. Therefore, if those people who come to the unction of the chrism and oil at the hour of death signify the Passion of the Son of God, how much more strongly do those people signify it who, through their love of Him, are anointed by the path of martyrdom with the blood of their body at the hour of their death, undergoing death to honor and serve the Son of God![79]

---

78. "The first sacrament," that is, Baptism (Ch. 23).

79. Just as the final sacrament is unction, for Llull the highest form of that final sacrament of unction is to be anointed with one's own blood in the act of martyrdom as Christ was anointed with his own blood on the cross.

On the Seven Gifts that the Holy Spirit Gives

30. On Wisdom

[1] Dear son, our Lord God is wisdom and God is Holy Spirit. Therefore, if God is wisdom and you have knowledge of God's wisdom, it follows that you have that gift of wisdom from God and from no other thing, for if you had it from something else, it would signify that wisdom was more in accord with something other than God, and that is impossible.

[2] Son, the wisdom that the Holy Spirit gives is different from the wisdom of this world, for, in the wisdom of this world, many men who are called wise with regard to this world commit sins and transgressions. But no man can commit a sin or a transgression with the wisdom that the Holy Spirit gives.

[3] Dear son, with the wisdom that the Holy Spirit gives, man has knowledge of God's goodness, greatness, eternity, power and His other virtues. For knowing God and His virtues is such a noble and excellent thing that no created thing is sufficient to give knowledge of God and His virtues without the work of the Holy Spirit.

[4] The glorious Holy Spirit, if you love Him and fear Him and honor Him, can give you wisdom through which you will wish to love, praise, honor, serve the God of Glory for all the days of your life.

[5] It is an unjust thing, son, for God to be known but not be loved, for God is such a noble thing that, through his nobility, love and knowledge come together in man to love and know God. Therefore, if you wish for love and wisdom to come together in you in knowing and loving God, ask the Holy Spirit to deign, in His mercy, to grant you light and charity so that you can know and love our Lord God.

[6] Through the wisdom that the Holy Spirit gives, man knows whence he came and who he is and where he is and where he is going, and he knows what he has done and what he is doing and what

he will do. Therefore, son, if you wish to have wisdom in all these things, strive as strongly as you can to love and honor and fear the Holy Spirit, who gives such gifts.

[7] This wisdom that the Holy Spirit gives makes men, who are on earth, know God, who is in Heaven, and makes them have contempt for the vainglory of this world, and makes them fearful of infernal fire, and makes them pleasing to God and to all the saints in glory.

[8] Ask the Holy Spirit for wisdom, son, for He gives it to all those who ask for it as they should, and He gives it to whomever He wants. But to those who do not love Him, He does not give it.

[9] And if the Holy Spirit did not give wisdom to those who love wisdom, He would be contrary to Himself, who is wisdom. And if He could not give wisdom to whomever He wanted, He would not have free choice in His giving. And if He gave wisdom to those who hate wisdom, He would hate Himself while loving those who hate God.

31. ON UNDERSTANDING

[1] The Holy Spirit, son, illuminates man's soul with understanding, just like the burning candle, which illuminates a chamber, or like the brilliance of the sun, which illuminates the whole world.

[2] Understanding, son, is the power of the soul that understands good and evil, and understands difference and concordance and contrariety in created things. Through understanding, man has knowledge of the things that are true and the things that are false.[80]

[3] Just as you see the streets down which you go, son, with corporeal eyes, your soul knows how to remember and love and imagine and see with the eyes of your understanding. And just as nature gives some men clearer vision than others, the Holy Spirit gives some men a clearer and loftier understanding than others.

[4] Dear son, the Holy Spirit gives a man a greater gift when He gives him a lofty and exalted understanding than He does when He

---

80. In addition to being a gift of the Holy Spirit, "understanding" is also one of the three powers of the rational soul (see Ch. 85 and Figure 2). Here Llull affirms that the understanding enables one to understand the essential principles of the very intellectual system deployed in the *DP*: difference, concordance, contrariety, truth, and falsehood, etc. These principles become increasingly important as the text moves from established tenets of the Catholic faith to the moral, social, natural and spiritual worlds.

gives him castles or towns or cities or kingdoms, for a king who does not have a subtle understanding cannot know God or himself or what God has given him, but the man who has a subtle understanding knows God and himself, and he knows and gives thanks to God for the goods that He has given him.

[5] In a place of shadows, son, a beautiful appearance and fancy clothes matter little. For men who are blind even smooth roads are dangerous and difficult. Therefore, pray to the Holy Spirit to illuminate your soul with subtle understanding.

[6] Many are the men who desire to have knowledge and cannot have it because they do not have a clear understanding. And many men have an infused knowledge through lofty understanding.[81]

[7] Dear son, the Holy Spirit gives to the understanding those things that enable it to understand Him. Therefore, if you understand God, it is because God is giving Himself to be understood by your understanding, and if you understand yourself and this world, the Holy Spirit gives both you and the world to your understanding, and it gives you your own understanding.

[8] Ah, son! And how many men are taken and deceived and betrayed and killed because they lack understanding! And how many men are rich and happy in this world and are in glory in the other for all time because they abound in lofty understanding by the grace of the Holy Spirit!

[9] The more you lift up your understanding to know and love and serve God in this world, son, the greater the understanding you will have in glory. For that reason, I advise you—as much as you can— to lift your understanding above all other things in order to honor, praise, know the One through whom you hold and possess your understanding, that is, glorious God Holy Spirit.

32. ON COUNSEL

[1] The counsel of the Holy Spirit, son, is the thing through which men do good works and have the will to cease from doing evil and to do good. Since the Holy Spirit is the counselor of all good, for that

---

81. The notion of "infused knowledge" is explained in slightly more detail in Ch. 34.3-5 as "knowledge given by the Holy Spirit." See also n. 88.

reason, in everything that you do or say, ask the Holy Spirit to counsel you and to illuminate the eyes of your thought with such works as may be pleasing to God.

[2] With the counsel the Holy Spirit gives, you cannot fail, for He knows all things and loves all goods and desires no evil. Therefore, son, you must pay heed to the counsel of the Holy Spirit if you wish to succeed in anything at all and avoid and flee the counsel of those who, in ignorance or with ill will, are counselors who counsel you to sin and error.

[3] Dear son, your bodily senses counsel you to love this world and to hold the other in contempt. And do you know why they give this counsel? Because they see the delights of this world and they cannot see the blessed glory of the other.[82] Because the Holy Spirit sees both this world and the other, He counsels you to despise the vanity of this fleeting world so that you can have the glory of the other, which will never end.

[4] If a bad woman counsels you to love her more than God, the Holy Spirit counsels you to love God more than all other things. And if you, son, believe the counsel of the wicked woman, know that you imprison your body in the infernal prison, from which you will never be set free.

[5] If infernal torments counsel you, through fear, to love God so that you can avoid their sufferings, the Holy Spirit counsels you to love God because He is good. And if the glory of Paradise counsels you to love God so that you may attain it, the Holy Spirit counsels you to love God because He is worth more than the celestial glory that you love.[83]

[6] In everything that you achieve, son, you succeed through the counsel that the Holy Spirit gives you, and in everything in which you fail, you go astray because you do not believe the counsel of the Holy Spirit.

[7] The Holy Spirit gives and counsels truth and good works in contrast to those who ask for payment for the evil counsel that they

---

82. Llull stresses again that our physical senses can only perceive physical (created) things. It is our spiritual senses (made keener by a "lofty intellect") that permit us to perceive spiritual things. Cf. Chs. 25 and 85.

83. That is, one must love God for Himself, not out of fear of punishment or hope of reward but simply because of his divine worth. Similar themes appear in Chs. 36, 39, 54 and 92.

give. For that reason, son, believe the counsel that God gives you and do not subject your understanding or your will to the counsel of an ignorant understanding or a harmful will.

[8] The Holy Spirit counsels the poor, the orphans, the dispossessed, the beset. And He counsels princes and honored barons not to submit themselves to the evil counsel of men who have contempt for the counsel that the Holy Spirit gives.

[9] At the moment of death, son, when all counsel fails, you need the counsel of God, which does not fail those who ask for it, for then, neither money nor honors nor friends nor knowledge nor arts nor any other thing can help you, but only the counsel of the Holy Spirit.[84]

33. On the Fortitude that the Holy Spirit Gives

[1] The Holy Spirit, son, gives courage to strong men with which to conquer and overpower their enemies and the delights of this world, which are the enemies of the glory of the other world.

[2] With the Holy Spirit, one is strong against the flesh and against this world and against the devil. And without the Holy Spirit's help no man can win any of these three battles.[85]

[3] The strengthening of faith, hope, charity, justice and the other virtues comes from the strength of the Holy Spirit, without which no man can combat or overcome the vices, which are contrary to the virtues just mentioned.[86]

[4] Dear son, the Holy Spirit gives diverse strengths, for to some men He gives physical strength, to others He gives strength of heart, to others He gives strength of lineage, and to others power in riches and so on for the other things like these.

---

84. It is worth remembering here that Llull calls his own system an "Art." Thus, implicit here may well be Llull's recognition that, like all "arts," that is, all human skills, even his own universal art of finding truth will fail at the moment of death when one will only be able to rely on the counsel of the Holy Spirit.

85. These are the three traditional enemies of salvation in medieval Christian thought. Llull mentions them again in the chapter on the created human virtue of fortitude (Ch. 57.2).

86. Here, under the topic of the fortitude given by the Holy Spirit, Llull first mentions the struggle between the virtues and vices, which will be an important theme throughout the remainder of the text (see Introduction).

[5] Physical strength and spiritual strength, son, both come from the Holy Spirit and for that reason, son, His strength is to be loved and feared above all other strengths and forces. If there were no Holy Spirit, everything that is created would not have enough strength to remain in existence for a single hour or a single moment, for everything that is would return to the nothing from which it came. But, by the Holy Spirit, all creatures are sustained.

[6] Many, son, are the demons who have so much strength that, if the Holy Spirit did not exist, they would put all the men of this world into Hell and would destroy the entire world. But the strength of the Holy Spirit is so great that no demon can do anything except what the Holy Spirit permits it to do.

[7] Since the Holy Spirit is so powerful above all other powers, if the Holy Spirit is with you, son, who is there who can succeed against your power? And who is the person who can separate you from the pleasing will of our Lord God?

34. ON KNOWLEDGE

[1] Knowledge is knowing what is. The Holy Spirit gave this knowledge to the Apostles and to other men who possess knowledge infused by the grace of God. This knowledge cannot be given without the grace of the Holy Spirit.

[2] Dear son, all Creation signifies and represents our Lord God's goodness and greatness, nobility and power to man.[87] Therefore, when the human understanding receives this representation that created things give about God, it is illuminated by the divine light of the Holy Spirit.

[3] Many a man, son, has knowledge through learning. But the knowledge that the Holy Spirit gives is infused knowledge, which is much greater and nobler than the knowledge you learn in school from a teacher.[88]

---

87. Here again, the idea of the Book of Nature: God's creation "signifies and represents" his virtues. See also Chs. 3 and 68.

88. In his "Book of the Lover and the Beloved," found in *Blaquerna*, Llull explains the difference between infused knowledge and learned knowledge thus: "The lover said that infused knowledge comes from will, devotion, prayer; acquired knowledge comes from study, understanding" (*Blaquerna* §234 [in other versions §241]).

[4] Son, if you dispute with someone in order to honor God and to spread the holy Catholic faith, entrust yourself much more strongly to the knowledge that the Holy Spirit gives than to the knowledge that teachers teach in school.[89]

[5] Acquired knowledge cannot inspire the hearts of sinners or of those in error. But the knowledge infused by the work of the Holy Spirit gives awareness to sinners of their sins and illuminates the darkened eyes of men who are in error.

[6] Do you know, son, why God has given you knowledge of Himself? So that you might love Him above all things. And if you love something more than you love God, the more you know Him, the greater your sin and the greater your punishment for it if you go to the infernal abyss bearing that sin.

[7] In heavenly glory, those who have greater knowledge of God have greater glory. But in the infernal fire, those who have greater knowledge of God will have greater punishment.

[8] The divine light of the Holy Spirit, son, has given you knowledge through which you know how to have knowledge of good and of evil. And do you know why? So that you love good and hate evil.

[9] If God shows you the things that you should do and those that you should not do, and you, son, do not do as you have understood, you blind the eyes of your soul and set it on the dark roads down which sinners go to eternal fire, where they are tormented by the justice of God.

35. On Piety

[1] Piety is a heart that suffers in the suffering of its neighbor.[90] Therefore, son, the Holy Spirit gives piety to men's hearts so that they may be loving and helpful to one another.

---

89. Here Llull may be slipping in a bit of propaganda for his own Art, which he believed to be a gift inspired by the Holy Spirit to provide a method for disputing with (and converting) non-believers (cf. "Disconsolation" ["Lo desconhort"], stz. 8 in Vega, 2003: 210). The implication would be that entrusting oneself to Llull's Art, which was infused by the Holy Spirit, will be more effective than the methods of disputation taught in the schools.

90. The term "piety" embraces both the common meaning of this word in English as well as the cognate English term "pity." The latter sense may be more useful for English readers in understanding Llull's text in this chapter and elsewhere in the *DP*,

[2] Piety makes men remember the holy Passion of our Lord Jesus Christ and the grievous pains He suffered for us sinners. And piety makes men reflect on the bitterness and on the tears and on the great suffering of Our Lady Saint Mary when they were killing and torturing her glorious Son before her very eyes.

[3] The blessed rich, poor in spirit, have piety when they have mercy on poor people who beg alms for the love of God. But those who have piety for the infidels—who, out of ignorance, go to eternal fire—and who subject themselves to suffering and death for the infidels' salvation have much greater piety.

[4] The greater the piety in your heart, son, the more pleasing you will be to the Son of God and the more you will assuage God's wrath at your transgressions.

[5] Dear son, have piety for your neighbor so that you can love and weep, for piety leads you to love and turns tears to sweetness.

[6] If the God of Glory had piety and, out of piety, was incarnated and tortured and hung and killed on the cross, who could be an enemy of piety? And who can exempt himself from having piety for his neighbor or for himself?

[7] When you sin, son, you have no piety for yourself. And when you hear it reported that, in some lands, the Son of God is blasphemed and dishonored and not believed in, you have no piety for the Passion of the Son of God or for those who are your neighbors who, because of the dishonor they show the Son of God, go to fire without end.[91]

[8] Piety makes a man give, pardon, pacify, love, have humility, help, and piety makes him trust in the gifts that the Holy Spirit gives, and piety conquers and overpowers cruelty and ingratitude.

[9] There is no avoiding it, son: either you love yourself or you hate yourself. If you love yourself, have piety. If you hate yourself, have cruelty.

[10] Do you think, son, that, at the end of your days when you come to death with the many sins that you have committed, it will be necessary for God to have piety for you? Do you think that the badly

---

but I have used "piety" here, both because it is the traditional name of this "gift" and because its use can help to deepen for English readers their sense of the word "pity."

91. The neighbors Llull refers to here are the Jews and Saracens and other non-Christians. See Ch. 72.3 for a full list of the peoples Llull believes to be in need of conversion.

clothed poor person, sick, hungry, needs to find your heart filled with piety when he begs for alms for the love of God?

36. ON FEAR

[1] Fear is recognizing your smallness and the greatness of someone greater than you, towards whom you have committed transgressions. Now, when such fear grows out of love, it has been given as a gift by the Holy Spirit.

[2] God is to be feared, son, so that you may possess Him and so that you do not lose Him and so that He does not give you enduring torments. But He is more greatly to be feared because He is good and worthy of love.

[3] If you have this kind of fear, son, your love will be like God's love, for God loves Himself for His goodness itself. And if you fear God out of fear more than out of love, you are a greater lover of yourself than of God's goodness. This kind of fear is not given by the work of the Holy Spirit, for if it were, the Holy Spirit would be contrary to His own goodness.

[4] The fear of physical death is a fear given by nature. And to fear to undergo suffering and death in praising and honoring God is not a fear given by the work of the Holy Spirit. Therefore, the fear that one might not die through serving God is a work that the Holy Spirit gives.[92]

[5] Answer me, son, and tell me which fear is greater in your heart: the fear of God or the fear of the criticism of the people? For if you fear people's criticism more than you fear God, the fear that you have is contrary to the fear that comes from the grace of the Holy Spirit.

[6] Dear son, the Holy Spirit gives fear so that you may know that He possesses all power, and knows all things, and is righteous in all times and in all places. Therefore, if you have greater fear of an earth-

---

92. This is a very good example of the logical processes and values that underlie much of the *DP*. 1) It is in our nature to fear death. 2) But it is not a fear given by the Holy Spirit if we fear to die while honoring and praising God, that is, to die as martyrs. Therefore, the only fear that is given by the Holy Spirit when we are honoring and praising God (that is, to infidels, who may martyr us) is the fear of not dying, the fear that we will not achieve martyrdom.

ly lord than of God, you deny the God of Glory, who is not afraid of anything. And you make an idol and a god out of your lord, who fears God and is His servant.

[7] Consider, son, how fearful is the God of heaven, for He can have the king that He has given you—whom He has created from nothing and who has to come before His judgment and His mercy—take everything you have away from you. And your king has many men who serve him who could bind you and torture you and kill you without your being able to defend yourself from them.

[8] If you do not fear God, son, then you do not fear the infernal fire. And if you do not fear the infernal fire, then you do not fear the fire of this world. And if you do not fear this worldly fire, go into the oven when it is all aflame and see if you can stay there for even a single moment.

[9] Do you know, son, why you fear death? Because you cannot escape it and you do not know when it will take you. Now, if you fear a death that can only kill your body, won't you then, son, fear God, who can put both your body and your soul in eternal fire?

[10] God would not be feared if He pardoned everyone. But because there are some whom He does not pardon, in order not to be among those, son, have fear. If you fear Him, you will not fear death, and the greater the fear you have, the greater your merits in glory will be and the more you will trust, in this world, in the mercy of God.[93]

---

93. Here Llull begins to introduce a theme that is essential to his understanding of human striving for salvation and of God's mercy: human beings cannot earn salvation, no matter how perfect their lives have been. Only God, through his mercy, can grant salvation. Human beings' best recourse, then, is to trust in the mercy of God. See also Chs. 39, 41, 53, 55, 59 and 67.

On the Eight Beatitudes[94]

37. On Reigning[95]

[1] To reign in glory is to possess the kingdom of Heaven as a gift from God. Our Lord Jesus Christ promised this beatitude, son, to the poor in spirit, as is told in the Gospels.

[2] Poverty in spirit is to despise the vanity of this world and to desire the kingdom of God. Therefore, those who are rich and despise riches, and the religious who, for the love of God, abandon the world and suffer poverty, those, son, are the poor in spirit and to them are promised riches in the heavenly kingdom.

[3] Dear son, those who are most honored and noblest in the kingdom of heaven are Jesus Christ and Our Lady Saint Mary and the Apostles and martyrs. Now, all these were poor in spirit in this world, and poor in worldly goods, and for that reason, you must willingly love poverty more than riches, so that you can possess the heavenly kingdom.

[4] You can have and possess the riches of this world, son, and still be poor in spirit, for if you dedicate the riches you possess to praising and honoring God, who has given them to you, and you give alms out of love for Him, you will be able to remain poor in spirit and still possess the riches of this world.[96]

[5] The person who considers himself satisfied with his worldly goods is poor in spirit. In him is signified the kingdom of heaven,

---

94. I have elsewhere translated "benauirança" variously as "blessing" or "bliss" according to the context, but in this section, I translate it as "beatitude" in accord with the context here of the Sermon on the Mount and the eight Beatitudes (Matthew 5:1-12). I cite the form of the text of the Beatitudes from *CCC* 1716, providing any variants important to the understanding of Llull's text in brackets.

95. Mt. 5:3: "Blessed are the poor in spirit, for theirs is the kingdom of heaven."

96. Note here that Llull is not opposed to wealth *per se.* If the wealthy use the riches God has given them in the proper fashion, they, too, can be "poor in spirit."

where all who are there find fulfillment. And the person who is not satisfied with what God gives him in this world signifies infernal captivity, in which sinners—who long for what they can never have—possess eternal poverty.[97]

[6] Think, son, on the vileness of worldly riches, which cannot satisfy the soul of the person who loves them, and think on the brief time that you possess them, and how you possess them in ignorance since you do not know when death, which takes away all the goods of this world, will come for you.

[7] The kingdom of this world is the virtues through which you will possess the heavenly reign. Therefore, if you want to have heavenly beatitude, hold the fullness of God in your heart in this world so that God fulfills the desire of your soul from Himself in Glory.

[8] Dear son, men who do not fill themselves with God in this world and who think they can satisfy their souls with worldly riches are despisers of God and praisers of earthly wealth, and for that reason, they condemn themselves to eternal suffering.

[9] If you want to be richer than the king, son, be poorer in spirit than the king. Now, if you, who are not a king in this world, can be richer than the king by despising this world, so much the more, then, can you, by poverty in spirit, be rich in the kingdom of God.

38. ON POSSESSION[98]

[1] The beatitude promised to those who are simple and meek is the blessed possession that the saints in glory have in the perfect kingdom.

[2] Dear son, meekness engenders peace, and peace is the reason for possession, and by this worldly possession is signified heavenly possession.[99]

---

97. That is, in Llull's analogical language of this world, the person who is fulfilled in the world represents the person who will find fulfillment in the next, as the person who is not satisfied in this world, will also be "dissatisfied" in the next.

98. Mt. 5:4: "Blessed are the meek, for they shall inherit the earth."

99. Llull understands the "this worldly possession" to "signify" the possession of the heavenly kingdom (cf. n. 22). "Meekness" allows one to possess this world, which, in turn, signifies the possession of heaven. In this paragraph and the following Llull equates "meekness" with "peacefulness" and, thus, identifies "wrath," "rebelliousness" and similar unpeaceable emotions with the failure to possess the heavenly kingdom

[3] The soul that does not rule the five corporeal senses is at war and in suffering, and the body rebels against the soul that does not rule its will. For that reason, man lives with suffering, possessed by the vanity of this world.

[4] Dear son, love meekness so that wrath does not move your heart to disobedience, from which follows servitude, and humble your thought by thinking about the vileness of this world so that your will is content in desiring the possession of infinite beatitude.

[5] The love that loves God makes the rebellious person simple and meek, and simplicity and meekness make humble men possess the proud. Humility pacifies the wrathful and, for that reason, son, charity and love are the beginning of the possession of peace.

[6] Meek was our Lord Jesus Christ, son, when He came into the world and when He let himself be taken and bound and whipped and crucified. And do you know why? So that the human lineage could recover its promised possession in the kingdom of God.

[7] Obedience, perseverance, patience assist meekness, which fights cruelty and rebelliousness to exalt the simple and meek man in the blessing of God.

39. ON CONSOLATION[100]

[1] Dear son, those who weep in this world to honor and serve and love our Lord God will be consoled because the Son of God will console them in Himself in heavenly glory in that He will give Himself to them to be their glory.

[2] Weep, son, for your sins and faults so that you are not disconsolate of heavenly blessings in infernal fire. This disconsolateness is felt by all those who do not console themselves in this world in the virtue of our Lord God and in His Passion.

[3] If you weep, son, because Christian sinners do not thank God, who has let His Son be crucified so that they can take consolation in Him, and if you weep for the infidels, who, out of ignorance, go to

---

promised in this beatitude. Such people cannot possess this world, but only its "vanity" (following paragraph), an empty possession.

100. Mt. 5:5: "Blessed are those who mourn [weep], for they will be comforted [consoled]."

the eternal torments that the demons give, take consolation in the justice of God, who does all His works righteously and as He has ordained.

[4] If, son, you desire to do something in service of Jesus Christ, and you cannot complete it, do not be consoled by thinking that the merits that you have from it are as great as if you had brought your work to completion and weep when you cannot fulfill your desire, for there is an insufficiency of love in those who are consoled by their own merits.

[5] Weep first, son, to honor and love God and then you can weep out of fear of infinite torments and from desiring heavenly blessings, which last for all time.

[6] To weep without love is not in accord with the pleasure that weeping makes agree with consolation. Therefore, so that you may be consoled, weep with love, which gives consolation to its lovers in tears.

[7] Ah, son, how great is the consolation of those who are filled with sighs and tears and weeping from love! Therefore, if you desire to be consoled and if you want to recover far greater things than those you have lost, learn to weep, for you gain more in the consolation you receive from the pleasure that you have in weeping than you lose in the vanities of this world.

[8] If you wish to weep and yet cannot weep, you do not know how to love or desire heavenly goods or how to despise the delights of this world, nor do you know how to have consolation from the goods that God has given you.

[9] Weep, dear son, for the torments that are prepared for all those infidels who do not have knowledge of God, for such tears prepare consolation for you in beatitude that has no end.

[10] This world is a place of tears so that we may learn how to console ourselves in the other world. Therefore, if you cannot weep, weep because you cannot weep, and love weeping so that you are consoled and so that you have relief from the sufferings that come from being disconsolate, for you cannot lose as much as you can gain from the consolation that weeping gives.

[11] So that you are able to weep, son, I advise you to leave your land and your friends and to cast all other things from your heart and to place God there. Go away into hermitages and into foreign lands and subject your body to poverty and suffering so that your life con-

sists of consolation and of the sweetness that comes from tears and from weeping in remembering the holy Passion of the Son of God.[101]

40. ON FULFILLMENT[102]

[1] Fulfillment, son, is the heavenly beatitude that satisfies the longing for justice, desiring works of hope, charity and the other virtues.

[2] God has promised the beatitude of fulfillment, son, to all those who desire justice. And do you know why? Because God—who is the fulfillment of the desire for justice—is justice.

[3] If you desire justice and you die for justice, death fulfills your desire, through which the fears and sufferings that death gives will be assuaged, and death will no longer be fearful.

[4] Dear son, the greatest and best foods give greater satisfaction than the lesser ones. Therefore, if your soul is satisfied because justice satisfies the injustice that someone did to you, how much more strongly the justice that you enact upon yourself to atone for your own wrong-doings must satisfy the desire of your soul![103]

[5] Dear son, if bread, wine, meat and other foods satisfy the body, and if beautiful sights give pleasure to the corporeal eyes, and soft voices and words are pleasant to hear, how much more can the delights of your soul find fulfillment in the beatitude that comes by the work of justice!

[6] If, in this world, you desire money, possessions, honors, son, or some other things unjustly, injustice will make you desire still more, without any possibility of satisfaction. Now, son, since justice is contrary to injustice, if you desire worldly things or heavenly things justly, it is fitting that justice give fulfillment and beatitude to your just desire.

---

101. Llull offers further techniques for provoking weeping in Ch. 84.19-21.

102. "Blessed are those who hunger and thirst for righteousness [justice], for they shall be satisfied [fulfilled]." Llull uses the word "compliment," which can be understood as "plenitude," "perfection," "fulfillment" (as I translate it here).

103. In this paragraph, Llull incorporates another meaning of the term "justice": the human system of justice or legal system. If the legal system (*justícia*) satisfies your desire for justice when someone who has committed a crime against you is punished, how much more, then, will the desire for justice in your soul be satisfied if you atone for your own crimes against yourself?

[7] The final reason for which you were created and redeemed is justice. Therefore, you cannot have the fulfillment of your desire by means of an unjust desire.

[8] If the greatest justice in man is to affirm and love unity and Trinity and Incarnation in God, the greatest injustice that exists is to deny and not believe in the unity, Trinity and Incarnation of God. Therefore, son, if you wish to have the greatest beatitude that man can have through justice, love to die for the greatest justice.

[9] Mercy and justice agree, son, in sinful men, whom mercy lifts up more strongly in this world and whom justice torments in that they do not have the fulfillment of their desire in this world, and in the other world they have damnation under the wrath of God.

41. ON MERCY[104]

[1] Mercy is the virtue through which faults are pardoned, and gifts are given to those who do not deserve them by their works alone. This mercy, son, is a beatitude promised to those who are merciful in this world.

[2] To signify that God wants to grant mercy, He promised the beatitude of mercy to those who, out of love for Him, are merciful to their neighbor. Now, if you, son, can grant great mercy to your neighbor from the goods that God has entrusted to you, how much more can God give you great beatitude if He grants you the mercy of Himself!

[3] If you did all the good that men in this world do and forgave all the wrongs, for all that, your works would not be sufficient for you to receive the beatitude that is in heavenly glory. But because God is mercy, He promises the kingdom of heaven to those who have some resemblance to Him in that they have mercy.

[4] To hate showing mercy to your neighbor is to hate the mercy of God, and to hate God's mercy is to hate the heavenly beatitude that cannot be granted by anyone else, but only by the mercy of God.

[5] Tell me, son, which is the greater harm: the harm to your neighbor if you do not grant him mercy or the harm to you if God does not grant you mercy?

---

104. "Blessed are the merciful, for they shall obtain mercy."

[6] God has granted you the mercy of being a man and the mercy of His Son, whom He sent to earth to become a man and die on the cross so that He could pardon the fault by which you came into this world. Therefore, if you are not merciful, you despise the mercy that God has granted you, and you despise the beatitude to which the merciful are called.

[7] Dear son, this world is the place for pardoning and for having mercy because, in the other world, you cannot pardon. For if all the demons and sinners who are in Hell could have the will to love mercy, all of them would escape their infernal torments, and, by their desire for mercy, they would be blessed in eternal beatitude.

[8] If mercy does not intercede for you with justice, who can save you? Nor is it in your power to condemn the person you do not wish to pardon. And because you did not pardon him, you are condemned to damnation. Therefore, so that you can have friends and so that your enemies are not the occasion for your damnation, have mercy.

[9] God has more things to pardon in you than you have to pardon in your neighbor. Therefore, since out of lesser pardon you can have greater mercy, if you do not love pardoning, then you hate greater and better things for lesser things. Such hatred makes you unworthy of the heavenly beatitude of our Lord God.

42. On Seeing God[105]

[1] Seeing God is the fulfillment of the beatitude that God has promised, son, to all those who have purity of heart. Such purity is found in the soul cleansed of sin.

[2] Just as a mote or rheum in the eye are obstacles to corporeal vision, blame and sin are obstacles in the eyes that see God. And for that reason, it follows necessarily that cleanness of thought is in accord with seeing God.

[3] Wash your corporeal eyes with the water of your body flowing from your eyes with tears and weeping, so that contrition and penance cleanse and purify your soul from vices and from sins and so that, through the cleanness and conscience of your soul, you have beatitude in eternal delights.

---

105. "Blessed are the pure of heart, for they shall see God."

[4] Dear son, if your mother takes great delight in looking at you, who are mortal and have come from nothing and who are in doubt regarding whether you will be called to heavenly glory or to eternal punishment, how much more can you have pleasure in seeing God, who is the Father and Lord of all that is.

[5] See how pleasant the stars, the sun, the moon, the sky and sea and earth and planets, birds, beasts, men, castles, towns and cities, clothes and statues and the other created things are to see. Therefore, if through your corporeal eyes you can have beatitude in seeing so many things, strive, then, to see the God of Glory, who has created all things and who can be seen with a clear conscience and innocence.

[6] To see God's goodness, greatness, eternity, power, wisdom, love, virtue, glory, fulfillment and the other virtues which accord with God with sure intelligence, such a vision, son, is above all beatitudes that exist in Creation, to which vision no eyes can rise without the cleanness of a pure and sanctified soul in which there are no blames or wrongs.

[7] In a clear mirror you can see your own features. Therefore, if you wish to see God, purify your soul so that it may be a clean mirror in which you see your Creator, your Savior, and let Him be the beatitude and glory of your soul.

[8] Dear son, lift up your eyes to the cross and see how the cross signifies the Son of God, who with His precious blood cleansed and purified original sin, and look at yourself and see if you are innocent of sinning against the commandments of God.

43. ON PATIENCE[106]

[1] Patience is restrained desire brought about through wrath converted into charity. For that reason, Jesus Christ promises in the Gospel that those who are patient will be the sons of God.

[2] Dear son, we are all God's sons through our creation, but through patience, a person becomes the son of grace and, through

---

106. "Blessed are the peacemakers, for they shall be called sons of God." Llull interprets the word "peacemakers" ("pacifici" in the Latin Vulgate version of Matthew 5:9) as "the patient" or "the suffering" ("pacients"). In this interpretation, those who actively make peace are interpreted as those who suffer "patiently" or "peacefully" (i.e., "with wrath converted into charity").

impatience, the son of blame and damnation. Thus, patience makes all those who are obedient and submissive to Him sons of God.

[3] The person who is patient in a foreign land is a son of God, and the person who is proud in his own land is a son of the devil. Therefore, to signify that it is better for you, son, to be poor and despised in a foreign land and to be patient than to be rich and proud among your family, God has promised Himself to be the Father of those who will be sons of God.[107]

[4] Do you know why God wants to be your Father if you have patience? Because patience makes the proud man patient and, with patience, the impatient are conquered and overcome.

[5] The impatient person is a son of wrath, which leads him through darkness in whatever direction it wishes, without discernment in his thought or contrition in his conscience, and offers him up to be the son of eternal death.

[6] The Son of God, Jesus Christ, had more patience on the cross than you can remember or than the cross can signify, for Jesus Christ was offered up to tremendous patience since man cannot torment or kill Him. For even if He had undergone still greater torments, His patience would have made him obedient to the will of God.

[7] Consider, son, which is better for you to be: the beloved and glorified, patient son of God, or the tormented, impatient son of the devil, a tormented impatient person, displeasing to the Son of God.

44. ON REWARD[108]

[1] Merit is a promised reward. The kingdom of the heavens is given as a reward to those who, out of love for God, suffer persecution, trials, humiliations and tribulations in this world.

[2] Dear son, just as creatures who are without reason are subjected to tribulations and suffering to serve man, all men are subjected and obligated to suffer tribulations to serve and honor the Lord of glory.

---

107. Another reference to the situation of the missionary who goes to foreign lands: they will have to give up their family and their parents, but God will step in to be their father.

108. "Blessed are those who are persecuted for righteousness' sake, for theirs is the kingdom of heaven."

[3] Therefore, since it is a fact that we are all obligated to serve God in order to demonstrate the great charity, generosity, grace and mercy, piety of God, the King of Kings promises that He will grant a reward to all those who undergo suffering in order to teach, praise and preach Him to the infidels, even though they are already obligated to do so.

[4] Great trials, great persecutions suffered to honor God are in accord with great rewards to demonstrate that not to undergo tribulations or suffer persecution for the love of God is not in accord with rewards.

[5] While rich men multiply their riches by multiplying money and possessions, the multiplication of heavenly gifts, son, is the multiplication of the torments and tribulations suffered in praising and serving the sovereign good.

[6] Is there any earthly man who is afraid of being rich or happy in the delights of this world? Then who could be afraid of multiplying his glory through sufferings pleasing to the One who rewards all merits with still greater beatitude?

[7] The sufferings of this world come to an end, but the rewards of glory are eternal. For this reason—because they could attain heavenly beatitude through them—the pains and the persecutions with which beatitude called the Apostles, martyrs to itself were most agreeable and pleasant to them.

[8] If you, son, desire to be blessed, do not fear to suffer tribulations or death to honor and serve God, for such a fear is contrary to the beatitude that is in those who, with desire and prayers to God, went to praise and serve the King of glory among His enemies.

[9] The lover of God, inflamed by the grace of the Holy Spirit, makes no distinction between his own land and a foreign land, or between honor and dishonor, or between one man and another, or between happiness and suffering, for everything is pleasant to him, so long as he can serve God.

[10] See how many men there are in this world who, for money (which is not God) and for vainglory (which makes a man God's enemy) and for earthly well-being, suffer so many trials and so many tribulations. And so, dear son, will you know how to or wish to or be able to endure suffering and humiliations to praise the name of God?

On the Seven Joys of Our Lady Saint Mary[109]

45. On the Salutation

[1] The first Joy of Our Lady Saint Mary came from the angel Saint Gabriel's salutation, when he greeted her, saying that she was full of the Holy Spirit and that from her would be born the Son of God, the Savior of all the world.[110]

[2] Dear son, you cannot calculate the great joy that the Queen of Heaven and Earth had when the angel Gabriel saluted her. For if you cannot grasp or understand the joy that your mother would have if all the nations chose you lord of this world, how much less can you reckon the marvelous joy that Our Lady had when the God of Glory elected her Queen of the Angels and of all the saints in Paradise and Lady of all the world!

[3] The Virgin Mary had greater joy beyond compare when she understood that her son would be united with the Son of God than she had from the fact that He is Lord of Heaven and earth and of everything that exists, for it is a much greater nobility to be one with God than to be lord of all the world.

[4] The honor that God granted Our Lady must be in proportion to the joy of our Lady, and, considering the degree of the benefit the human lineage received from the conception of the Son of God, that joy must be great. And so, incalculable is Our Lady's joy.[111]

---

109. The recounting of the "joys" of the Virgin was a tradition popular throughout the literatures of medieval Europe. In some versions there are as many as fifteen "joys." The survival of this theme in the English language tradition is seen in the well-known Christmas carol: "The Seven Joys of Mary."

110. For Gabriel's salutation, see Ch. 6.2-3.

111. Since the joy felt by the Virgin Mary at her Son's conception will be in proportion to the benefit the human race derived from that conception (which is incalculable), it follows that her joy will be incalculable, too great for us to calculate or imagine. And therefore, the honor that God granted her must also be incalculable.

[5] If there were a single fire that engulfed the entire world, it would follow necessarily that you were in that fire, for if you were not in that fire, you would not be in the world. Now, if the joy that Our Lady had is greater than the whole world, it follows necessarily that the nobility of Our Lady and her happiness and her glory and honor are greater than all the world.

[6] The marvelous joy that Our Lady Saint Mary had was so great that each man, for all he may lose and for all the many tribulations that he encounters and the many sufferings that he endures, can be consoled and made happy and receive benefit in the joy of Our Lady.

[7] The sun cannot illuminate, nor the fire heat, as much as the saints in glory can rejoice in Our Lady's conception.[112] Nor is everything that the creatures in this world do as great a source of joy as it is for Our Lady to remember and to understand and to love that God wished to be one with her Son. Therefore, since this is so, from this so great and glorious joy of Our Lady you can learn, son, how to be joyful about the conception of her Son so that you may be pleasing to Our Lady.

46. On the Nativity

[1] When the Son of God was born of Our Lady Saint Mary, a son was born who is true God and true man. Therefore, with regard to divine nature, Our Lady gave birth to infinite goodness, greatness, eternity, infinite power, infinite wisdom, love and the other virtues that pertain to God. And, with regard to human nature, Our Lady gave birth to a son who was a better man than all men and all women and all Creation.

[2] Dear son, when this most glorious and honorable Son was born of Our Lady, the Queen of Heaven was so joyful that the heart of man cannot reckon it nor angelical intelligence understand it.

[3] Since Our Lady is closer in nature to her Son than are the other created things, it follows necessarily that she was more joyful in the Nativity of her Son than men or angels can understand. And if this were not true, it would follow that the possibility of understand-

---

112. Here, of course, is meant by "Our Lady's conception" her conception of Jesus Christ.

ing is greater in angels and in men than is the closeness of Our Lady to her Son, and that is impossible.[113]

[4] Joy and being Lord of all the world are not in agreement or concordance as strongly as are joy and giving birth to the Savior of the world and the God of the world. Therefore, if you want to contemplate the joy that Our Lady had in the Nativity of our Lord Jesus Christ, consider what great joy you would have if you could create a world as big and as beautiful as this world.

[5] So great and marvelous a thing was the great joy Our Lady had from her Son when her corporeal eyes saw a man born with all his sense and with all His power and the eyes of her soul saw Him as the God of Heaven and earth and of everything that is that her joy ought to be called by a different name that could signify greater joy and greater happiness than all the joy and all the happiness that can exist in this world.

[6] Do you believe that a queen would feel joy when she has a son who will become king? Nevertheless, she will not have complete joy until she sees him actually become king. But the Queen of Heaven, as soon as she had given birth to her Son, immediately saw Him King of Heaven and of earth and of all that is.

[7] When the sweet queen Our Lady had given birth to her beautiful Son and held Him in her arms, and her merciful eyes looked at Him, and her glorious Son looked at His mother with His pious corporeal eyes, and His divine nature showed itself to the understanding of Our Lady, the joy, the happiness, the pleasure, son, that filled Our Lady cannot be understood completely—in this world or in the other—by any other creature, but only by Our Lady and her Son, who is man and God.

47. ON THE THREE KINGS

[1] The holiness and celebration of the Nativity of the Son of God was so great that—by the power of God—on the thirteenth day of His life, as Our Lady held Him in her lap, three kings came from faraway lands to adore Him.

---

113. This is an example of a form of argument found often in Llull's works: the *reductio ad impossibile.*

[2] Those three kings were guided by a bright and shining star that went before them and guided them until they came to the Son of God.

[3] When the three kings saw Our Lady Saint Mary, who held our Lord Jesus Christ in her arms, they got down from their horses and offered incense and gold and myrrh to the Son of God, to signify that He was God and man and that He would die to save the human lineage.

[4] Dear son, when Our Lady saw the three kings coming and saw the star that guided them and saw the gifts that they offered to her Son, she felt joy equal to the lordship that the gifts and the star signified about her Son.

[5] Consider what great joy is signified in being the lord of the stars, which was signified by the star. Consider the joy that a mother would have in her son who is shown by incense to be Lord of Heaven and by gold to be Lord of the earth and by myrrh to be a man, the Lord of death and of the devil, through whom the human lineage had been lost.[114]

[6] When the three kings had offered their gifts to the Son of Our Lady and had made that reverence that a creature must make to its Creator and had gone to sleep, the angel Gabriel came to the three kings and told them they should not go to the court of King Herod, who wanted to kill Jesus Christ and who killed the Innocents. And when Our Lady understood that her Son had been delivered from the power of Herod by the ministrations of the angel, she took very great joy in the deliverance of her beloved Son of God.

48. ON THE JOY THAT OUR LADY HAD IN THE RESURRECTION

[1] So that you can better understand, son, the great joy Our Lady had from her Son when He was resurrected and appeared to her and to the Apostles, I want to tell you the suffering and the pain and the passion that she felt on the day when she saw her Son taken and bound and whipped and saw Him die on the cross.

---

114. The three gifts were interpreted allegorically as follows: incense, used in the church, represents Christ's spiritual kingship; gold, the sign of material wealth, represents his earthly kingship; myrrh, traditionally used to embalm the dead, represents Christ's human nature, his mortality.

[2] On the night the Jews took and bound Our Lady's Son and took Him away, mocking Him, Our Lady was there and followed her Son as best as she could. And because of the size of the great crowd, Our Lady was not honored with the honor that was due her, and she was pushed and mocked by the Jews.

[3] When Our Lady saw her Son stripped and bound and whipped so fiercely that the precious flesh and blood He had taken from her was torn and destroyed, she had such sorrow that it needs no telling—nor is there anyone who could tell it.

[4] If you, who are a serf and are obliged to obey the Commandments of the glorious Son of Our Lady—and not just you, but so are all the angels and all the men and everything that was created—, if you were taken and tormented and killed in front of your mother although guiltless of any crime, you can well imagine that your mother would feel great sorrow and great pity for you.[115] Therefore, if your own mother—who is capable of error—would have such great displeasure from your suffering, how much more the Virgin Mary—who cannot err—had great sorrow in the suffering of her Son![116]

[5] Consider, son, the pain that your mother would have if someone put sharp nails through your hands and feet and nailed you to the cross, and you looked at your mother with piteous regard as if asking for her aid and she could not help you. Through such thoughts and such imaginings, son, you will be able to grasp how great was the sorrow that Our Lady felt at the Passion and death of her Son.

[6] And if you imagine what great joy your own mother would have if you were resurrected, you can imagine how great was the joy Our Lady felt when she saw her beautiful Son resurrected in an immortal body, incorruptible, invulnerable, glorified in eternal beatitude.

[7] Unless you contemplate the much greater excellence, nobility that the Son of God has (greater than you have) and that Our Lady possesses (which is greater than your mother's), and unless you count all the pain you can imagine for the suffering your mother would

---

115. I translate "pietat" ("piety") as "pity" here in line with the emphasis on Mary's sorrow (cf. Ch. 35, n. 90).

116. Your own mother, who might be mistaken (or, perhaps, harbor some doubt) about your actual guilt or innocence, would still be greatly upset if you suffered the fate that Jesus suffered. Since the Virgin Mary cannot err, there was no possibility of doubt concerning her Son's innocence and, therefore, her suffering was that much greater.

have in your passion and death, you cannot contemplate as you should the great suffering and pain Our Lady endured at the death of her Son, nor the great joy she had from the Resurrection of our Lord God Jesus Christ.

49. ON THE JOY OUR LADY HAD WHEN HER SON APPEARED TO HER

[1] Son, the mother of God was with the Apostles and with the other disciples of Jesus Christ at an inn, and they were speaking about the Passion and death that the Son of God had suffered. And as they were speaking these words and Our Lady was full of pain and sorrow for the death of her Son, at that very moment, Jesus Christ appeared as the Son of God to cheer and console Our Lady and those who were with her.

[2] No man could tell the joy and happiness that filled Our Lady when she saw her glorious Son before her, whole and alive in a glorified immortal body. For just as the pain Our Lady suffered for the Passion of her Son is beyond my words, which could not speak it, so the joy of Our Lady is beyond my understanding, which cannot understand it, and beyond my words, which cannot tell it.

[3] Son, this name "Jesus Christ" is the same as naming God and man together and this word "apparition" is the same as saying "manifestation." Now, if a man, much loved and missed, who has been in a foreign land for a long time makes his mother very happy when she sees him coming, and he stands before her, how much the more Jesus Christ, who is God and man and who returned from death, made joyful Our Lady, who is His mother!

[4] So great was the joy the Queen of Heaven had in the apparition of her Son that it is enough to make every other joy joyful and enough to console every sadness, and anyone can be made happy by it, and by that joy every man can be blessed.

[5] Rejoice, son, in Our Lady's great happiness and in the virtue you can have through the virtue Our Lady had in her joy for her Son, for by such joy you will partake in the agreeable pleasure that Jesus Christ has from Our Lady. And every time you pray to Our Lady, remember the joy she had in the apparition of her Son and your prayers will be heard.

[6] If you are under the protection and benediction of Our Lady and you feel pain and sadness for any reason, do not think of it as a negative thing, for Our Lady is so overjoyed in her glorious Son that the happiness and bliss that fills Our Lady is so greatly sufficient for those who serve her that they become pleasing to the blessing of God.

50. On the Quinquagesima, Which Is Called Pentecost

[1] In the year there is a day called "Pentecost," that is to say, "the fiftieth day."[117] On that day the Holy Spirit came down upon Our Lady and upon the Apostles and illuminated them with knowledge and with diverse languages and comforted them with the grace and blessing of God.

[2] On that day, Our Lady and the Apostles were filled with such great joy that, through the abundance of great happiness and great joy, the beginning was begun when the Apostles began to preach the coming and the Passion of the Son of God. And, with the grace and blessing they had on that day, they spread throughout the world and converted the world to the path of salvation.

[3] Just as a piece of iron is heated in the fire so intensely that it is all aflame and full of fire within and without, on that day when the Holy Spirit came down from Heaven and came upon them in the semblance of tongues of flame, Our Lady and the Apostles were all inflamed in fervor and devotion and charity and joy.[118]

[4] When the Apostles were thus filled and inflamed with the grace of the Holy Spirit, they went to preach God's Gospels, which they could not preach until the Holy Spirit, who illuminated them and filled them with love so that they were able to and knew how to and desired to preach the faith of God, had descended upon them.

---

117. It seems likely that it is by Llull's design that the fiftieth chapter, and the middle chapter of the entire book, deals with "the fiftieth day" after Christ's Resurrection: Pentecost, the day on which the Apostles began their mission of evangelism throughout the world. This arrangement would, then, illustrate, once again, the quite literal centrality of the Apostolic missions for converting non-believers to Christianity to Llull's entire world view: at the close of the chapter, he promotes, once again, his primary goal of founding schools for the training of missionaries and for instruction in the foreign languages they will need to use in their preaching.

118. Acts 2:1–31.

[5] With the great devotion and great desire that filled the Apostles for converting the world, and through the death and passion they suffered out of love for the Son of God, they worked miracles and converted men to the way of salvation.

[6] Far away now, son, is that day when the Holy Spirit descended upon the disciples, and for that reason, son, devotion and charity for preaching and converting the infidels—who are in error—is almost dead and the fear of death has returned, which had filled the Apostles before the Holy Spirit descended upon them.

[7] Human understanding is lifted up in men by customs and writings, and the infidels ask insistently for necessary reasons and proofs to show the truth of the Catholic faith.[119] And we are called upon to work with great charity and fervor to learn diverse languages and to gain the necessary training since we are not worthy to work miracles, which unworthiness we have through our lack of charity and fervor and through the fear we have of undergoing suffering and death for the love of God.

51. ON THE ASSUMPTION OF OUR LADY

[1] For a long time, son, Our Lady's presence in the heavenly kingdom—which is her due—was desired by her Son and the angels and all the saints in glory, and great was the desire Our Lady had for a long time to be there. However, so that the Apostles and disciples who went throughout the world to preach the holy Catholic faith were stronger and more devoted to suffering tribulations for Jesus

---

119. Jews and Muslims reject arguments based on Christian authorities (that is, authoritative texts like the New Testament and the authoritative Christian interpreters of these texts) and, similarly, Christians reject Jewish readings of the Old Testament and the Qu'ran. Therefore, the only way in which the "infidels" can be convinced of the truths of Christianity is by agreeing before discussions begin to a set of "necessary reasons": self-evident premises that can be accepted as true by people of all belief systems. As the unspecified wise man (was it the Jew, the Christian or the Muslim sage?) in the Prologue to Llull's *Gentile* exclaims: "And since we cannot agree by means of authorities, let us try to come to some agreement by means of demonstrative and necessary reasons" (*SW* 1.116). This is a fundamental idea in Llull's thought and the prime impulse for Llull's development of his Art (see Ruiz Simón 1999: 358-366; and, especially, Bonner 2007).

Christ through the virtue and the holiness of Our Lady, it pleased our Lord Jesus Christ that she remain in this world for a long time after He had risen to the heavens.

[2] Now, when it pleased our Lord God for Our Lady to pass from this world to the other, on the day of her death, a procession with our Lord Jesus Christ and all the angels and archangels and all the saints of Paradise went out from Heaven to earth. With songs of great sweetness and with many great honors, they raised Our Lady to the sovereign Heaven, to the glory of our Lord God.

[3] When Our Lady remembered the misery of this world, which she had left behind, and saw her God and her Son, who had raised her to the Heavenly Father, before her, and she saw her Son Lord of all the saints in glory and saw that all of them praised Him and honored her Son, and that all had come together to honor and praise her, whether Our Lady was joyous or happy it is not even necessary to say. Nor, if there is anyone who seeks to measure it, will he be able to conceive or think of all the joy Our Lady had.

[4] Our Lady was raised and lifted above the moon and the sun and the stars, son. Therefore, as her Assumption was lofty and excellent and honored, so her happiness and joy must have been as well. Therefore, since her honor is inestimable, who is there who can say or write or signify, reckon the great joy the Queen of Heaven had when she arrived in glory?

[5] In the heavens there are two crowns that are better and nobler than all the others among the saints in glory. The first belongs to our Lord Jesus Christ and the other to Our Lady Saint Mary. Now, when her Son had crowned Our Lady and Our Lady saw her Son so nobly crowned and saw the nobility of the crown with which her Son had crowned her, the joy of Our Lady was equal to the crown. Therefore, since the glory of the saints in Paradise is so great, see how great was the joy of Our Lady.

[6] Dear son, if the sweet, divine and human regard with which Jesus Christ looked at Our Lady in heaven as mother and as Queen of Heaven and earth gave joy and sweetness to Our Lady, you may think I fall short in telling and writing such great and glorious joy. Therefore, since the joy of Our Lady Saint Mary, Glorious Virgin—may she be blessed!—is so great and so marvelous, I beg you, son, that Our Lady be the joy and hope and consolation and desire and love of your soul above all things.

[7] In your cares and in your prayers, remember Our Lady. Honor Our Lady's Son, as much as you can in all things if you wish to honor Our Lady and make her joyful, for the greatest honor that you can do Our Lady is to honor and serve her glorious Son God Jesus Christ.

On the Seven Virtues, Which Are Paths to Salvation[120]

52. On Faith

[1] The Catholic faith is to believe true, invisible things in accord with the Christian religion. Through faith, son, man perceives what is true without reason having to prove the things that he believes.

[2] Just as by the light that illuminates your corporeal eyes you see physical things, so, by the light of grace, you see the things you believe about the heavenly God of Glory and His works. And because the light of understanding is not sufficient for understanding everything that man requires in order to believe in God and His works, God illuminates the soul of man to believe in invisible things by the light of grace.

[3] Dear son, by the light of faith, the understanding rises up to understand, for, just as the lamp goes before you to show the way, so faith goes before understanding. Therefore, if you wish to have a subtle understanding, do not be an unbeliever, and believe so that your understanding can rise high enough that it understands the things that faith illuminates.

[4] Just as man earns merit by loving God and his neighbor and by being just with himself or others and by doing good works, so God has given man faith so that he earns merit by believing things he does not understand. Just as you ought to be thankful if someone makes you a loan without surety and without collateral and without a written contract but believes your word, if you believe those things you do not understand about God and His works, you have earned God's pleasure for what you believe, and through that pleasure you have merit and, through merit, glory. Thus, so that God can have the opportunity to give glory, He has given men faith.

---

120. On the role of the virtues and vices in the *DP*, see the Introduction.

[5] Son, Jews and Saracens, heretics, idolaters do not have faith, nor do they wish to have it. Thus, all of them together do not have as much light for believing in God and His works as you alone have if you believe in the fourteen Articles about which we have already spoken.[121] Therefore, since these people are lost by their lack of faith and, through faith, they can have salvation, remember and understand what a dear thing faith is and what a great gift our Lord God gives those to whom He gives faith. Since faith is such a great gift and so dear and so noble, hold the faith that God has given you dear and do not cast it from your heart for any other thing.

[6] God has given man two hands so that one can help the other and God has given man two lights: the light of faith and the light of understanding. So, if one cannot have the light of understanding, let one have the light of faith and believe what one cannot understand. Now, this light of faith is more necessary to farm laborers and artisans and men who do not have a lofty understanding. By this light, they help themselves from errors and temptations against the demons, who strive to make man disbelieve the things that understanding cannot understand.

[7] Faith rises above understanding in this world, for you can love God more through faith than you can remember Him through understanding. And faith sees God without intermediaries, and understanding cannot rise up to God without the demonstration of other things.[122] Faith retains things for the understanding at one time so that the understanding can understand them at a later time. By faith, you will understand in the other world—when you are there—what you cannot understand about it now. Just as nothing can conquer truth, so, too, your faith, if you love it, cannot be conquered.

[8] The bad Christians who deny and disbelieve God when they become Jews and Saracens would not give the eyes in their head for any amount of money. But from disloyalty and out of fear of death and in order to become noblemen, they cast faith from their soul, which remains in darkness and cannot, without faith, see God.[123]

---

121. See Chs. 1-12.

122. Through faith, we can experience God directly. We can only know God via the understanding by using proofs, and "necessary reasons," which are not God, but can lead our understanding and our memory to Him (see n. 119).

123. Here Llull suggests some of the motivations that, from his point of view, might cause someone to convert to Islam or Judaism. We do not have any clear idea of

53. ON HOPE

[1] In hope is our salvation. God has given man hope so that by doing good works he may have hope in God's justice and so that, if he commits sins or transgressions, he may be contrite and have hope in God's mercy.

[2] Dear son, when men hope for God's justice and mercy they fear falling into error. For if through hope for justice and mercy men who do good works and who repent their sins have hope of having glory, by doing bad works and by not being contrite in their hearts, they are contrary to God's justice and mercy, by which contrariety, they are worthy of being in the eternal infernal fire.

[3] Because you are my son and are the son of your mother, you hope to possess our worldly goods after my death and the death of your mother.[124] Now, if you have hope in heavenly glory, it behooves you to believe you are the son of the heavenly Father, the spiritual God of Glory, and you must fear his wrath, and you are subject to obedience to his commandments. And, if you act contrary to this, there will be no need for you to have hope in heavenly goods.

[4] You would do a great injustice to God's justice, son, if you did good works and yet despaired of God. And you do a great injustice to God's mercy if you despair of God's mercy because of sins that you commit. Therefore, since the hope of doing good is a reason for hoping for good, and hope makes you hope for pardon and reward, look! and see what a good thing hope is.

[5] God has ordained that you must eat and drink to sustain the body, and God has given hope, through which you have recourse to God and trust more in God than in yourself or in any other thing. For just as foods sustain the body, hope that trusts in God's power is the

---

how many Christians, in Llull's place and time, actually converted from Christianity to Judaism or to Islam, though it seems safe to assume that there were more cases of the latter than the former. It should be remembered that these are Llull's Christian views of the reasons for apostasy and are not necessarily the actual motivations of converts from Christianity to Judaism or Islam. A century and a half after Llull writes the *DP* another Majorcan Christian, Friar Anselm Turmeda, will tell the story of his own conversion to Islam in Tunis (Epalza 1994: 208-222 and 226-228). For this and other narratives of conversion, see Szpiech 2012.

124. Here we glimpse again a slightly more personal view of the father-son relationship than that suggested by the traditional trope of "dear son" (cf. Chs. 12.12, 53.3, 87.6, 88.6).

reason for which God helps you in your worries and in your needs and in the other things in which no one can help you, but only God alone.

[6] Many a man who cannot eat because he has nothing to eat would like to eat, and many a man would get well and would live if he had something to eat. And because every man can have hope, if he dies in eternal fire, it is not the fault of hope or of God, who allows all men to take of hope as much as they need.

[7] If you call heavily upon the man in whom you trust, son, because you have hope that he will help you, how much more do you call upon God if you trust in Him! For if you did not call upon God through hope more strongly than upon any other thing, it would follow that God does not have greater justice, power, wisdom, charity, mercy than man. And if He did not have these things, man would be God.

[8] Remember, son, the Incarnation and grievous Passion of our Lord God Jesus Christ, and understand how He has placed you under great obligation to have hope. For if God, without your having asked Him for it and without your having deserved it, was incarnated and suffered death for you, how much you, then, should have great hope in the justice, mercy, power, wisdom, charity and in all the virtues of God!

54. ON CHARITY

[1] Charity is to love God and your neighbor, which lightens the heavy labors and perils that come from love. Charity strengthens and multiplies nobility of heart against the enemies of love and worth.

[2] Dear son, charity gives pleasure from the goods and from the ills that one suffers for love. Charity exalts the will to desire great and noble things and exalts the understanding to understand great and lofty things, and charity brings man closer to God. Charity causes God to give great and noble gifts and allows God to pardon great transgressions and great sins. Charity consoles men from great misfortunes and makes poor men rich in their hearts.

[3] I could not tell, son, all the nobility that is in charity and for that reason I advise you to have charity in your heart so that you may have God, who does not enter into the heart of a man without charity.

The more charity you have in your heart, the more you will have God there. And, since you can have as much charity as you want, if you wish to have much God in your heart, have much charity in your soul.

[4] This world is a place where you can gather and multiply charity and love. The more charity and love you have in this world, the more glory you will have in the other. And do you know why? Because you are more loved by God through greater charity than through lesser, and God's will and His charity are accustomed to give greater glory to those who are more beloved by Him and who have loved Him most in this world.

[5] True charity, son, is to love God because He is good, and false love is if you love God more so that He will give you Paradise and worldly goods than for His goodness. False love is to love anything without God. Therefore, before you love anything else, love God, and love everything else you would love less than the love you have for God. And do not lift up your will to love any other thing above the love that you have for God.

[6] Have the intention of loving God in everything that you love, for if you do not, you will have charity in nothing that you love, and if you do not have charity, you will be unloved by God, and all those unloved by God are under His wrath, which torments them in eternal fire.[125] Therefore, because you are capable of having charity, dear son, wish not to be under the wrath of God.

[7] Love what God's will wants if you wish to have charity. Do not be impatient with anything desired by God's will. Love, son, all those whom God loves and love all those who love God, and hate everything that is hated by God and by those who love God. Before you love or hate anything, consider whether that thing is loved or hated by God and by those whom God loves and those who love God.

[8] Many a man, out of fear for his body or wealth or some other thing, is afraid to love God. Therefore, love so that you are loved by God, for the person who is loved by God suffers no harm, and there is no wealth and no profit comparable to the bliss of men who are loved by God.

[9] Son, charity—if you know how to have it—will gladden your heart every time you hear love and what you love spoken about. Whenever you see what you love, you will be happy and have pleasure

---

125. Cf. Ch. 92.

from it. Charity will protect you from wrath, sadness, despair, which are things that cause man great tribulation and great suffering.

[10] Just as you can see nothing if you have no eyes, so, without charity, you cannot have any virtue or any agreeable pleasure. The more you love, the more you will be able to understand, and the more you understand, the greater the love you can have. Therefore, if you do not wish to love greatly, then you do not wish to understand greatly, and if you do not wish to understand greatly, then you do not wish to love greatly. And if you hate loving greatly and understanding greatly, then it seems that you are capable of desiring neither to love nor to understand. Therefore, remember: if you would give your will for nothing, so that you desired nothing, or give your understanding for nothing, so that you would understand nothing, and if you gave your will or your understanding for something, then you would give yourself for something and you would love that thing more than to be in being. And if you were nothing, what thing could you have or possess?[126]

[11] Many a man has a cloak he does not know how to wear; many a man has a horse he does not know how to ride; and many a man has wealth he does not know how to use. So, ask yourself if you have the will and know how to love because a will that knows how to love is a greater thing than all the things just mentioned.

[12] Consider, son, how much the will that always wants and never has what it desires and always has what it hates has lost, when it could have had what it would love forever all the time. Consider what deep suffering the understanding gives to the will when it understands that the will will always want what it will never have and will have what it hates all the time, and that it has lost God, whom it could have loved

---

126. This is an example of one of Llull's arguments by *reductio ad absurdum* (Bonner 2007: 198 and n. 25). Joan Santanach i Suñol has explained it thus in a personal communication (2015): "After emphasizing the importance of desiring to love and to understand as much as one can, Llull [illustrates this point] by taking the contrary situation to absurd lengths, that is: what if one went entirely without loving and understanding—actions of the will and the understanding, respectively? The possibility of doing without the will and the understanding, in exchange for something else would be the same thing as giving oneself to oneself since one would have ended up without a will and without the capacity to understand. As a result, one would love whatever thing one had obtained in exchange more than one's own existence. And, if one were nothing [having giving oneself to oneself], one could not possess the very thing that one had given in exchange for the powers of will and understanding."

and possessed for all time. Know, son, that such understanding torments the will of the people who are in Hell because, in this world, they did not have love for God.

55. ON JUSTICE

[1] Justice is to render to each person his right.[127] Therefore, son, since God has given you so much, and you hope for so much mercy from God, it is just that you not take yourself or the goods He that has entrusted to you away from Him, for if you do not serve God with yourself and with what you have, you take from God what is His.

[2] All power, knowledge, righteousness is in God and His will loves justice and hates injustice and wrongs. For that reason, God's justice is fearful, for by injustice man cannot defend himself before God's might, nor by injustice can he hide the crimes he commits against justice from God's wisdom, nor by injustice can he pacify or restrain God's wrath.

[3] God's justice is worthy of love because God is good. Therefore, if you love God, you must love His justice. And if you hate God's justice, you hate God, who is His very justice, and you are hated by God and by all the saints in glory and by all the damned in Hell. Therefore, if you love God's justice, do not be angry at what God does with you, for you are His, nor should you be angry at what He does with the goods that He has entrusted to you, for they are His before they are yours.

[4] If divine justice punishes your body and punishes you in your goods, and you love it, you have greater love for divine justice than you would have if you loved God's justice because He punishes your enemy in his person and in his goods. The more you love God in His justice, the more you love mercy, which is God, and the more you love God's mercy, by that much more are your guilt and your sins pardoned.

[5] Ah, son! And how useful it is to be a lover of God's justice in this world, for if the damned in the other world—who will be in eter-

---

127. Llull plays with the various meanings of "dret" ("right/law") in this chapter on "justice." It could be interpreted as to render each person his due, his just deserts, what is his by right. See also Ch. 76, n. 208.

nal fire for all time—could love God's justice for even one moment, they would have glory for all time. But because they are not in a place where they can love God's justice, they will suffer punishment without end. Therefore, since this world is a place where you can love divine justice, son, love divine justice with all your soul, as much as you can.

[6] God's justice is fearful since it is a fact that mercy does not pardon all sinners, for if it pardoned all of them, it would be greater than justice, which would then damn no one.[128] Therefore, if you do not fear God's justice and you are among those whom mercy does not pardon, if you want to be among those whom it pardons, fear divine justice.

[7] If you bless God's justice when it gives you some suffering, you will bless justice with your mouth and with your mind, but justice will bless you in heavenly glory, which lasts for all time. And if you bless God in His justice when He does some good for you justly, why do you blame Him when He punishes you justly? Do you know, son, when it is that you blame God for His justice? When your will is resistant to what divine justice does.

[8] Justice and knowledge are in accord, and the person who judges without knowledge is like the blind man, who walks in darkness. Therefore, if you wish to live righteously, temper your will between your memory and your understanding, because, through too much desiring, the understanding is disturbed in its understanding, through which disturbance it comes into accord with ignorance, which is in disaccord with justice.[129]

[9] Do you know, son, why men who are involved in a legal dispute are given a judge? Because the judge can have a will more tempered between memory and understanding concerning what he is to judge than the men who dispute have, for each party wants to have what he is demanding or what he is defending so strongly that his abundance of will corrupts his understanding. Therefore, if you are a

---

128. Since "justice" and "mercy," as attributes of God, are equal in "virtue," one of them cannot be greater than the other. If God's mercy were greater than his justice, that would mean that mercy would always override justice and everyone would be pardoned. This is an excellent example of one of Llull's favorite forms of proof: the *demonstratio per aequiparantiam* (proof by equivalence). See the *Ars Demonstrativa, SW* 1.318 and Bonner 2007: 65-67; Ruiz Simón 1999: 238-295.

129. For the concept of "tempering," see Ch. 58.1.

judge, take care not to corrupt your understanding by taking bribes. And, if you want to be judged rightly, do not corrupt the understanding of the judge with gifts or by pleas, and entrust your case to justice, so that justice can commend you to the mercy of God.

56. ON PRUDENCE

[1] Prudence is a virtuous act of the will that loves good and avoids evil, and it is the act of an intelligence that knows how to choose between good and evil. Through this virtue, son, men have certainty and know the way to do good works and cease from doing evil.

[2] Prudence is to choose the greater good or the lesser evil, and prudence is to bring time and place, quantity and quality, into concordance, and prudence is to dissimulate in order to preserve secrets. Prudence is to gather when others scatter, and prudence is to scatter when others have nothing to spend, and prudence is to have both this world and the next.[130] And things contrary to prudence are those that are contrary to the ones just mentioned.

[3] Dear son, have prudence so that you are not deceived and so that you do not deceive, for deceiving and being deceived are not in accord with prudence. However, being deceived and prudence are in accord if you mix in patience and pardon.[131]

[4] Prudence lies between wisdom and knowledge, for, through wisdom it is a lover of the good and hates the bad and through knowledge it knows what is good and what is bad. For that reason, prudence brings wisdom and knowledge together, and wisdom and knowledge constitute prudence, and prudence does not exist without wisdom and knowledge.

[5] Would you be able to tell me, son, which is the greater good: to be loved by God or to be loved for being the lord of money, castles, cities, kingdoms? If you know how to answer and you love God more, you have knowledge with prudence. If you know how to answer and you love money, castles, cities, kingdoms more than God, you have

---

130. Perhaps Llull is thinking here of Ecclesiastes 3:5-6: "A time to scatter stones, and a time to gather...a time to keep and a time to throw away."

131. If one learns that one has been deceived and, instead of, say, taking revenge, one reacts prudently, with patience and pardons the deceiver then one has made being deceived and prudence come into agreement.

knowledge without prudence. And do you know why? Because you put the contrary of wisdom in concordance with knowledge, which is the contrary of prudence and wisdom. And if this were not so, it would follow that money, castles, cities, kingdoms and other worldly goods were worth more than God.[132]

[6] The fool in his wrath pursues wisdom, which is in concord with peace.[133] Therefore, if the fool in his wrath destroys your peace and makes you resemble him, ask yourself what you have done to prudence, which protects the patient wise man with a strong and firm heart against foolishness, wrath, suffering, which are in agreement in a disturbed will and a blinded intelligence.

[7] Precaution, mastery are in accord with prudence in trade and in the other mechanical arts, as long as there is no deceit or trickery involved.[134] These are contrary to prudence. Therefore, son, if you are a lover of prudence, have wisdom and knowledge, through which you desire and know how to bring prudence and precaution, mastery, into concordance, without falseness and deceit.

[8] To know how to deceive and to hate deception is to love prudence, which knows and hates deception and knows and loves charity, justice. Therefore, if the cobbler and the merchant know how to have prudence and earn worldly riches with dead flesh, will you, son, know how to earn heavenly life with your living flesh by making a virtue out of your death, which will happen in any case?[135] That is to say, that you can know how to die and desire to die giving glory and praise to your God.

---

132. The meaning of this argument is clearer if we understand the phrase "if you know how to answer" to be the equivalent of "if you have knowledge and your answer is that you love God more (or love money, castles, etc. more)..."

133. Cf. Proverbs 12:16 and 29:11.

134. The word Llull uses for "precaution" here, "cautela," had a double force, which Llull makes use of here: it could mean "taking precautions" in the normal, prudent, sense, or it could mean "precautions taken deliberately with the intention of deceiving someone" (DCVB).

135. The cobbler with leather and, perhaps, a merchant who is a butcher or a seller of skins or furs, prudently earn wealth by working with or selling dead flesh. Your living flesh is worth far more and can be prudently "merchandized" by you by dying a martyr's death—since you have to die one way or the other—in order to earn the far greater wealth of God's glory.

57. ON FORTITUDE

[1] Fortitude is strength of heart that strengthens the spiritual powers of the soul. And fortitude is the strengthening of the soul that vivifies bodily strength. And fortitude is nobility and sureness of courage.[136]

[2] Dear son, if you want to be strong in the battle against your flesh, the world and the devil, have strength in your heart, because fortitude is such a noble virtue that it conquers and overcomes in every battle. There is no fortitude in anything that can be conquered and overcome spiritually.

[3] The soul strengthens physical strength with its virtue and, with the objects that it perceives, it strengthens its own powers, for when the soul remembers and understands and loves God, it is strong against sins and evil thoughts. Therefore, in remembering and understanding and loving the goodness, greatness, eternity, power, wisdom, love and the other virtues of God, the soul's memory and understanding and will are so fortified by these objects it takes from God that evil remembering, understanding and willing have no power against the nobility of its heart.

[4] Do you know, son, what an object of the soul is? It is the representation of something made to its memory and understanding and will. Just as color is the object of the corporeal eyes when the eyes see colors, and just as flavor is the object of taste and odor for the sense of smell and voice to hearing and feeling to touch, and all these objects are corporeal, the soul has spiritual objects that it perceives through remembering and understanding, loving or hating.

[5] Just as the colors blue or green fortify corporeal sight and seeing red fortifies a man's courage, remembering and understanding and loving God and His power and the other virtues that pertain to God, and remembering and understanding and loving faith, hope, charity, justice, prudence, temperance and the other virtues which are appropriate to man reinforce the strengths and powers of the soul, through which strengthening, nobility of heart comes into its strength.[137]

---

136. For the psychological system referred to in this chapter, see Ch. 85 and Figure 2.

137. That is, we must engage all three powers of the rational soul—memory, understanding and will—with God's uncreated virtues as well as with the "created" virtues (that is, the theological virtues and the cardinal virtues) that pertain to men in order

[6] You know well, son, that some foods give greater strength to the body than others, and for that reason, you can know that the soul, by remembering and understanding and loving certain things more than others, can be stronger against sins and vices than by remembering and understanding and loving other things. For just as the noblest foods give greater strength to the body, the noblest memories, thoughts, desires, give greater force to the soul.

[7] Do you know, son, how nobility in remembering and understanding, loving takes root? In frequently remembering, understanding, loving great things and noble things and things of great nobility. Therefore, if you want to have strength of heart, know how to remember and understand, love noble things often, for many a heart is conquered and turns toward evil and deceit by remembering and understanding, loving vile things and from remembering and understanding and loving noble things too little.

[8] Dear son, if you are weak with the fear of death, recognize that you must die. If some delight seeks to subject you to itself, know that you will get tired of it. If you cease serving God because it is hard, imagine the hardships of Hell. If you are tempted to some evil out of poverty, desire to have poverty of spirit, which is richness of heart. If the beautiful appearance of woman inclines you to lust, consider and imagine the filthiness that issues from man and from woman. And if you have such thoughts and such imaginings, you will be strong against the vices, which are disagreeable to God.

58. ON TEMPERANCE

[1] Temperance is the will restrained between two extremes that are contrary in quantity. Therefore, son, if you wish to have temperance, you must increase the lesser and diminish the greater, and raise the lesser up toward the greater, and lower the greater toward the lesser until you make them equal in virtue.

---

to fortify these same powers. Llull gives a rationale for engaging all three powers in rehearsing these virtues in the next paragraph.

At the beginning of this paragraph, he offers an interesting glimpse of medieval ideas on the ways in which specific colors can affect physical sight, mood and emotions.

[2] Much remembering and understanding make for a tempered will. Much remembering and willing and little understanding mortify the understanding and exalt faith and belief. Therefore, if you want to understand with a tempered will, make your will equal in loving, hating memory and understanding.

[3] Love temperance, son, before you are full from eating and drinking, for loving temperance when you cannot eat or drink any more is not as good a time for loving temperance as is loving temperance when you feel the urge to eat and drink. You should not love temperance less during the times when you can be temperate easily than in the times when temperance best demonstrates its power.

[4] Temperance gives greater pleasure to the soul than eating or drinking does to the body. Temperate men are healthier and happier and live longer and are richer than men who stuff themselves by eating and drinking. Therefore, son, if you know how to make a comparison between good and better or between bad and worse, you are to blame if you do not have temperance.

[5] By eating and drinking you will have pleasure for as long as you eat and drink, and from eating and drinking too much, you will have pain and suffering and illness, which will bring about your death. If you are temperate in eating and not eating and in drinking and not drinking, you will have pleasure and bliss.[138]

[6] Dear son, poor men do not suffer from fasting as much as rich men suffer from eating too much, and poor men cannot gain as much merit through temperance as rich men can. Therefore, do not wish to be rich so that you can eat a lot and do not wish to be poor so that you can have temperance.

[7] Just as your body requires temperance so that you do not weaken it too much by eating too little or corrupt it by eating too much, your wealth and your rank and your age require temperance in your dress, in your speech, in your sleeping, in your spending and in all the other things that are necessary to you for praising and serving our Lord God.

---

138. That is, you will have both worldly pleasure and heavenly bliss.

59. ON SALVATION[139]

[1] Salvation, son, is the bliss of a male or female saint chosen by our Lord God in glory without end, for which salvation the seven virtues just discussed are the light in this world by which saintly men and saintly women see the roads down which they go to chosen bliss.[140]

[2] The seven virtues discussed above are great and noble things, son, but salvation is a greater thing beyond compare. And do you know why? Because the seven virtues are created things and salvation is to see God, who is the salvation of the saints in that they are saved and blessed and glorified in Him. Thus, created virtue alone is not enough for the salvation of man: uncreated virtue is also necessary.[141]

[3] There is no man, for all the good that he may do, who deserves salvation, but God grants salvation to those who have virtue and saintliness against vices and evil deeds. The person who thinks himself worthy of salvation because of his virtue is less worthy of it than the sinner who, because of his transgressions, believes himself to be worthy of damnation.

[4] Salvation is so lofty and noble a thing, son, that the Son of God, in order to save mankind, was born to be a man and to suffer terrible anguish and a painful death in His human nature. Therefore, since our Lord Jesus Christ had to do and undergo so much in order to give salvation more perfectly to man, who, for all the virtues that he may possess, can do enough to deserve salvation?

[5] Ah, son! And how many men who think they are worthy of salvation are damned! And do you know why? Because they think their works are equal to the works of God, which are greater than anything that a man can do for God. God gives more to a single soul when He gives it salvation than all the creatures that exist could possibly give to God.

---

139. As Joan Santanach points out in the Introduction, the sequence of the seven virtues is closed with a chapter on "Salvation," just as the sequence of chapters on the seven vices is closed by a chapter on "Damnation."

140. Llull again stresses that it is entirely by God's choice that we are saved, however saintly we may be. This is what Llull refers to at the beginning of this chapter as "chosen bliss."

141. Again, in this summary chapter on the virtues, Llull refers to the distinction between the seven created virtues just discussed and the necessity of God's uncreated virtues if one is truly to be saved. See Ch. 1 and n. 5.

[6] Hypocrisy and salvation are more strongly contrary in those who think they merit salvation by their works alone than in sinners who consider themselves unworthy of salvation because of their sins.[142] That is because the works that one does are not salvation, and the opinion that one has that by works alone one may be saved is the cause of one's damnation. And the unworthiness that the sinner recognizes in himself is in concordance with the mercy of God.

[7] Dear son, God's will is greater than your will, and for that reason, it follows that God loves your salvation more strongly than you do. Thus, His will is in accord with His power, which can give salvation to whomever He wishes. Because your will does not have the power to give salvation to yourself or to anyone else, if God did not love your salvation more than you do, He would be lesser in will than in power, and that is not true.

[8] God has given you free will so that you may be a lover of salvation and a hater of damnation. Just as God has given your body all the members appropriate to the body of a man and has given your soul all the powers appropriate to a soul, God has given your free will everything necessary for desiring salvation and hating damnation, so that you desire to receive salvation solely through the gifts of God.

---

142. Llull devotes portions of an entire chapter to the theme of hypocrisy below, Ch. 89.

On the Seven Deadly Sins

60. On Gluttony

[1] Gluttony is intemperate desire in eating and drinking, that is, eating and drinking more than is necessary.[143] This vice makes men desire to live so that they can eat and drink. It causes them to fear death, hunger and thirst while serving God, who makes men live so that He may be served by the man who undergoes suffering, perils, hunger, thirst and even death, if necessary, out of love for Him.[144]

[2] Therefore, son, since gluttony causes man to stray from the reason for which God created him, it is a mortal sin. And because man, according to the course of nature, wants to eat and drink every day, the contrary of gluttony can be an opportunity for salvation for him every day. That contrary is temperance, abstinence, continence and the other virtues that are appropriate for countering the sin of gluttony.

[3] Dear son, when infants are small, and you get them used to eating bread spread with oil and roasted meats and other such things frequently, they become gourmands. And when they are big, they become gluttons and eat and drink so much that they stuff themselves and sin by eating and by drinking too much, for which sin they are worthy of having hunger, thirst that will never end, in fire and in boiling water.

[4] Through gluttony, men make a god of their belly and of the things they wish to eat and drink. For just as the soul's desire should be to think continually about how a person can serve, love, praise,

---

143. Llull links the discussion of specific virtues to the discussion of specific vices across the intervening chapter on "Salvation:" the last of the virtues Llull discusses is temperance; the first of the vices is due to intemperance.

144. Here Llull shows the seriousness of the sin of gluttony in that it can cause men to avoid what Llull sees as the maximum expression of human love for God: martyrdom.

honor God, in gluttony, man obsesses continually about how to be full and how to obtain the foods he takes delight in eating and drinking.

[5] You never saw so bad a lord as the vice of gluttony, son, for it tortures you continually and often makes you suffer many hardships in seeking foods. And when you are full and cannot eat any more, it makes you obsess about how to eat more. From eating too much, you get indigestion and are sick and sad, and gluttony impoverishes and debases you, and you suffer when you fast.[145] So guard yourself as much as you can from being a slave to your belly.

[6] If you are tempted by gluttony, have recourse to temperance and abstinence, continence and prudence, for temperance will give you health, sufficiency and measure. Abstinence will give you the use of reason, and it will give you conscience and sense, for when you abstain, you understand and love reason and have conscience. Continence, son, will give you satiety of the will. Prudence will enable you to earn merit through temptation, by which you will be pleasing to God.[146] Therefore, consider and reflect on which gifts are nobler and better: the gifts given by the virtues mentioned above or the stuffed feeling and fullness that gluttony gives?

[7] Do you know, son, when you are being tempted by gluttony? When you have eaten and drunk enough and you still want to eat and drink something more in which you might find some pleasure. And do you know why you are conquered by gluttony? Because you remember the delights you find in eating and drinking, and you forget the dangers that come from eating and drinking too much. And do you know why temperance, abstinence, continence, prudence do not help you? Because you do not have fortitude against temptation and you do not remember the virtues mentioned above, which are pleasing to God.

[8] It is the custom of a good warrior to remember his enemy before he engages with him in battle. And do you know why? So that he can be prepared to fight and is not taken by surprise. Thus you, son, before you are full, remember your enemy, that is, gluttony. And do

---

145. That is, if you are used to being full, the days on which Christians are supposed to fast are especially onerous.

146. That is, you will gain merit by prudently resisting the temptation to eat too much. See Ch. 56.

you know why? So that you do not stuff yourself and are not the captive and subject of gluttony, which has so many subjects whom it brings under the wrath of God.

61. On Lust

[1] Lust is an insatiable desire contrary to the order of matrimony. Such a desire is hateful to God—who created the order of matrimony—because all those things, son, that are against God's will are against what He has ordained and created.[147]

[2] Lust is such an evil sin that it does not die in old age, for in lustful old men, their body is no longer up to lustful activities and, in their will, they continue to lust. Lust is such a stubborn vice—so deeply rooted—that without prayer, devotion and without punishing the body you cannot cast it from your imagination or from your desire.

[3] Dear son, lust defiles the soul in its remembering and understanding, willing, for the thing that it makes the soul remember and understand, love, is such a foul thing and so ugly that I dare not name it or write it. And lust fouls the body with that thing I do not dare to say. Therefore, since lust has so much filthiness in having its deeds named, how much greater is the filth of the deed itself!

[4] The best remedy one can have for a bad lord or a bad land is to flee them, and the best remedy one can have against lust is to flee the occasion for sinning and for imagining the delights of lust, and to forget them and to remember other things that are not like lust.

[5] The moment your imagination imagines the delights man has through lust, imagine, son, the filthiness that is in man and in woman through lust. And do you know why I command you to imagine it right away? So that you can turn and bend your imagination to some other thing through which you can forget lust and so that lust cannot take root in your memory. For when the lust puts down roots in the memory by being remembered often, through that rooting it also puts down roots in the will, which then desires it.

[6] Painting and coloring one's face and ornamenting one's clothes are signs that signify lust. Now, if the signs of corporeal death are terrifying, how much more so are the signs of lust, which is the

---

147. See Ch. 28.

death of the soul, by which death the soul of the lustful man dies, eternally suffering punishment without end!

[7] Lust and jealousy are in accord, and scorn and suffering and death every day are in accord. Lust does not give delight every day or every hour of the day and, for that reason, lust and damnation are in accord.[148] Therefore, son, if you wish to flee the suffering and death that man suffers continually through jealousy, flee and do not be subject to lust.

[8] The more sense and reason men have, the more they fear and flee great dangers. Therefore, since lust is such a bad lord, son, see under what obedience religious men and women place themselves and see how they flee lust because they are lovers of chastity, virginity, which are virtues through which they are pleasing to God.

62. ON AVARICE

[1] Avarice is to hoard things that are more than you need for yourself and are necessities for the poor. These things are denied to the poor by the insatiable greed of the avaricious, through which denial, the poor suffer hunger, thirst, cold, nakedness, illness, sorrow and death.

[2] Dear son, the miser collects money in his coffers and possessions in the land where he is, and he casts charity, hope, generosity, justice and the other virtues from himself. For that reason, he collects vices contrary to the virtues discussed in the preceding section in his heart.

[3] Your shirt is closer to your flesh than your tunic, and the skin on your back is closer to your bones than your shirt. And so you can understand, son, that man can bring hope, charity, justice, generosity and the other virtues closer to himself—and to what man is—than are money, possessions and other riches, which are not like man in their nature. And because man, by being covetous and avaricious, distances the virtues that are pleasing to God from himself and draws the vices that are hateful to God closer and places them within him-

---

148. Llull's argument is: lust does not give delight every day or every hour; eternal damnation, since it is eternal and perpetual, also does not give delight every day or every hour (in fact, it never gives delight); and so, lust and damnation are "in accord."

self, if you are wise, cast avarice far from your soul so that you are not under the wrath of God.

[4] Covetousness is the same whether it involves money, bread, wine, meat, fine fabrics, horses or other things like these, for with each one of these things man can be covetous if he does not use it in the appropriate way. Now, even by giving away money, horses, clothing and by accumulating the honor that should be given to God for oneself, one can be covetous and avaricious of honor and fame and social status. For just as rich men are covetous because they do not want to give to those to whom they should give, they are covetous when they want to have the honor and worthiness that man should attribute to his Creator and his Lord.

[5] Dear son, do not be covetous, for a covetous man always feels deprived because his will cannot be satisfied. And do not have so much generosity that you have to be covetous and take from another what God has given him, and consider yourself satisfied with what you have, for you do not know how long you will live or when death will come for you, nor can you take what you have in this world with you to the other, for you will have to leave it behind in this world.

[6] There is no man in all the world who desires to have riches as much as the covetous man. Nor is there any man in all the world who is as poor as the man who is covetous, for every man who is not covetous possesses at least something, and even if he does not have anything, at least he has fulfillment in his soul in that he considers himself satisfied in not having anything. But the covetous man possesses nothing. Rather, he is a slave and captive of that which he thinks he should have.

[7] Just as many maggots swarm together in a lot of meat, many an envious man and many malicious gossips and many enemies gather around the avaricious man. And do you know why? Because they need the riches that he possesses, riches that he makes no good use of, either for himself or for others. Therefore, be assured, son, that many an avaricious man dies early from his riches, either because his enemies kill him or because God kills him so that his riches, which He has created, can bear some fruit.[149]

---

149. That is, God kills the avaricious man so that, once his hoard of wealth is released at his death, it can pass on to others who will put the wealth to better use.

[8] Avarice makes a man forget God and loyalty, and makes him remember betrayal and deceit. Avarice makes the body labor and go from one land to another and from one place to another. Avarice makes the soul struggle in its remembering and in its understanding and in its will. And for that reason, the body—which is not of the nature of the soul and does not have the same needs—cannot help the soul and causes it to fall under the malediction of God.

63. ON SLOTH

[1] Sloth is sadness of the soul made worse by the well-being of one's neighbor. Know, son, that this vice signifies damnation more strongly than any other vice, and salvation is better signified by sloth's contrary than by any other virtue.[150]

[2] Son, be not slothful, for it is a sin contrary to what God does. For if God gives something to a man, sloth makes the man feel displeasure in the good that God gives; and if God punishes him in this world, sloth makes the man angry that God does not punish him more strongly.

[3] Sloth keeps its subjects upset and unhappy all the time. For that reason, son, avoid and hate its lordship and be a lover of good and do not let evil please you. For if you love good, you will be happy when you see and understand the good that you will love, and if you hate evil, you will have piety and you will fear the justice of God.

[4] Sloth makes men always full of ill will. Ill will is a disease of the soul, and the sickness of the soul mortifies the body, and, by the mortification of their body, men get sick and die early. Therefore, son, since all this harm comes from sloth, if you are the lover of your own harm, be slothful.

[5] If God were slothful, He would not have created the world, nor would He have taken human flesh in Our Lady Saint Mary, glorious Virgin, nor would He have suffered the Passion to redeem the human lineage, and He would destroy everything that exists. If you, son, are slothful, then you would love God if He were slothful, for one

---

150. Lull leaves it to the reader to work out what the "contrary" of sloth is. For medieval texts that offer a specific schema of vices and opposing virtues, see the Introduction.

like loves another. And if you loved God for being slothful, you would hate Him because He does not take what He has given you away from you. And you would love Him if He destroyed you. Therefore, since these things follow from one to the other, you can imagine what a serious thing it is to be slothful.

[6] The man who is slothful is like the devil, for the devil is slothful because of all the good that he remembers and understands, and he is sad when evil is not greater than good. And for that reason, the slothful man strives as much as he can to diminish good and multiply evil. He receives suffering and blame in this work, by which blame, he multiplies his own punishment and torment, from which multiplication, he has wrath and sadness, and, for that reason, he has suffering, damnation and punishment in all possible ways.

[7] If you are slothful, you will speak disparagingly, for sloth will make you say negative things, and you will be a liar. You will never be far from deceit, betrayal, falseness. You will be in danger from your enemies and, because of sloth, no one will help or defend you.

[8] Ah, son! So many men are unaware that they are in sin because of sloth, and so, among the other evils that come from sloth is that it does not reveal itself. And for that reason, sloth is more dangerous than any other sin, for you receive more damage from the harms you least suspect than from those that are evident.

[9] The devil had sloth because of the good that God gave to our father Adam and to our mother Eve in the earthly paradise, and for that reason, he advised them to eat of the fruit, by which Adam and Eve fell under the wrath of God.[151]

64. ON PRIDE

[1] Pride is the belief and vehement desire in the heart for what is vile to be noble and what is noble vile. Pride is the contrary of humility, which resides in a nobility of heart that favors less noble things so that it can give them greater nobility.

---

151. In this chapter, Llull offers a remarkably keen analysis of the state of mind we might identify as "depression" today. In the final paragraph of this chapter, Llull finds the devil's sloth to be the cause of the most cataclysmic event in the history of humankind: the Fall and the expulsion from the Garden of Eden.

[2] Know, son, that pride flees equality and seeks solitude and uniqueness, and it finds no peer or equal. And humility always seeks its like. Therefore, since the King of Glory is unique and has no peer or equal in nobility, if it were possible, a proud man would make himself God.

[3] God has divided His entire Creation into three states: greater, equal and lesser. Pride is contrary to each of these three, for the proud man is contrary to greater in that he wants to be above greater and wants to diminish that which has greatness above him. The proud man is contrary to equal in that he wants to be greater and for his equal to be beneath him through inferiority. And the proud man is against lesser in that he does not want it to be greater and does what he can to make it less than it is. Thus, the proud man is contrary to what God has created.

[4] Out of pride, the demons wanted to be like God and, if they could have climbed so high, to be the equals of God. Since they were like God, they wanted and desired to be greater than God. For that reason, God cast the demons down into the infernal abyss, which is the lowest place that exists and the place that has the most evil and suffering. And for that reason, God—may He be blessed!—created man and wants man, through humility, to rise into the glory from which the demons fell.

[5] Know, son, that proud men will not rise into Paradise, for if the proud were allowed to rise there, God would not have cast out the demons. Therefore, if you prefer the companionship of demons in eternal fire for all time and you hate the company of God and the angels in glory without end, be proud.

[6] In this world, proud men act like the demons when they were created as angels, for the poor proud man desires to be equal to the rich man in riches and honors. And when he has risen to that wealth and to that honor, he despises the person who is equal to him and wants to be above him in nobility and wealth, and he desires to be equal to another man who is further above him in riches and honors. Thus, he is engaged in nothing but wanting to climb and in looking down on his equal. And for that reason, such men are like the demons who despised the benign angels in that they wanted to be nobler than the angels—in that they wanted to be like God.

[7] Dear son, if you are a proud man and you are a cobbler, you will want to be a draper. When you become a draper, you will want to

be a burgess, and when you are a burgess, you will want to be a knight, and from knight, you will want to rise to count, and from count to king, and from king to emperor. And if it were possible to climb higher, you would want to climb higher. Now, God would permit you all this, and you would not be committing a sin in this, as long as you were not proud and did not despise those beneath you or above you or those equal to you in riches and nobility.[152]

[8] The proud man not only has pride in his own rise and in knocking down others, but also has pride in his children, for the cobbler wants to marry off his daughter and his son to spouses who are more noble than he is, and a draper will want the same, and so on for all the other steps mentioned above. As a result, inappropriate marriages are made and, because of the inequality between them, husbands are despised by their wives and wives by their husbands. Many sins are committed so that great dowries can be given, and, through inappropriate unions, many a father is dishonored and many a mother is dishonored and vilified, and there is great discord between husband and wife.

[9] In a proud man there is no charity or piety, nor does he have any virtue. However rich, honored, powerful, or however handsome his appearance, he is not pleasing to anyone else, nor does he take pleasure in anyone else. Therefore, since pride is the cause of so much evil in this world and of so much suffering in the other world, know, son, that the person who casts humility from his heart for pride knows little about making trades.

[10] Dear son, when you look at your features and you think about your wealth and having honors, if the temptation of pride comes over you, immediately remember and understand what you were born from and through what place you were born and what the clothing in which you were born was like. And remember, son, what you have in your belly beneath your tunic and what comes out of you through your nose and your mouth and other places. And do not forget the worms that will gnaw your ribs and your face, nor the dirt in which you will be laid. And if, son, you hold all these things in memory so

---

152. Here and in the following paragraph, Llull offers a vivid view of social climbing in medieval society, which is so often seen as socially static. In Llull's view, God does not oppose social mobility as long as it is not done out of pride or with the result that one despises those beneath one. For the meaning of the term "burgess," see Ch. 79 and n. 242.

that you are not proud, you will be humble, pleasing to men and to God.[153]

65. ON ENVY

[1] Envy is to desire the goods of others without deserving, through merit, to possess them. Avoid this vice, son, as much as you can so that you do not deserve to be possessed by demons in eternal fire.

[2] To envy the goods of others is a mortal sin through which the envious soul dies under the wrath of God. God's wrath makes the envious soul live in painful death without end, in which death the miserable soul desires what it will never have.

[3] Just as man has knowledge through words of what the soul wants and understands, through envy and the other sins he has knowledge in this world of the infernal punishments. For just as the envious man desires what he does not have and does not do the things by which he could have what he wants without harm to his neighbor, the damned in Hell will forever envy the heavenly glory of the blessed in glory and will not do anything to earn glory for themselves. Rather, they will want God to take the glory away from the saints and give it to them, who do not deserve it.

[4] According to the course of nature and according to what the philosophers explain, form is the manifestation of matter. Therefore, just as matter shows itself through form, so, according to the quality of the mortal sins, infernal punishment is revealed. For that reason, God has ordained that those who practice sin recognize in their sin the punishment that is prepared for them for that sin.[154]

---

153. Here, as in Ch. 61, Llull offers some practical ways for using the memory, understanding and will to resist the temptation of the vice under discussion, in this case, pride. The process described here is that for keeping a venial sin (those we may commit impulsively before the intellect has a chance to intervene) from becoming a mortal one (one taken with the full consent of the soul's free will). The same process is also described in Ch. 92.10.

154. In this and the preceding paragraph, Llull observes that the specific nature of a specific sin in this world prefigures the punishments one will receive for that same sin in Hell. Thus, like words, our acts and any negative consequences in this world are signs we can and should read that are indicative of far greater suffering to come. In this particular case, the envious person's desiring of things he cannot have is the "form" which reveals the "matter" that will be the envious person's eternal desire in Hell for a

[5] Envy is contrary to charity, hope, justice and the other virtues. Therefore, since man merits having worldly goods by being a lover of virtue, if man could have worldly goods through envy, it would follow that, in order to have virtues, he should not possess that which God has placed in the service of man. Therefore, since it is not this but the contrary, the envious man is not worthy to be the possessor of any good, in order to signify that the damned have no blessing.

[6] The envious man does not give thanks to God. And if there were another god, he would believe in that god—if it gave him what he desires—and he would deny the God who created him. For that reason, envious men are impatient and hate God when He takes things from them. And if He gives them worldly goods, they love Him more for the things He gives them than because of the nobility, goodness that God has in Himself.

[7] The envious person takes and does not give, and destroys and kills and does not forgive. The envious man is never without sadness, worry, falseness and deceit. He is more inclined to treachery than any other man. Therefore, son, since envy contains so much evil in itself, do not be envious if you wish to be in heavenly bliss with the angels and with God.

66. On Wrath

[1] Wrath is a disturbance in thought that destroys the connection between will and intelligence. And because God has given man understanding so that he understands Him and has given him will so that he loves Him, it follows that wrath, which destroys the order that God has established in the soul, is a sin, by which sin man falls under the wrath of God.

[2] Son, do not be subject to wrath and do not obey it if you are moved to wrath, for wrath blinds the eyes of the understanding and makes a person hate what he should love. And wrath makes men speak like fools and puts them in danger of losing this world and the other.

---

salvation he can never possess. This idea is more fully and explicitly developed in Ch. 99.

[3] The wrathful man pays no attention to good beginnings or middles or ends. Whatever he does, he does it rashly, and if he has killed men or said vile words or committed some other sin when wrath has left him he scarcely remembers what he has done, and he regrets what he has done. For that reason, son, take care not to do anything while you are full of wrath.

[4] Reason shows that a man should not do anything at all in anger, for if what he does is bad if he were not wrathful, he would not act as badly. And if what he does is good, if he were not wrathful, he would do it better than he does it while wrathful. Therefore, just as the crazy man must be tied up so that he does not throw rocks, the wrathful man should be tied up so that he does not do anything at all.

[5] A person can protect himself from a false man, but who can protect himself from a wrathful man, since it is a fact that one wrathful man makes another man, or other men, wrathful? Therefore, son, if you wish to protect yourself from a wrathful man, keep wrath from your heart and fight wrath with patience, abstinence, hope, charity, justice, fortitude, for with such arms man can defend himself from wrath and from those who provoke it.

[6] You wake a sleeping man by shaking him and shouting. So, son, when you are wrathful, wrath will shake your heart so that you wake up and have abstinence, patience, charity. The more wrathful you are, the better you will be prepared to have great abstinence, patience, charity, and, the greater the virtue you have in your heart, the nobler your heart will be and the more pleasing you will be to our Lord God.[155]

67. On Damnation[156]

[1] Damnation is losing eternal heavenly glory and being subjected to enduring infernal punishments without end. Know, son, that men are damned by the seven deadly sins mentioned above.

---

155. This is an interesting analogy, in which the experience of an episode of great wrath can "shake" you up (as one shakes a sleeping person) and actually "awaken" you to be more receptive to the virtues, especially those of abstinence, patience and charity.

156. Just as Llull has closed the series on the virtues with a chapter on salvation (Ch. 59), he closes the series on vices with a separate chapter on damnation.

[2] Dear son, our Lord God has created man so that he can achieve salvation. When man subjects himself to sin and is disobedient to God, he strays from the reason for which God has created man, and, because God is just, He punishes man with infernal torments.

[3] God damns whomever He wants, but His will does not wish to damn any man without reason. And do you know why? Because reason and justice are in accord and because God's will and God's justice are one and the same thing. For that reason, our Lord God does not damn any man without the man's being to blame.

[4] Do you know, son, why no man merits glory no matter how virtuous he is? Because God is glory and God is greater, beyond compare, than man is in himself or through any virtue or virtues that he may possess. Thus, it is signified that every sinful man deserves infernal punishment. And do you know why? Because losing God is infernal punishment. No sinful man merits having God, for if just men, for all the virtues that they may possess, do not merit God, how much less do sinful and unjust men deserve Him!

[5] In your soul, son, you can sense free will, which God has given to your heart so that you can do good or evil. If you do good, God has reason to give you salvation, and if you do evil, you are destined for damnation. But, since salvation is a nobler thing than your will and than any good that you can desire to do or do on your own, without God's grace you cannot have salvation. And because your will has the power of desiring and of doing evil, for that reason, you, by yourself (and any other man by himself), can choose damnation without the assistance of God.[157]

---

157. It is important to note that Llull closes his section on the virtues and vices and, indeed, the entire catechetical portion of the *DP*, with a mention of free will and its role in salvation. Despite its importance, free will is limited in its reach, however. As an excellent example of the intellectual moves Llull intends to inculcate in the *DP*, he argues that since salvation is nobler than the human will or any good works a human being might do, free will's power cannot reach as high as salvation. Ultimately it can have no influence there: God alone determines whether we are saved. The will and good works are superior, however, to damnation and so, although we cannot choose salvation (which depends on God alone), we can, in fact, choose damnation of our own free will.

ON THE THREE LAWS[158]

68. ON THE LAW OF NATURE

[1] Natural law is a commandment intelligible through rational discretion, understood in order to be obedient to God. The patriarchs and prophets from the time of Adam until Moses lived under this law.[159]

[2] This law is signified to human understanding by the actions that the elements, plants, beasts, birds, men and all the other created things perform. For the things they do according to the course of nature signify how man should use his reason and be obedient to God and how he should act so that he can accomplish the purpose for which he was created.

[3] Dear son, it is natural law to honor one's lord, one's elder, one's benefactor and to love one's neighbor. It is natural law to want for one's neighbor what one wants for oneself and to hate in one's neighbor what one hates in oneself. It is natural law to love good and to avoid evil.

[4] Some elements are naturally obedient to others in the generation and corruption they undergo.[160] Plants and trees, according to

---

158. This section is a transitional section in which Llull moves from the "catechetical" first part of the *DP* to the more "encyclopedic" second part. Nevertheless, as Joan Santanach points out in the Introduction, moral and spiritual topics are by no means abandoned in the second part. By "law," Llull understands the various sets of divinely given rules governing human conduct. For him, there are three: 1) natural law; 2) Judaism, the Old Law; and 3) Christianity, the New Law. In the latter two cases, the term "law" comes to coincide for us with the idea of a specific "religion," but this term does not carry quite the same meaning in Llull's day (see Ch. 82). In this section, Llull also treats the beliefs of Gentiles, who, he says, live "without law" (Ch. 72). See Romano & De la Cruz (2008: 432-459) for a useful guide to Llull's attitudes toward non-Christian faiths over the course of his career.

159. Ch. 97 situates these "laws" within a Christian scheme of history.

160. For an explanation of the generation and corruption of the elements, see Ch. 77 and Ch. 94 and Figure 1.

the season, bear leaves and flowers and fruits. And some beasts bow down before others. All this signifies, son, that you should be obedient to God and to your earthly lord according to the course of nature and that each man should follow the nature of his understanding. The philosophers that compiled the science of philosophy lived under this law.

[5] Natural law is the same as saying, "according to the natural order." Therefore, since God created everything that exists in order to demonstrate His great virtue and His great power and to be loved and known and served, obeyed by man, all Creation signifies and reveals God to the human intelligence in ordered fashion according to the course of nature. However, because sinful men stray from the order of natural law and love the vanities of this world, they do not understand the signification that created things give concerning our Lord God, and thus they are disobedient to God and to nature.

[6] It is a natural thing to see the sky and the stars, the sea and the lands and all the other things with your corporeal eyes, and to hear voices and sounds with your ears, and to smell odors with your nose, and so on for the other physical senses. And it is a natural thing that the soul, using the imaginative power, gathers all the things that the physical senses perceive and passes them to the human understanding in the phantasy, which is located between the forehead and the back of the neck, and that the understanding lifts itself above the phantasy in order to understand what is presented to it concerning God's nobility and greatness, and so that the will loves and obeys God.[161]

69. ON THE OLD LAW[162]

[1] The Old Law consists of written statutes, commanded and given by God to Moses. It is such a necessary and reasonable thing, son, to

---

161. In this final paragraph on natural law, Llull shows how the process of perception of the natural world through the senses and the powers of human psychology leads ultimately to an understanding of God's greatness and, thence, to love and obedience for God. For a fuller explanation of human psychological powers as understood by Llull, and for the spelling "phantasy" that I use here, see Ch. 85 and nn. 290 and 291.

162. For Llull's understanding of Judaism, see Book 2 of the *Gentile*, in which a Jewish sage argues for the beliefs of the Jews (*SW* 1.151-190).

obey God's commandments that natural law alone was not sufficient. It was also necessary for our Lord God to speak to Moses and to give him a written law so that His commandments had more force and so that man was more obligated and more responsible to God's command.

[2] Moses was a prophet, which is the same as saying "a person inspired and illuminated by the Spirit of God," through which inspiration and illumination he had knowledge of things present and past and future beyond the reach of human understanding. So, God gave the Law to this man on Mount Sinai, in which are written the Ten Commandments, as we have already discussed.[163]

[3] Know, son, that Moses was a Jew and was lord and ruler of the people of Israel, who were Jews. Moses was a man of such saintly life that our Lord God showed Himself to him and spoke with him and revealed to him how He had created the world and how He had put Adam and Eve in the earthly paradise and how Adam was disobedient to God and how Noah went in the ark and how the flood happened. And God revealed all the other things to Moses, as is told in the first book of the Old Law.[164]

[4] In that time, Moses, by the grace of God, brought the people of Israel out of the power of Pharaoh and out of the land of Egypt and led them to the desert where they lived on God's manna. And among that people were many holy men who were prophets and friends of God. And that Law lasted until the coming of our Lord Jesus Christ, who gave the New Law to renew the Old. The New Law is the Gospels you hear read in the holy Church.

[5] In the Old Law, son, there were many rules and many customs that prefigured the New Law and, because the Jews who live now believe that they keep and follow those statutes and do not understand what they truly mean, they live in error and they are contrary to the New Law.[165]

---

163. Cf. Chs. 13-22.

164. The "first book of the Old Law" is, of course, the biblical book of Genesis. Llull uses this chapter, in part, to review the basic Bible stories of the Creation, the Fall, and the Flood, just as he told the story of the Creation in detail in Ch. 3.

165. In this and the following paragraphs, Llull refers to the "typological" Christian reading of the Old Testament, in which events, people, prophecies and expressions of the Old Testament were seen as "prefiguring" elements of the New. The meaning of, say, Abraham's willingness to sacrifice Isaac, must be read as a prefiguration of the sacrifice of Christ upon the cross. It is only with belief in Christianity that this full

[6] The Old Law was made to be the beginning and foundation of the New, and the New Law was made so that it could be the fruit and the fulfillment of the Old, and that, son, is how it is with all things according to natural law, for it is fitting that what is first be the foundation and that what comes after be the fruit and the fulfillment.

[7] The Jews who have lived from the time of Jesus Christ forward believe that they keep the Old Law. But they do not really keep it (except in the literal sense), and they are contrary in belief to the signification that the Old Law conveys about the New and to the concordance that exists between both the Laws. And because they are in error and because they plotted the Passion of the Son of God, God has condemned them to be the slaves and captives of all peoples, and they are the most debased and cowardly people who exist.

[8] There are no men who commit more evil deeds than the Jews, nor do they have kings or princes, which all other peoples have. And because of the servitude in which they live, they cannot keep the Old Law or the rules established by it.[166] Just as God honored them above all the other peoples in the beginning, for the blame and the vileness in which they live—which are greater than among any other peoples—they are held in greatest dishonor by the justice of God.

---

meaning of the Old Testament event can be understood. The Jews, of course, rejected such notions and from this stemmed the frequent characterization of Jews as being blind to the true, fulfilled, meaning of their own sacred texts. As Llull continues below, the Jews only understand the literal sense of their texts; they do not understand their deeper meaning as prefiguring the coming of Christ. See nn. 38 and 343.

166. In Llull's day this idea was becoming one of the rationales for increasing intolerance and, ultimately, for the expulsion of Jews from Christian lands: Augustine had argued that Jews could be tolerated in Christian society. However, in Llull's century the mendicant friars (see Ch. 82) had begun to argue that current Jewish intellectual activity "distorted the true biblical Judaism whose observance theoretically entitled the Jews to remain in Christendom" (Cohen 1982: 14-16; see also 19-22). Cohen reviews other theories for the increasing intolerance toward Jews in Western Christendom, including "the notion of Jewish servitude or serfdom, as it was expressed in the papal and imperial legislation of the period, [which] did much to degrade Jews socially, to deprive them of basic civil rights, and to make them the objects of popular disdain and hostility" (15). Llull strongly echoes such ideas here.

70. On the New Law[167]

[1] The New Law is the grace of God founded upon natural law and on the written Old Law. The most important foundation of the New Law is the joining and the binding together of the Son of God and the human nature taken from Our Lady Saint Mary, Glorious Virgin.

[2] Dear son, Jesus Christ came into the world to give a New Law, which He gave by enduring death and suffering for us sinners. For just as God gave the Old Law to Moses in writing, Jesus Christ gave the New Law in suffering and death, charging His people to obey, love, fear and serve Him.

[3] Strong, son, are the commandments given in the Old Law because God commanded them, but, because, with the New Law, Jesus Christ—who is God and man—obligated His people so greatly to serve Him (because He wished to die for them), those who break the ordinances of the New Law are more culpable than those who broke the commandments under the Old Law before the New Law came into existence.

[4] Son, the New Law is founded on the Seven Sacraments of the holy Church, which we have already explained to you and which are ordained in the holy Church by the authority that our Lord Jesus Christ gave to Saint Peter the Apostle.[168]

[5] The apostles Saint Matthew and Saint John, and Saint Mark and Saint Luke, who were disciples of Jesus Christ, are the four evangelists who wrote the New Law, that is, son, the four Gospels you hear read in the holy Church.

[6] In those four Gospels are written the words our Lord Jesus Christ spoke when He was in this world. And in that book are the deeds and the miracles Jesus Christ performed and the blessings He promised.[169] The instructions He gave to His disciples are written there, and you can find the doctrines He gave them in that book.

---

167. See also Book 3 of the *Gentile*, in which a Christian sage argues for the beliefs of the Christians (*SW* 1.191-257).

168. Cf. Chs. 23-39.

169. Llull may be referring to the blessings promised by Christ in the Gospels in general or, more specifically, to the eight Beatitudes promised by Christ in the Sermon on the Mount found in Matthew and presented by Llull in Chs. 37-44.

[7] Do you know, Son, why the New Law is the fulfillment of the
Old Law? Because you can have more faith by believing the New Law
(because of the Trinity and because of the Incarnation, which are set
forth more clearly there) than by believing the Old Law.[170] And if you
understand the New Law as well as the Old Law, you will have greater
understanding by understanding the New Law than the Old. Therefore, because through greater faith you can have greater merit and
through greater understanding you can have greater charity, the New
Law is superior to the Old.

[8] Take care, son, when you swear on the four Gospels, not to lie
knowingly, for if you do, you are renouncing all the benefits promised by the New Law and are disobeying all the rules and commandments of the New Law, by which disobedience you will be displeasing
to God.

71. ON MOHAMMED[171]

[1] Mohammed was a deceitful man who wrote a book called *The
Koran*, which Mohammed said was the law given by God to the Saracen people, of whom Mohammed was the beginning.

[2] Mohammed was from a town called Yathrib, which is ten days
journey from Mecca, where the Saracens worship, just as Christians
worship at the Holy Sepulcher in Jerusalem.[172]

---

170. Llull again affirms that the Incarnation and the Trinity were already a part of
the Old Law, and contained in the Old Testament, figurally, but that in the New Testament these things are set forth "more clearly" and explicitly.

171. In this chapter, Llull does not treat the specific beliefs of Islam (which Llull
no doubt knew rather well) as a "law." See Book 4 of the *Gentile*, in which a Muslim sage
argues for the beliefs of Muslims (*SW* 1.258-293). For Llull, Islam is not a part of the
succession of "laws" given by God that form the core of human history from the Christian point of view (see Ch. 92). Rather, Llull treats Muslim beliefs as, at best, a rough
compilation of the Old Law and the New Law taught Mohammed by the hermit Micolau (see n. 173), together with things Mohammed "invented" on his retreats to the
mountain. This chapter, then, omits the topic of specific Islamic beliefs and talks about
two things: the life of Mohammed and Llull's ideas of the ways in which it might be
possible to convert Muslims to the Christian faith. On Llull's treatment of the life of
Mohammed in the *DP*, see Fidora 2011: 145-149.

172. Llull gives the form "Tripe" for "Yathrib," the pre-Islamic name for the town
renamed "al-Madīnah" ("the city") in Mohammed's lifetime.

[3] Yathrib and Mecca and all that province, son, were full of peoples who believed in idols and worshiped the sun and the moon and the beasts and the birds, and they had no knowledge of God, nor did they have a king. And they were peoples of very little discretion and very little understanding.

[4] In that time, it came to pass that Mohammed, who was a merchant, went to Jerusalem on business. On the road near Jerusalem there was a false Christian named Micolau, who was a recluse. He knew a lot about the Old Law and about the New, and he taught Mohammed how he could raise himself up to be king and lord of the town of Yathrib.[173]

[5] Know, son, that the learning that the deceitful recluse showed Mohammed was composed of many citations from the Old Law and the New because he could make money from it.[174] And Mohammed went away to a mountain near Yathrib and was there for 40 days in order to represent the 40 days that Jesus Christ was in the desert and that Moses was on Mount Sinai.

[6] When Mohammed came down from the mountain, he went to the town of Yathrib and pretended to be a prophet and said that God had sent him to the people of that city. And he promised them that in paradise they would have the company of women and would eat butter and honey and would drink wine and water and milk, and that they would have beautiful palaces of gold and silver and precious stones, and that they would have any kind of clothes they desired.[175] And he promised them many other benefits so that they would believe him. He would throw himself to the ground and twist his hands and roll his eyes like a man possessed. And afterwards, he would say

---

173. This refers to the Christian monk mentioned in some versions of the life of Mohammed under the name "Sergius" or "Bahira" or "Sergius Bahira" (Roggema 2009). "Micolau" is the Majorcan variant of the name "Nicolau," that is "Nicholas," and Llull's usage here, it has been suggested, may be related to a popular identification of Mohammed with the beliefs of the Nicolaites and their "deacon" Nicolas, identified already in Apocalypse 2:6 and 15 as heretical. See De la Cruz 2002 and Fidora 2011: 145-149. Or it may be related to a contemporary Western version of the life of Mohammed, the *Liber Nycholay*, which identified Mohammed as a disgruntled former Christian cardinal named "Nicholas" (González 2004).

174. The idea seems to be that Micolau took ideas from the Old and New Testaments and sold them to Mohammed.

175. Compare Llull's negative reference to what he believed to be the idea of paradise in Islam in Ch. 5.5 and see n. 17.

that Saint Gabriel had come to him and brought him the words of
God, which are in the book that is called *The Koran*, and that, because
of the great holiness of Saint Gabriel and his words, he had been unable to remain standing and that for that reason he had fallen on the
ground. And it was the custom to cover him up as he lay on the
ground. And when he had been that way for an hour, he would get
up and report what had occurred to him.

[7] The people, who were ignorant and had no belief that they
would be anything after death and who heard what Mohammed
promised them about paradise and that they would be resurrected,
were pleased to hear what he told them, and all the people in that
town converted to him. The people of Mecca did not want to convert
to the sect of Mohammed until he went there with many men and
took Mecca by force, and every person who refused to become a Saracen was killed. And thus Mohammed became lord of all that land.

[8] Mohammed was a very lustful man, and he had nine wives,
and he had relations with many other women, and he made the rules
of the sect very loose. And because of the latitude that he gave, people believed in him and in his words, and after his death, they followed his sect.

[9] Devotion and charity cooled among the Christian people in
the land of Ultramar.[176] And the first Saracen king, who was called
Abu Bakr, Mohammed's advisor, who had *The Koran* written down in
beautiful words dictated to seven troubadours, came into the lands of
Egypt and of Jerusalem and conquered all that land.[177] And then other Saracen kings conquered Barbary and Spain, which belonged to
Christians.[178]

---

176. Literally, "the land beyond the sea," but generally used to refer to the Levant
or the Holy Land.

177. Llull's account appears to conflate two different persons with the same name.
One is the first Muslim caliph following the death of Mohammed: Abū Bakr al-Ṣiddīq
(d. 13/634). A widely held idea attributes the "compilation" of the Qu'ran to him (EI3;
EI2, "al-Ḳur'ān"). The second is Abū Bakr b. Mudjūhid (d. 324/936), who resolved the
issue of arriving at an authoritative text of the Qu'ran by declaring the readings of
seven earlier Qu'ranic scholars (Llull's "seven troubadours"?) to be the only ones possessing divine authority (EI2).

178. Barbary refers to portions of North Africa inhabited by Berbers, extending
roughly from present-day Libya west to the Atlantic Ocean. In using the word "Spain"
("Espanya") to refer to the entire Iberian Peninsula, Llull invokes the Roman name for
its province "Hispania."

[10] So vile and filthy are the deeds of Mohammed, and his words and his deeds are in such discord with the life of a saint or of a prophet that, especially those Saracens who know a lot and have a subtle intellect and an elevated understanding do not believe that Mohammed is a prophet. For that reason, the Saracens have made an ordinance that no man among them should dare to teach logic and natural science so that their intelligence remains untrained. For this reason, they are of the opinion that Mohammed is a prophet.[179]

[11] Dear son, such Saracens as have a subtle understanding and do not believe that Mohammed is a prophet would be easy to convert to the Catholic faith if there were someone who would teach them that faith and preach it to them, and who would love the honor of Jesus Christ so greatly and would remember His passion so strongly that he would not hesitate to suffer the struggles a man faces in learning their language and would not fear the danger of death. And by the conversion he would effect among them through the power of martyrdom, and because they are all already of the opinion that Mohammed is not the messenger of God, the other Saracens would convert if they saw their greatest sages become Christians.[180]

[12] Know, son, that the Apostles converted the world by preaching and by shedding tears and blood and through great suffering and terrible deaths. And they had converted the land that the Saracens now hold. For that reason, Jesus Christ signified through the cross and by stretching out His arms that the blessed sages who are among the Christian people should come and remember His holy Passion and that He will embrace them if they preach to the Saracens and to the infidels.

[13] Dear son, if it pleased the God of Glory and those who are so well rewarded and honored by Him and indebted to Him, then would

---

179. This seems to be a surprising assertion, given that Muslim sages were the primary transmitters of logic and natural science to the West. Llull explains this assertion with more nuance in the *Gentile* (*SW* 1.292 and n. 27) where he says that the prohibition is against teaching these subjects *publically*. The fear, he explains, is that the common people will come to believe certain heresies taught by Muslims who have studied these subjects.

180. In this paragraph, Llull outlines two of his major strategies for the conversion of non-believers to Christianity: the need to learn their language in order to be able to dispute with intellectuals of other faiths and the conviction that these intellectuals, once they had been convinced of the truth of Christianity, would convert to Christianity and that others would follow their example.

be the reason and the hour for the fervor and devotion that used to
exist for converting and correcting those in error to return so that
they were not sent to Hell and could have glory, and so that they
loved and knew and served, obeyed God.[181]

72. ON GENTILES

[1] Gentiles are people without law who have no knowledge of God.
Now, because of their ignorance of God and because, according to
the course of nature, every man should have knowledge of his Creator, the gentiles—although they do not know God—at least show
some reverence to certain created things, in signification that there is
something that is nobler than they are.

[2] Dear son, because of the gentiles' ignorance of God, they have
diverse errors and opinions, and for that reason they are diverse peoples: some worship idols and some worship the sun and the moon
and the stars, and others worship beasts and birds, and others worship the elements, and each of them has a practice different from the
others according to what they believe.

[3] Mongols, Tartars, Bulgars, Hungarians from Lesser Hungary,
Cumans, Nestorians, Russians, Genovians and many others are gentiles, and they are men who have no law.[182] Just as a river of water al-

---

181. Although this is certainly a blanket call to Christians to dedicate themselves
to the conversion of non-believers, the remarks seem aimed in particular at the clergy,
who enjoy all the rewards and honors of their position in society but are also obligated
by it to continue the work of the original Apostles. On the responsibilities of the clergy,
see Chs. 27, 81, 82 and 87.

182. Here Llull surveys the mission fields of his day. This list can provide us with
only an approximate idea of the actual groups of contemporary "gentiles" Llull had in
mind as it is based, on the one hand, on Llull's information on these groups, which
may have been outdated or inaccurate in some cases and, on the other, on the difficulty we have in identifying precisely which groups Llull was referring to. "Tartars" refers to the Tatars, that is, in general, the Mongols. On the Mongols and on Latin Christian missions to them, see Jackson (2008). Romano and De la Cruz suggest that by
"Tartars," Llull probably understood some combination of Mongols and Turks (2008:
440). In his list of gentiles Llull surprisingly includes Nestorian Christians. The Russians [*rosogs*], too, were Christians, but of the Orthodox variety. Marco Polo, telling the
story of his journeys around the time of the composition of the *DP*, says of the Russians
that "they are Christians and hold the Greek faith…. They give tribute to no one, except sometimes to a king of the West who is [a] Tartar" (Polo 2016: 212). Llull may
have placed them in this list, then, because he saw them as entertaining the same, for

ways flows downhill and does not stop until it runs into the sea, all these peoples run downwards and do not cease to lose God and to go to eternal fire.[183] And there is scarcely anyone to be their advocate or to help them by showing them the eternal path.

[4] Greeks are Christians, but they sin against the Holy Trinity of our Lord God because they say that the Holy Spirit proceeds from the Father alone. They have many good customs and, because they are so close to the Catholic faith, they would be easy to bring to the Roman Church if there were those who would learn their language and their writing and who had such great devotion that they did not fear dying to honor God, and who went to preach among them the excellent virtue that the divine Son has in giving procession to the Holy Spirit.

[5] Ah, Son! Why do we fear suffering and death, which would honor the Holy Spirit among those who dishonor Him by disbelieving the excellent virtue which is in Him because He issues from the Son of God? And why are we afraid to cast off riches and goods and wife and children or even kingdoms to offer such great honor to God the Father who engendered such a glorious Son, from whom issues such a glorious person as the Holy Spirit?

[6] Since the Holy Spirit proceeds from the Son of God, who, in order to save us, became flesh and died on the cross in His human nature, who can be afraid to die to honor the Son of God by preaching to the Greeks that the Holy Spirit, who is such a noble person, proceeds from Him? And if a man fears to undergo such a death, where is his gratitude to the Son of God?

---

him, mistaken notions as the Greek Orthodox Christians, whom he discusses in the next paragraph. The Cumans or Comenians were a people of Eurasian origin who moved into Eastern Europe before and after the Mongol invasions of the thirteenth century. Some remained pagans and were the object of intense missionary efforts in the decades just before and after Llull's life (Rowell 2008: *passim*). The "genovins" of the Catalan text have not been satisfactorily identified. Both Georgians and Guineans (or Ghanians) have been suggested as possible identifications; it seems unlikely that Llull is referring to the Genoese. With "Bulgarians" (*bulgras*), Llull might be referring to Bulgarians, more or less as we identify this group today, but he might also be referring to members of a particular dualist Christian sect, considered heretical, that had been prevalent in the area of Bulgaria: the Bogomils. Members of this group were known in Western Europe as "bougres," that is, "Bulgars."

183. Cf. Ch. 99.

[7] The Holy Spirit is God, who breathes the blessed to glory without end.[184] Therefore, whoever knows how to honor such a God in the way just mentioned in the places and the lands and in the thoughts in which He is dishonored, think, son, how great would be the blessedness into which he would be breathed by the Holy Spirit?

---

184. Since "spirit" means breath, the idea seems to be that the breathing, the "exhalations" ("espirar") of the Holy Spirit blow the blessed to glory. Cf. John 20:22. The term "spiration" (which may be in Llull's thoughts here) refers to that particular form of "breath" by which the Holy Spirit proceeds, eternally, from the Father and Son.

On the Seven Arts[185]

73. On Grammar, Logic, Rhetoric

[1] An art is a system and set of rules for learning the subject about which one wishes to have knowledge.[186] Grammar consists of speaking and writing correctly and, for that reason, it was chosen to be the common language among the nations who, because of the distances between their lands and lack of contact, are varied in their spoken language.[187]

[2] Son, if you wish to learn Grammar, you must know three things: construing, declension and vocabulary.[188] You can learn these three things in this book, which should be translated into Latin, since, because you already know it in Romance, you will more readily be able to construe meanings in this book than in any other. And

---

185. This is the final section title in the *DP*. In the final twenty-eight chapters, Llull returns to some of the pedagogical ideas already seen in the Prologue. Technically, however, the section title refers only to the following two chapters, on the Trivium (grammar, logic and rhetoric) and the Quadrivium (geometry, arithmetic, music and astronomy). These seven subjects were known as the "Seven Liberal Arts" and formed the curriculum for the degree of Master of Arts in medieval universities. In the chapters immediately following, Llull goes on to discuss the higher university faculties: theology, medicine and law.

186. For medieval understandings of the term "art" as "a practical science, like medicine, one intended for the production of concrete results, one that offered a system of precepts and rules for attaining a given end" and Llull's use of the term, see Bonner 2007: 293.

187. "Grammar," of course, meant "Latin," the only language whose grammar had to be studied, in contrast to the vernacular languages, which one learned naturally, and which, for the most part, had no formal grammars in Llull's day.

188. Here Llull lays out some additional details of the pedagogical program he announces in his Prologue. "Grammar" consists of "construcció, declinació e vocables." I interpret "construcció" as a form of the "construing" explained in n. 1. In modern linguistic terms, we might think of this as "syntax." "Declension" refers, of course, to the declension of nouns, but Llull may also be including the conjugation of verbs and other morphological features of Latin under this rubric.

because this book deals with many diverse things, you will learn declension and come to know many words.

[3] When you have learned Grammar in this book, then study it in *The Book of Definitions and Questions* so that you can learn the other sciences more readily.[189] If you wish to enter into any art or science, you must first pass through this art of Grammar, which is the gateway to learning the other sciences.

[4] Logic is the demonstration of things true and false, through which one learns to speak straightforwardly and sophistically.[190] And Logic is the art through which the human understanding is made more subtle and rises upwards.

[5] Dear son, through Logic you will learn to recognize the genera, the species, the differences, the properties and the accidents, which are called the Five Universals.[191] With this knowledge, you will know how to descend from general things to specific things, and from the specifics, you will know how to lift your understanding up to general things.[192]

[6] Through Logic you will know how to begin and support and conclude what you say, and with Logic you will protect yourself from being deceived by sophistic words, and through Logic you will be more subtle in all the other sciences.

[7] All created things exist, son, through ten things, that is: substance, quantity, relation, quality, action, passion, position, habitus, time, place. These ten things are the Ten Predicaments, which you

---

189. *Llibre de definicions e de qüestions* (1274-1283?). No surviving copy of this work is known. Llull mentions it again in Ch. 91.19 as the *Llibre de definicions e de començaments e de qüestions*. The *DP* is the only place in which Llull cites this work. It may have formed a part of Llull's larger pedagogical program connected to the *DP*, as with his inclusion of vernacular "rhymes" on logic at the end of the book (see five paragraphs below). In the case of the *Llibre de definicions*, the goal was to move the student from the knowledge of Latin ("Grammar") to the knowledge of other "sciences."

190. For the meaning of "dretament e sufismadament" I have used the first of two possible meanings for the passages suggested by Johnston (1987: 45-46): this one restates the idea of distinguishing between true and false speech from the first part of the sentence. For those surprised that Llull seems to promote the use of sophism, that is, untrue speech here, Johnston (1987: 46) points out: "It is typical of Llull's early accounts of Logic that he does not denounce its sophistical subtleties, but rather proposes to improve its efficacy...."

191. The Five Universals are also known as the Five Predicables.

192. Cf. Prologue.

will come to know through Logic.[193] And through that knowledge, you will know how to have knowledge if you know how to bring them into concordance and to combine them with the Five Universals mentioned above using the Ten Predicaments, for from the combination of one statement with another, you will have the meaning you seek.

[8] Before you learn Logic in Latin, learn it in Romance, in the rhymes found at the end of this book.[194] And do you know why? So that you may then learn it more quickly in Latin and understand it better.

[9] Rhetoric is speaking beautifully and in ordered fashion. Through Rhetoric words are listened to pleasantly and the speaker is often listened to with approval.

[10] Rhetoric shows how you ought to speak and which words you should say first and which at the end and which in the middle. With Rhetoric, long speeches seem short.

[11] If, son, you wish to speak using Rhetoric, give beautiful examples of beautiful things at the beginning of your words, and the best material in your speech should be at the end so that you leave a desire to hear more in the hearts of those who are listening to you.

[12] Time, place, truth, status, the appropriate amount of time, necessity and other things like these pertain to Rhetoric. Whence, son, if you want to speak using Rhetoric, it is necessary for you to bring your words into concordance with all the things just mentioned so that you will be pleasing to men and to God.[195]

---

193. The "Predicaments" Llull refers to here are perhaps more commonly known as "Categories" today.

194. By "Romance" Llull means a vernacular Romance language, in this case, Catalan. Perhaps Llull is referring here to the rhymed *Lògica del Gatzell* (Logic According to Al-Ghazālī), Llull's very first known Catalan work, or to some adaptation of it made especially for the *DP*. In any case, these "rhymes" do not survive in any known copy of the *DP*. The *Lògica del Gatzell* can, at least, give us some idea of the *type* of material Llull might have intended for the "rhymes found at the end of this book." For the *Lògica del Gatzell*, see Johnston 1987: 31-44 and *passim*. The Catalan text and an extensive study are found in Rubió 1985: 111-166.

195. For Llull's theories of rhetoric, see Johnston 1996. For an English translation of Llull's *Rhetorica nova*, also by Johnston, see Llull 1994.

74. ON GEOMETRY, ARITHMETIC, MUSIC, ASTRONOMY

[1] Geometry is the study of immovable forms multiplied in number in human thought.[196] Now, son, if you take a measurement with the rectangle that is on the astrolabe on a high wall, from your eyes to your feet and to the bottom of the wall and you are as far away from the wall as is the distance from your feet to your eyes, you have taken the first measurement in geometry.[197]

[2] Then you should take another measurement on top of the first and see where on the rectangle the straight line comes. After that, move away from the tower twice as far and see where the line comes on the rectangle, and here, take another measurement. Thus

---

196. In the paragraphs on Geometry, Llull describes a technique for what is called "indirect measure," in this case, determining the height of a wall that is too high to be measured directly. But Llull's first sentence in this chapter should not be ignored: he is primarily interested in the ways in which concepts, here "immovable [or immutable] forms," "can be multiplied in human thought." The process described, then, is much more about learning how to recognize the greatness of God—although our minds can never *measure* this greatness, we can at least "recognize" it when our "multiplications" fail—than it is about learning the height of a wall. The specific techniques of indirect measure necessarily take second place to this goal and are only presented in the most schematic form. This interest in the multiplication of numeric concepts can be seen again in Chs. 99 and 100. Although Llull refers to the astrolabe here, he is not using the instrument for astronomical measurements or as a navigational tool. Rather, he is using the separate set of measuring tools for surveying and measuring purposes found on the back of the instrument, specifically, the "shadow square" (see the following note). See Lewis 2001: 67-71 and 253-255. In this discussion, Llull is essentially using his "son"'s eye height as a standard to be "multiplied." Despite the focus on intellectual multiplication here, one could, in fact, use the method described here to determine the rough height of the wall as a multiple of one's own. See also Badia 2004: Section 6.

197. The "rectangle that is on the astrolabe" or "shadow square," was often found on the backs of astrolabes beginning in the 9th or 10th century (and was rectangular in form, despite the name). It was primarily used to calculate heights using the proportional lengths of shadows, as its name implies (Lewis 2001: 254). Kiely (1947: 63) describes the shadow square as "the most important part, so far as surveying is concerned, of the three predominant instruments of this [medieval] period: the astrolabe, the geometric square, and the quadrant" (see also 68-70, 292-293 and *passim*). It was also frequently used, however, as here, in measuring inaccessible heights, depths or distances using similar triangles. Sixteenth-century engravings showing uses of the shadow square similar, but not identical, to those described by Llull here are found in Webster & Webster 1998, Ch. 1, figs. 14-17, Ch. 2, fig. 6, and the text on p. 19. Millás Vallicrosa (1931: 163) provides a drawing of a case of using the shadow square on the back of the astrolabe to calculate heights indirectly that is quite similar to the one Llull describes here. For photos of an astrolabe bearing the shadow square, produced in the Iberian Peninsula in Llull's lifetime, see Pingree 2009: 6-7.

you can double your measurements. And the space between you and the tower should be flat so that your feet will be at the same level as the tower in a straight line.

[3] Through this art, you can know the height of a tower and how far away high mountains are. And by the measurements that human thought can multiply in the imagination, you can recognize the greatness of God, who is greater than all the world.

[4] Arithmetic, son, is multiplying sums upon sums, and many sums into one and dividing one into many. This art involves multiplying an even number with another even number and an odd number with another even number so that the result can be even. For an even number can be multiplied more easily than an odd number.[198]

[5] This art exists so that men can better know how to hold a number in memory and in physical sight, for the nature of memory is that it forgets many things more readily than a single thing. For that reason, sums were created, that is: X, XX, XXX, C, M, MM^a, CM^a. And when these sums are not sufficient for writing what you need to, you can turn to ciphers and to the numerals of the algorithm and the abacus, which are more easily read and understood.[199]

[6] Music is the art in which we learn how to sing and play instruments correctly, fast and slow, raising and lowering and matching the notes and the voices so that the different voices and sounds are in harmony. This art was invented, son, so that man can praise God with singing and with instruments, and the clerics who sing in church to praise God possess this art. And the minstrels who sing and play instruments before princes for the vanity of this world exist in opposition to the principles of this art.[200]

---

198. Lull is talking, once again, about "multiplying 'forms' in number in human thought," that is, doing multiplications in your head, and he may be thinking of techniques such as multiplying by powers of 2 or doubling and halving, which both involve the manipulation of even numbers to create simpler multiplication problems for easier mental solutions.

199. With "CM^a" Llull indicates "100,000," not "900." The words "algorithm" and "abacus" both mean here simply any calculation made using Arabic numerals as opposed to Roman numerals. I thank Stephen Chrisomalis for his important clarifications of the sense of this passage.

200. Music exists only for the purpose of praising God. Worldly court entertainments do not follow this purpose and therefore they exist in opposition to the principles on which music was founded. Llull's final sentence in this paragraph links us to one of the most important, and interesting, aspects of his socio-moral world and his own self-image. "Joglar," which I translate here as "minstrel," has no precise equivalent

[7] Astronomy is a demonstrative science through which man comprehends that celestial bodies have lordship over and effect upon terrestrial bodies in order to demonstrate that the power that resides in celestial bodies comes from God, who is sovereign in the heavens and in everything that exists.[201]

[8] Know, son, that this science functions through the properties of the twelve signs and the seven planets according to the ways in which they are in concordance with and oppose one another in heat, dryness, coldness, humidity, for they have an effect on earthly things according to these properties.[202] But because God—who is sovereign above all powers—has power over all powers, He often prevents celestial bodies from working upon earthly ones in the ways that their properties would dictate. For this reason, this science can fail and what happens in reality is not what should have happened according to the rules of this art.

[9] Dear son, I do not advise you to learn this art, for it is very difficult and you can easily go wrong. It is dangerous because the men who know the most about it use it badly, and, favoring the power of celestial bodies, they are ignorant and disdainful of the power and the goodness of God. Nor do I advise you, son, to learn Geometry or

---

in English but generally refers to traveling performers who entertained either the public in the streets or a higher class audience at courts with music, skits and acrobatic feats (cf. the English word "juggler"). In *Felix*, Llull criticizes the minstrels at court for having "praised what should have been blamed, and blamed what should have been praised," no doubt in order to increase the rewards they will receive from the king for their performance. At this moment, a figure "poorly dressed and with a long beard" (a likely stand-in for Llull) appears and calls for there to be someone at court whose job it is to "reprove what is reprovable… [and] praise what is praiseworthy," a sort of anti-minstrel. Llull calls for (and perhaps sees himself as) an *ioculator Dei*, a "joglar" of God, who will go about promoting faith rather than the vanities of this world as the regular minstrels do. See also *SW* 2.971 and 885, n. 86. *Blaquerna*, Ch. 48, also calls for a "Minstrel of Worth." For a fierce indictment of *joglars*, see Llull's *Llibre de contemplació*, Ch. 118 (cf. n. 304 on this text). It is important to remember that this issue is at the very heart of Llull's "conversion to penance" and his life's work: he was composing a worldly love song of the type a *joglar* might perform on the nights the crucified Christ appeared to him, eventually triggering his conversion (*VC* §2-§5).

201. On astronomy as a demonstrative science in Llull, see Rubio 2008: 359-362.

202. Cf. Figures 1 and 3. Yates (1954: 118-128) discusses Llull's ideas of astronomy as found in a slightly later work, the *Tractatus novus de astronomia* (1297). Yates's Fig. 1 (119, based on several manuscripts of Llull's work) and the explanation of the meanings of the letters that is found on the following page, which bases this system on the qualities of each of the four elements, offers a useful visualization of the astronomical-astrological ideas Llull is discussing here.

Arithmetic, because they are arts that absorb all of a person's mind, which should be dedicated to loving and contemplating God.

75. ON THE SCIENCE OF THEOLOGY

[1] Theology is the science for speaking about God. Now you should know, son, that this science of Theology is nobler than all the others. And because this science is more generally practiced and loved by men of religion, they are, therefore, worthy of very great honor.

[2] This science, son, has three types: the first is when one has knowledge of God; the second is when one has knowledge of God's works; the third is when one has knowledge of those things by which one can go to God and escape infinite sufferings.

[3] Dear son, clerics were established in the world so that they can learn Theology and teach it to men so that they can be lovers of God and know how to guard themselves from sin. For that reason, clerics who love another science more than they love Theology do not follow the principles for which they are clerics.[203]

[4] Theology, insofar as it is founded on faith, may be found in the words of holy men who have written and spoken about God and His works. You should believe their words so that you can hold God and His works in memory and in love.

[5] Because God has given nature and properties to created things—which signify and demonstrate Him to the human understanding in nature—, Theology agrees with Philosophy, which is the natural science that, by means of necessary reasons, demonstrates God and His works, so that if one wants to lift his understanding to God using Philosophy, one may do so.[204]

[6] Faith and reason come together in the science of Theology so that, if faith fails, one can help oneself using necessary reasons. And

---

203. Llull may be referring here to clerics who became students of Medicine or Law, as did many in his day, including his sometime mentor Ramon de Penyafort, a Dominican who became an authority in law and adviser to kings (see Ch. 76, n. 207) and Llull's contemporary Arnau de Vilanova (c. 1240–1311), a famous physician (see Badia, Santanach & Soler, 2016: 252-263).

204. For "necessary reasons," see Ch. 50.7 and n. 119. Here, too, Llull stresses that God is "demonstrated" to the human mind in the things that he has created, in the "Book of Nature," if one reads it correctly.

if reason fails in the human understanding, one can help oneself with faith, believing those things about God that the understanding cannot understand.

[7] Aristotle and Plato and the other philosophers who sought, without faith, to have knowledge of God were unable, son, to lift their understanding high enough to have clear knowledge of God and His works or of the things by which man goes to God. And that is because they did not wish to believe or to have faith in those things through which the human understanding, by the light of faith, rises up to understand God.

76. ON THE SCIENCE OF LAW

[1] Law is divided into two parts: canon law and civil law. Canon law is divine law, and civil law is earthly law and customary law. Civil law pertains to the practices of rulers so that they can maintain justice.

[2] Just as canon law is given to clerics so that they follow the rule through which they are in the clergy, civil law is given to rulers so that they follow the rule by which they were established and lifted up above other men.

[3] Know, son, that there is one more type of law, which was created for putting an end to greater evil. And this law does not agree with divine law because it contains within itself some defects where theory and practice conflict within this law. The reason for this discrepancy is to overcome the malice of the people and to consent to a lesser evils. Thus, under this law, a man may be excused by his earthly lord, and he is not exculpated before his heavenly Lord.[205]

[4] The fourth type of law is canon law, which conflicts between theory and practice, for in canon law one thing is right in theory and the opposite thing is right in practice. For that reason, clerics judge one thing according to theory and another according to practice.[206]

---

205. That is, that in order to avoid the "greater evil," "lesser evil," perhaps as a means of putting down political upheaval ("the malice of the people"), a ruler may bend the law and forgive those who are, in fact, culpable of breaking the law. But these individuals are still answerable to God for the laws they have broken.

206. After announcing that law is divided into "two parts" (civil and canon law), Llull ends up with four "types" (*maneres*) of law. The latter two seem to be imperfect

[5] Dear son, if you want to learn law, you must learn the four types just mentioned if you wish to practice it well as a secular person. For you must bring earthly law into concord with heavenly law, and, when you find that the law contradicts itself, you will have to make a judgment.

[6] Canon law, son, is found in the *Decretum* and the *Decretals*, which are the sayings of saints and the rule and ordinations of the holy Church and its sacraments.[207] Civil law is based on common sense and on laws and customs, for the latter of which you need not learn law because they are not established under law.

[7] I do not advise you, son, to learn civil law, for few are those I see who practice it well. For that reason, it is dangerous to learn such a science when almost all of those who learn it use it badly. However, I do not absolutely disadvise you from learning it, for you will earn great merit if you seek to practice it well.

[8] If, son, you study law so that you can do wrong, you love wrong and want to know law, and if, using the patrimony of the holy Church, you learn civil law, you do canon law a wrong.[208] And if you learn law to defend the poor who have nothing to give to lawyers, you will be marvelously pleasing to men and to God.

77. On the Science of Natures

[1] Nature is the beginning of everything, and it is the occasion for there being something natural. Know, son, that the principles of na-

---

applications of civil and canon law respectively, cases in which there is a significant difference between the letter of the law and practice.

207. The *Decretum* or *Decretum Gratiani* was compiled by Gratian (fl. 1140) from findings of Church councils, papal letters and works of Church Fathers such as Augustine, as Llull states here. The *Decretals* or *Decretales Gregorii IX* were completed in 1232 by the Catalan Dominican Raymond of Penyafort (1180/85-1275) at the request of Pope Gregory IX (Brundage 1995: 190-194, 196-197, 212, 215, 222-223). According to the *VC* §10, Llull met Penyafort not long after his "conversion to penance," perhaps around the year 1265.

208. Here, as in other sections of this chapter, there is a play on the Catalan word "dret" meaning both "law" and "right." So Llull is saying that "if you study law/right so that you can do wrong, you love wrong and want to know law/right, and if, using the patrimony of the holy Church, you learn civil law/right, you do canon law/right a wrong."

ture are five.[209] The first is primordial matter. The second is the four simple elements, and this is divided into three parts, which you are not yet of an age to understand.[210] The third principle is the four compound, sensible elements. The fourth is in the bodies engendered by nature, which are of three types: vegetable, animal, metal. The fifth is in corrupted, unnatural things like rot, feces, sweat, rust, death and other things like these.

[2] Dear son, the first principle is prime matter, which the word "nature" suits better than it does all the other principles because it is more general. And the other principles, in that they refer to specific things, are more in accord with the word "natural" than the first principle.[211]

[3] One cannot see or touch or hear prime matter, son. And do you know why? Because it is a confused and mixed natural corporeity, without being a body having form. In it are located all the elemented corporeal bodies that have form.

[4] Just as the soul and the body of a dead man have human nature without being a man, prime matter is of corporeal nature without being a body.

[5] Prime matter seeks to conserve the genera and the species and the individuals and has a natural desire for its particulars to have the properties that are appropriate to them. For that reason, the second principle composes itself in prime matter: fire and air and earth combine, and water and air and earth combine, and from these two compositions, they all combine together in the third principle, in which is engendered the fourth.[212]

---

209. That there are five types of nature discussed in this chapter is the reason for which the title speaks, not of "nature," but of "natures" plural.

210. Llull is referring to "strange" terms such as those that will appear in the *Tree of Science* (1295-1296), where, for example, he refers to the three parts of fire as "the ignificative, the ignificable and the act of ignifying" ("ignificatiu," "ignificable,"and "ignificar"; "The Twigs of the Human or Rational Tree"; Llull n.d.a. 1: 106). On Llull's "paraules estranyes" ("odd words"), see Badia, Santanach & Soler 2016: 70-75.

211. Prime matter, undefined, is "nature"; the other principles, which can be broken down into specific things like "elements," or "animals" or "metal" or "sweat" or "rust" are better referred to with the derivative "natural."

212. "Elemental theory" is basic to the conception of Llull's Art in this period, referred to as the "quaternary" period, in part, because of the role the four elements play in its elaboration. "Elemental theory" also constitutes a fundamental set of ideas that Llull wishes to communicate to his "son" in the *DP*. In addition to the discussion of the elements in this chapter, see also the chapter on medicine (Ch. 78), the chapter on the

[6] Just as prime matter is invisible because the first and second principles are invisible, secondary matter may be sensed because it belongs to the third and the fourth and the fifth principles, which are sensible.[213] Just as prime matter is a general power in all forms, secondary matter is a specific power in all sensible natural forms, according to the diversity of their genera and species.

[7] Know, son, that, because of the contrariety of the four elements in the fourth principle, there is a fifth principle, in which nature becomes corrupt. For that reason, those things that are in the fifth principle do not belong to nature. But because the first principle seeks the conservation of its genera and its species and its individuals, it returns that which is in the fifth principle to itself. And when the first principle has received it, and each element has returned to its simple form, the first principle, by means of generation, gives it to the second, and the second to the third, and the third to the fourth, and the fourth casts it from itself by way of corruption. And in that way, the movement and course of nature is a wheel that never stops moving through generation and corruption. This movement is in secondary matter, which is sensible.

[8] The reason fire and the other elements combine themselves in the fourth principle is because each element, in that it is simple, desires to have its own simple body. And because matter, without form and a joining between it and form, cannot be a body, it desires form and joining. And because no element can achieve joining in the third or the fourth or the fifth principle, the elements compound themselves in the second principle, without contrariety, and then they pass contrarily to the other principles as is explained above.

[9] If the four elements, son, had something to move toward or possessed what they desire in the second principle, they would not move to the other principles, in which they are contrary to one another, and if they were violently and forcefully moved there, their movement would not be natural.

[10] When water is a simple body in its own region, fire, which is above air, cannot receive dryness from the earth, which is below the

---

body (Ch. 85) and the full chapter devoted to the elements (Ch. 94). See Yates 1954; Pring-Mill 1962; Bonner 2007: 57-60; Rubio 2008: 333-45.

213. Prime matter and the "simple elements" are invisible, but "secondary matter," that is, the elements in compounded form, the vegetable, animal and metallic bodies, and the various forms in which these decay may be sensed, are "sensible."

water, which water is below air.[214] Nor, if a simple part is taken from simple fire as a body passing through the region and the sphere of water (as long as it is simple and a continuous body), will the part of fire be stronger against water than all the water against the part of fire.

[11] Do you see, son, the bubbles in the water that rise upwards in a spring? These signify that some simple elements pass through others, for if simple fire desires to pass through simple water, it will combine itself with air, which is in accord with water, and it will pass through the middle of the water. And the same thing happens with the other elements.

[12] For the above-mentioned reasons, son, there are diverse opinions on whether the simple elements are, or are not, a body in the second principle. But it is certain that, together, they are a compound body in the third and fourth and fifth principles, and that one passes to the other by means of the middle. For, if fire wants to pass through water, it will put itself in the middle and it will put air, which accords with water, around itself and it will pass through water to take dryness from earth, which agrees with fire and with water. In this way, the elements compound and mix themselves one with another.[215]

[13] Many are the things I could tell you, son, about nature, but because I am speaking to you in abbreviated form and because I would have to use some strange words that I cannot explain to you, I will just tell you briefly the intention the philosophers had in their books and then we will speak about something else.[216]

---

214. Each of the elements also had its own region or circle, starting with fire as the highest region, followed by air as the next highest, then water, then earth as the lowest region of the elements. See Figure 3.

215. This discussion is more easily understood by referring to Figure 1 on the "Circle of the Elements." The passage of one element through another can take place as a result of the fact that each element possesses, at least in the third principle, both a "proper" quality and an "appropriated" quality. The proper quality of fire is heat; its appropriated quality is "dryness." As we move around the circle counterclockwise, we find that heat is the appropriated quality of air. That fire and air share the quality of heat, although in different degrees, allows fire to "put itself in the middle" of air and, in this sort of disguise, pass through water (which shares the quality of wetness with air) to take the quality of dryness from earth, which agrees with water in its appropriated quality "cold" and with fire in its proper quality "dryness."

216. Here again, as in the mention of the "parts" of the "simple elements" above, Llull detours from discussing his own Art, in part because of the difficulty of the terms ("vocables escurs") he would have to use to introduce it. See n. 210.

[14] In the book on *Metaphysics*, the Philosopher intends to show all the things that are common among the sciences and treats the principles that are appropriate to being, that is, the spiritual substances, describing their order and nature and being.[217] He does so hoping to come to discover a primary spiritual substance that is eternal, infinite, perfect, that is the first cause and end of all things, for which and by which all things are ordered, and that is God.

[15] In the book on *Physics*, the Philosopher intends to determine the natures and properties of all natural things in general in order to give universal knowledge of all of them. And for that reason, he seeks one eternal, regular movement and a prime movable and a prime mover and moved, and a single immovable mover that moves everything that is movable.

[16] In the book *On Heaven and Earth*, he investigates the natures and properties of the heavens in general and studies their movements. And he inquires into the four elements from which the world below the moon is composed.[218] He studies this in order to prove that there is but one world alone.

[17] In the book *On Generation and Corruption*, he investigates how to determine the nature and properties of those things that are engenderable and corruptible, and he studies how some elements are active and others passive. His intention is to show the nature of the elements that compose elemented bodies for the knowledge they give about compound bodies.

[18] In the book *On Meteorology*, he speaks about rain, snow, wind, thunder, lightning and earthquakes, and about the stars, comets and the other signs like these.[219]

[19] In the book *On the Rational Soul*, he speaks about the substance of the soul and about its spirituality and incorruption, and about its powers, and how it orders the body and how it perceives

217. "The Philosopher," the name by which Aristotle was commonly referred to in Llull's day. The list of Aristotle's works that follows is unusual in the Lullian corpus, for Llull seldom refers to other "authorities" in his works (see Introduction).

218. The sub-lunar region of the universe is composed of the four elements in their circles or regions as described in Ch. 94, n. 329 and Figure 3.

219. Comets, in particular, were believed to be signs of disasters to come. Isidore of Seville (1982-1983: 1.476 = *Etymologiarum* 3.71.16) says that "this type of star, when it appears, signifies either pestilence or famine or war." Aristotle believed that comets appeared in the sub-lunar realms and were atmospheric phenomena (Heidarzadeh 2008: 1-3), hence their treatment under the topic of meteorology.

objects. And he speaks about how it is different from the other, irra-
tional, souls. And he does this in order to know the nature of the rational soul.

[20] In the book *On Sleeping and Waking,* he speaks about the nature and properties through which animals sleep and wake.

[21] In the book *On the Sensing and the Sensed,* he discusses how
man senses using the five corporeal senses and the ways in which
physical things are sensible to the five corporeal senses.

[22] In the books on animals, he speaks about the properties and
genera and species and differences that they have through nature,
and he studies the same things in the book *On Plants and Herbs.*[220]

Now, son, the philosophers investigated all this so that they could
have knowledge of God.

78. ON THE SCIENCE OF MEDICINE

[1] Medicine is the science of putting together what is natural for preserving nature and for returning nature to its accustomed state in the
animate body.[221] Now, son, this science has three principles: the first is
natural, the second is non-natural, the third is contrary to nature.[222]

[2] The first principle is divided into seven parts: elements, complexions, humors, members, virtues, operations, *spiritus.*[223] The sec-

---

220. The book "On Plants" (*De plantis*) is not today considered to be one of Aristotle's authentic works.

221. Compare Llull's definition to the classic definition of medicine in the medieval West, found in the *Canon* of the Persian philosopher and scientist Ibn-Sīnā (c.
980-June 1037), known in medieval Europe as Avicenna: "Medicine is the science by
which we learn the various states of the human body, in health, when not in health, the
means by which health is likely to be lost, and, when lost, [the body] is likely to be re-
stored to health" (Avicenna 1930: 25, with minor modifications). The underlying principle is that the body's natural state is one of health so that the physician has the task
both of maintaining the body's healthy state and that of restoring the body to a healthy
state when health is lost. Siraisi 1990 is an excellent general introduction to medieval
medical ideas; McVaugh 1993 offers thorough information on medicine as practiced
in the Crown of Aragon in Llull's day.

222. Llull gives the "textbook" definition (as found, for example, in the *Isagoge* of
Hunayn ibn Ishaq, an Arab Nestorian Christian known in the West as Johannitius, 809-
873) of the principles of medicine here and in the following paragraphs (Siraisi 1990:
101).

223. This list of the "naturals" is, again, a very standard list. "*Spiritus*" is not "spirit"
in our current sense. Rather, it "was supposedly a substance manufactured in the heart

ond principle is divided into six parts: breathing, exercise—that is, working and resting—, eating and drinking, sleeping and waking, filling and emptying—that is, that sometimes one eats and drinks a lot, and at other times a little. The final principle of the second principle concerns the accidents of the soul, that is, joy and sadness.[224] The third principle is divided into three parts: illness, the cause of illness, accident.[225]

[3] Each of these parts is divided into many further parts and the science of medicine is composed of all of them together. And because we wish to show this science briefly, son, we will say just a few things about the first principles as briefly as we can.

[*The first principle (the seven naturals): elements, complexions, humors, members, virtues, operations,* spiritus][226]

[4] Know, son, that the human body is composed of the four elements, and when their properties are tempered, the body is healthy, and by their distemper, it is ill.[227] For that reason, physicians artifi-

---

from inspired air and transmitted through the body via the arteries" (Siraisi 1990: 101).

224. The list of six "non-naturals" is also very standard. It included, as Llull does here, the "accidents of the soul," meaning "passions and emotions" (Siraisi 1990: 101-109; McVaugh 1993: 144-150). Referring to Llull's contemporary, the physician Arnau de Vilanova, McVaugh (1993: 146-147) explains the connection between the body and the emotions: "The emotions..., because of their fundamentally somatic character... originate in a judgment by the brain's cognitive faculty that some object is desirable or harmful, a judgment that causes a corresponding physical reaction in the heart. For example, something terrible that cannot be avoided or withstood evokes sadness, which is a constriction of the heart that leads to a diminution of blood and spirits diffused to the internal and external members, thereby chilling and drying the whole body; it can no longer digest food, and so wastes away. Joy, anger, shame, distress— every emotion corresponds to a particular physiological process."

225. Since it is "natural" for the body to be in a state of health, illness and its causes are "contrary to nature."

226. Because of the complexity of this lengthy chapter on medicine, I have added headings not found in the text to clarify the structure of Llull's treatment of the topic.

227. That is, when the four elements—fire, air, water, earth—are in their proper balance, the body is healthy. This idea of balance (or "temper") does not mean that all four elements are present in equal quality in the natural state, however. Each individual has his or her own unique balance based on such things as the time and place of birth, as Llull notes two paragraphs below. These constitute, in fact, that person's "temperament." These are factors the physician had to take into consideration in seeking to restore the natural balance (Siraisi 102-103; McVaugh 1993: 141).

cially vivify some elements and mortify others so that a tempered virtue can be created in them, by which one can be well.

[5] There are four complexions: bile, blood, phlegm, black bile.[228] Bile or cholera belongs to fire, blood to air, phlegm to water, and black bile or melancholy to earth. Bile is hot by fire and dry from earth. Blood is wet by air and hot from fire. Phlegm is cold by water and wet from air. Black bile is dry by earth and cold from water. When these complexions are disordered, physicians try to find a way to put them in order, for if they are disordered, one becomes ill.

[6] Son, the four complexions mentioned above are found in every person, but each person is judged to one complexion more than another, and for that reason some people are choleric and others sanguine and others phlegmatic and others melancholic.[229]

[7] The concordance of these four complexions is brought about in two ways: the first is when the complexion that is strongest in a person is preserved and fortified in its power so that it has the other complexions that serve it ordered below it. The second way is when the complexion that takes command so strongly that it destroys the others is reduced and mortified by its contraries. For that reason, son, physicians make two types of cures: the first is when they cure and heal the illness by like things in nature, and the other is when they cure it by contrary things.

[8] When the cure is made by likes, it is necessary for the lesser degrees to be like the complexion that is too strong in its power and

---

228. Llull seems to erase here the distinction he establishes above in the list of "naturals" between complexions and humors. He is referring to what are more commonly known as "humors" here, and he was by no means the only medieval writer to use the term "complexion" in this way (cf. OED, s.v. "complexion"). Bile, blood, phlegm and black bile are more generally called "humors" and it is the prevalence of one or the other that determines a person's "complexion," as is explained in the following paragraph. "Bile" was also known as "choler," or "red bile" or "yellow bile." "Black bile" was also referred to as "melancholy." See Siraisi 1990: 104-106. Figure 1 will be of help in understanding the description of the humors in their relation to the four elements in this paragraph.

229. When Llull says that each person is "judged" to have a greater quantity of some humors than of others, he is referring to the idea that each person's peculiar "temperament" (their individual balance among these humors) is determined at the moment of birth by the "judgments" of the stars, the particular astrological point at which one is born. Note that the four terms Llull uses here do, in fact, correspond to words still used to refer to a person's temperament in the modern sense of the word. Cf. Siraisi 102-103; 110-112; 135-136; 149-152.

the greater degrees to be contrary to it. [230] When the cure is made by contraries, it is necessary for the lesser degrees to be in the first degree against the two greater degrees. Physicians make these cures, son, with herbs and with seeds, and they order the four degrees found in medicinal things.

[9] Dear son, there are two types of mixtures: the first is that of the four humors, which takes place in the human body; the second is of things that are mixed outside the body. Physicians mix the latter in an infusion, an unguent, or a poultice or an electuary so that they can then mix in the body to vivify the complexion that needs help and mortify the complexion that is too strong. [231]

[10] Members are the places in the body in which the humors are mixed. [232] Each member, depending on how it differs from the others, needs a different cure. For that reason, physicians must have knowledge of the differences and the qualities of the members so that they know how to act on each in a way that is appropriate to that member. [233]

---

230. In the use of the term "degree" (*grau*) here, Llull is referring to the theory that medicinal materials possessed the qualities of hot, dry, cold and wet in four varying degrees and that by choosing the medicinal plant or seed with the correct degrees of these characteristics, according to whether one wishes to cure by likes or by contraries, one can restore the body's balance with regard to these qualities and effect a cure. A few examples may help to clarify this point. From the *Arbre de ciència* (*Tree of Science*), pt. 2, "De l'arbre vegetal" (On the Vegetal Tree) 7: "fire...rules in pepper and in garlic, which are hot in the fourth degree, dry in the third degree, wet in the second degree and cold in the first degree.... Cinnamon in which fire is in the third degree of heat, earth in the second degree of dryness, air in the first degree of moisture while water is not assigned a degree...." (Llull n.d.a: 1, 56 for translation; I have made minor modifications). Much of this seems intuitive: in the same work, *Arbre de ciència*, pt. 6, "On the Flowers of the Tree of Exempla," 2.8, Llull explains: "Wine comforts the heart with heat and destroys the brain with dryness" (Llull n.d.a.: 1, 380). Gayà (1995: xxviii-xxx) provides a detailed explanation of how Llull's application of the theory of degrees might work in compound medicines. Such complex calculations probably remained in the realm of theory and were not fully deployed in actual medical practice (Siraisi 1990: 145-146 and n. 52).

231. An electuary was "a medicinal conserve or paste, consisting of a powder or other ingredient mixed with honey, preserve, or syrup of some kind" (*OED*).

232. Llull now continues with his treatment of the seven parts of the "first principle" of medicine, which has been taken up at length with the discussion of the first three: elements, humors and complexions. He discusses in relatively abbreviated form members, virtues, operations and *spiritus* or the "vital spirit." See n. 223.

233. By "member" Llull simply means "distinct parts of the body," which might include organs as well as limbs. Siraisi explains: "The heart was always hot...the brain was always cold...Medical textbooks provided four long lists of bodily parts arranged in order of hotness, dryness, wetness and coldness" (1990: 102).

[11] Virtue, son, is found in all the parts and each part, joining with another, has operative virtue through the mixings, through *spiritus* and through operations. For that reason, the virtues of the herbs mix one with another and the substances yet remain distinct one from another.

[12] Natural operations are those that each element carries out by its own nature and by the nature of the other element with which it is compounded and mixed. For that reason, physicians imitate natural operations as best they can, and to the extent that the work of some physicians is more like natural operation than the work of others, some physicians are better than others.

[13] The vital spirit, son, is the means by which the vegetative and sensitive powers and the rational power come together, and the soul preserves matter with its powers, with the vegetative receiving its virtue from elemented things. For this reason, physicians order the body with medicinal things so that the spirit is ordered through all the members, which are an ordered instrument for the spirit, which is the conjunction of the body and the soul.

[*The second principle (the six non-naturals): breathing, working and resting, eating and drinking, sleeping and waking, filling and emptying, joy and sadness*]

[14] Without breath, the complexions cannot be tempered or mixed, for without it one would immediately destroy the other. But because breath casts that which is too hot or cold or wet or dry out of the body in the form of vapor and draws and brings from outside and puts what is necessary for the mixing of the four qualities into the body, breathing is in accord with preserving the natural state and for that reason physicians give scents and the appropriate air to sick people and they avoid places where the air is corrupt.

[15] Exercise, son, is an opportunity for health, for if you work while fasting, natural heat will fortify the digestion and will multiply in the members and will consume any bad humor engendered by indigestion, which it will purge through sweat and vapor.[234]

---

234. In the *Proverbis de Ramon*, Llull defines "vapor" as "the combination of bodies that are so subtle that they have no definite color or shape" (cf. Bonner & Ripoll 2002, s.v. "vapor").

[16] Without eating and drinking, the human body could not be sustained, for by eating, the gross matter is preserved and, by drinking, the subtle. By eating and drinking cold things and wet things the gross matter is fortified, and by eating and drinking hot things and dry things the subtle matter is fortified.

[17] If you are sick, son, and you understand the nature of your illness—whether it is from cold or from heat or from dryness or from humidity—, learn to eat and drink according to what is discussed above, multiplying or diminishing what you are eating or drinking according to what is appropriate to preserving the matter that is required for health and to mortifying the matter that is making you ill.

[18] Frugal eating and drinking engender a subtle understanding and subtle matter, and it gives great space to the vital spirit and to breath, which cools it from the heat that is contrary to it. Too much eating and drinking creates gross matter. And do you know why? Because natural heat cannot cook the food that the vital spirit needs for the members so that the virtue and the operation that are necessary can be present, without which the vital spirit cannot be in the members in its power or in its strength.

[19] Waking and sleeping are necessary to man. And do you know why? So that through sleeping man can rest and through waking he exercises, for by sleeping the spirit recovers natural heat when the body rests and by waking men work in carrying out what the powers of the soul command and the spirit's natural heat is multiplied and preserved by the movement of the body heated by its movement.

[20] Too much sleep destroys the spirit in that it deprives it of natural heat, which is necessary to it for work and for movement. Too little exercise has the same effect. And too much work and too much staying awake destroy natural heat because they take away the humidity and the heat that the spirit needs in the form of vapor.

[21] By eating and drinking, one fills the intestines and fortifies natural operation, which lessens when the natural heat fortified by repletion wanes. By emptying, the expulsive acts are carried out. And natural heat, through frugal eating and drinking, consumes some of the unnatural superfluity.[235]

---

235. That is, in addition to the act of expulsion, natural heat itself burns off some waste products in the body, as long as there is not too much food and drink for it to burn.

[22] By the accidents of the soul, son, the body is vivified when one experiences joy and satisfaction and pleasure.[236] Through sadness of the soul and through brooding too much and by suspicion and fear and jealousy and anger and other things like these, nature is mortified in the human body.

[The third principle: illness, the cause of illness, accident]

[23] Dear son, the physician's intention is to cure the illness, and he looks for the cause of the illness in the accidents that show themselves through the illness.[237] And, when he learns the cause, he cures the illness by a contrary cause.

[24] The accidents that signify the cause of the illness, son, are the various fevers, urines and pulses and coloration and cravings for certain foods and other things like these.[238] And the cure is worked, son, by the properties and the degrees in herbs and in the simples of medicine, from which one makes infusions and syrups, electuaries, unguents, poultices, emetics and other things like these.

[25] Bleedings, diets, emetics, baths and many other things, son, are contrary to the cause of the illness, which things are surer than the recipes or electuaries or syrups or other things compounded from simple medicines.[239]

[26] Son, if you are sick, do not entrust yourself to a physician who is of the opinion that hot and dry can be in the same degree in me-

---

236. See n. 339 for the general idea of "accident" (and of "substance") that Llull is employing in specific contexts here and in paragraphs 23-24 below when he discusses "accidents of the soul" and "accidents that signify illness."

237. We might most readily understand Llull's technical term "accidents" in this context as "symptoms," but we should keep in mind that Llull was working with very different concepts of the nature of illness than the term "symptom" might suggest to us.

238. The term "color," which Llull uses here is most often associated in medieval medicine with determining an illness by the color of urine. But since Llull has already mentioned urines, it seems likely that he is using this word (translated as "coloration" here) to refer to various external colors the skin takes on in illness such as being pale, jaundiced or flushed.

239. Here Llull recommends, in preference to complex medicines mixed (and sold) by physicians and apothecaries, seeking to restore the body's balance of humors by using relatively simple means such as controlling, say, an excess of the humor blood by bloodletting and by using specific diets, specific foods, as a means of restoring the body to its previous humoral balance.

dicinal things. For if hot is in the fourth degree, dry must be in the third, and if hot is in the third degree, dry must be in the second, and if hot is in the second degree, dry must be in the first. That is because fire is hot in itself and it is dry from earth.[240]

[27] The same thing follows, son, with air and fire because air is wet in itself and is hot from fire, and water is cold in itself and is wet from air, and earth is dry in itself and is cold from water. Therefore, a physician who is ignorant of the degrees I have just mentioned and who is more interested in profit than in knowing the cause of the illness is not contrary to the illness, nor is he in concord with the will of God.

79. On the Mechanical Arts

[1] A mechanical art is a lucrative manual science that provides sustenance to bodily life. Artisans, that is, farm laborers, blacksmiths, carpenters, cobblers, drapers, merchants and the other occupations like these, son, participate in this science.[241]

[2] Dear son, men work physically in this science so that they can live, and one trade helps the other, and without these occupations the world would not be ordered, nor could burgesses, knights, princes, prelates live without the men who have the occupations just mentioned.[242]

---

240. Llull is referring here, again, to the "proper" and "appropriated" qualities of the elements. See n. 230 on the theory of degrees and Figure 1.

241. Here Llull includes "llauradors," that is, "plowmen" (or, more broadly as "agricultural workers," or simply "farmers"), among the list of artisans, which seems unusual. In Ch. 52.6, however, Llull clearly distinguishes "llauradors" from "artisans," though both pertain to the class of men "who do not have a lofty understanding."

242. Llull has a very specific class of townspeople in mind when he uses the term "burgès." One usage of the English term "burgess" comes closest to that meaning: "Any of various officials exercising judicial or executive authority in a town or borough" (*OED*). Llull defines this class in the following way in his *Arbre de ciència*, Book 7, "On the Imperial Tree" (or "The Tree of Government," 3.3). "Burgesses are men who rule cities and receive their privileges from them, and, for that reason, they are excluded from having any other occupation, that is, they cannot be knights or merchants or practice a mechanical art. They are necessary to a ruler to govern according to the laws of the cities and to keep the trades in order. And for this reason, burgesses deserve some honor above the merchants, for they have broader responsibility, and because of this honor they should have horses, and they should be wealthy so that they can live off the income and maintain their position" (cf. Llull n.d.a.: 1, 157; I have made minor

[3] An artisan can live in whatever land he finds himself in. Now, the Saracens have a very good custom, for, however rich a man may be, for all that, he does not fail to show his son some trade so that if he loses the wealth, he can live by his trade.

[4] Many sons of the high nobility die of hunger in foreign lands because they do not have a trade.[243] And many men leave their son rich, who then comes to poverty and death because he squanders the wealth and has no trade to live by.

[5] Many a man would like to know some trade by which he could live when he has spent all he has, and many a man would be wise if he had the means to be wise, and many a man could live by his trade if he knew how to get one. Some men show their sons how to spend when it would be better to teach them some trade.

[6] Enriching your son with some trade is a more secure form of wealth than leaving him money, possessions, for all other wealth abandons a man, except for a trade. Therefore, son, I advise you to learn some trade by which you can live if you should need to.

[7] All trades are good. But just as everyone can take whatever name or mark he wishes, everyone has the choice of selecting a good trade.[244] For that reason, I advise you, son, to choose a good trade.

[8] Almost all the men in the above-mentioned trades desire to be in the class of burgesses, and they would like for their sons to be burgesses. But there is no estate in all the world that is more harmful or that lasts so briefly.

[9] The burgess arises from the above-mentioned trades, for, at the beginning, his ancestor will have engaged in some trade and will have earned enough so that the heir can be a burgess. And in the burgess, the lineage will begin to decline. And do you know why? Because the burgess spends and does not earn, and he has sons and all of them are lazy and want to be burgesses, and his wealth is not sufficient for all of them.

---

modifications: the original version uses "city governors" to translate "burgueses," another good solution).

243. I translate the term "ric-hom" as "noble" or "nobleman." This was a specific class of nobleman: the highest. "Ric" does not refer, then, to wealth but to high social status. The *DCELC* explains that "ric" here retains its etymological sense from the Gothic "rīks": "powerful" (cf. modern German "Reich": "kingdom," "empire") and does not necessarily imply material wealth.

244. Llull is probably referring here to the often elaborate identifying marks that notaries and other professionals used to sign documents.

[10] Men in the above-mentioned trades, son, move just like the wheel, which turns in a circle. Those who are in the least honorable trades desire to climb each day until they are at the very top of the wheel, where the burgesses are. And because the wheel must turn and circle downward, the status of the burgess must also fall.[245]

[11] No men live so briefly as burgesses. And do you know why? Because they eat too much and suffer few hardships in life. No one pesters his friends as much as a burgess who is poor and there is no more disgraceful poverty than that of a burgess.

[12] No man earns so little merit from giving alms or from doing good as the burgess. And do you know why? Because he suffers no hardship for what he gives. Because man was created to work and to suffer hardship, the person who makes his son a burgess acts against the reason for which he was created, and for that reason, this occupation is punished more than any other by our Lord God.

80. ON PRINCES[246]

[1] A prince is a man who has been chosen for lordship over other men so that he can keep them at peace through fear of his justice. Such men, who are obliged to keep justice, hold the people who are less noble than they are under their protection, for which protection they bear more responsibility than other men.

[2] Know, son, that no man is under so much obligation in his office as a prince or a prelate, for you or I or another person are only obligated to one person, who is our king, and the king is obligated to me and to you and to that other person, that is to say, to all the people who are under his rule.[247]

[3] Just as the prince has more responsibility than any other man, so princehood is less desirable. And, just as a prince has more things

---

245. Here, again, as in Ch. 64, Llull gives us a view of medieval social climbing, this time with a view of the downside as well.

246. By "prince," Llull understands, of course, "any person having the status of ruler or lord over other men" (see *OED*).

247. A "prelate" would be the equivalent of the prince within the religious establishment. In Ch. 81.4 he lists the following ecclesiastical ranks as "prelates": bishops, archbishops, cardinals and the pope.

to answer to than any other man, so he ought to be assisted more than any other man.

[4] Dear son, just as the soul directs the body, so a good prince guides his people. And just as the body dies when the soul leaves it, so a bad prince is the death and destruction of his people.

[5] A prince is one man alone, like any other man. But God has honored him by making him the lord of many men. Therefore, son, when you realize that the prince is a man like any other, do not look down on him. Rather, love him because he is of your own like nature. And fear him because he is your lord and the lord of so many men, and honor him because God has honored him above you and above so many men who are better than you.

[6] The soul keeps the body in order throughout its members.[248] And do you know why? So that the body may be aided by its members when it fails. And for that reason, the prince, to protect himself from losing power, should keep his realm ordered through good men who help him rule his house and his kingdom.

[7] Sick members are the destruction of the body, and bad officials and counselors are the destruction of the sovereignty and honor of the prince, and the destruction of the sovereignty and honor of the prince is the destruction of the prince. And the destruction of the prince is the destruction of the land and its people.

[8] If the body can fall ill in its members, the same can happen to the prince through evil counselors and evil officials. If an evil people make for an evil lord, a good people make for a good lord, for if it did not work this way, it would follow that evil was more strongly in accord with evil than good with good.

[9] No man has to deal with so many thieves or robbers, traitors, detractors, enemies, deceivers, as the prince. Therefore, the person who would be a prince is not afraid of the dangers that come from men like these.

[10] Know, son: if you hate your lord because he imposes his justice on you, then hate the cobbler who has made your shoes and hate the tailor who has made your tunic, for the king is more obligated to impose justice on you than is the cobbler to make your shoes or the tailor to make your tunic.

---

248. For the meaning of "members," see n. 233.

[11] God has placed an earthly lord between you and Him. And do you know why? So that by loving and honoring and fearing your earthly lord you can be the lover and honorer of God and fear His power.

[12] Dear son, if you are in the good graces of your earthly lord, you will be loved by his subjects, honored and feared. And if you are under his wrath without blame and you still love him and honor him and respect his officials, the more will you be loved for it and pleasing to the justice of God.

ON KNIGHTS[249]

[1] A knight is one noble warrior selected from one thousand to defend justice and to preserve the honor that pertains to the prince.[250] The knight exists to put fear and trembling of death into those who love evil and deception and oppose truth, humility, mercy, peace and patience.

[2] Dear son, a knight should be the son of peace, justice, fortitude, humility, boldness, charity, hope and the other virtues like these. A knight is given the order of knighthood, son, so that he may be obedient to all the honors that pertain to the order of knighthood.[251]

---

249. In one of the Latin manuscripts of the *DP* and in the French translations, there is an additional chapter in this place on knights. Although this "extra" chapter breaks the original design of 100 chapters, there are reasons to think that Llull himself may have decided to include this chapter at some time after the original form of the book began to circulate (see Introduction). In any case, the language of this chapter is very similar to that of the *Book of the Order of Knighthood*, which Llull composed in 1274 and could easily have been composed by him or by someone close to him. I translate this chapter from the Latin version edited in Llull 2005: 287-289. Llull's *Book of the Order of Knighthood* was among the first books printed, by William Caxton, in England, as *The Book of the Ordre of Chyvalry or Knyghthode* (1484). There are recent English translations by Fallows (Llull 2013b) and Cortijo (Llull 2015), which also contains Caxton's text.

250. The idea that the knight is "one noble warrior selected from one thousand" derives from an etymological understanding that the Latin word *miles* meaning "soldier" (or, in the Middle Ages, "knight") derives from the number *mille*, "one thousand." This idea can be traced back at least as far as the 6th-7th century in Isidore of Seville (1982-1983: 1, 770 = *Etymologiarum* 9.3.32).

251. Knighthood is an "order," just as are the monastic orders (Ch. 81), or the clerics (Chs. 27, 80 and 87) or matrimony (Ch. 28). See n. 73.

[3] The horse is a good animal: strong, swift, not wild or proud. For this reason, son, the horse was given to the knight: so that with it he can conquer and overcome evil, proud men, faint of heart and vile of habits, friends of sloth and enemies of the virtues.

[4] Son, the knight was given a castle to keep the roads to a city that might rebel against or disobey its prince secure. But just as the bad knight is proud upon his horse, so, in his malevolence, the proud man in his castle is the enemy of the peace of the city, of orphans, widows, merchants, farmers and the rest.

[5] The knight was given insignia so that he can be recognized and feared. And a shield, armor, sword, lance and other accoutrements befit the knight. And do you know why? So that he can protect himself from death and blows with his armor and shield, and so that he can kill and hunt down thieves, traitors, the proud and others worthy of death with sword and lance.

[6] Son, the knight was given a squire to serve him. And beautiful clothes, white breads, good wines and noble foods befit the knight, and honors, liberties and many other privileges also pertain to him. And do you know why? Because the knight is ordained to be the victor and warrior who undergoes great trials and dangers so that the people who are under the protection of the prince can have peace and justice.

[7] The knight was given a prince to be the lord under whom knights are ordered and supported, through whom the prince can rule his kingdom. And the prince, too, should be a knight so that there is greater likeness and friendship between him and his knights.

[8] On account of goodness and nobility and the other pertinent things, the knight should be given great gifts and should have a wife honored by noble birth. And do you know why? So that in that line there may be honor, wealth and nobility of soul so that the knight does not fear to undergo suffering or death and does not fear proud men so that, rather, he can be so bold that he maintains the honor that befits knighthood.

[9] Knighthood is such a privileged order because it comes from a wealthy and honored ancient lineage. And do you know why? So that knighthood can maintain itself in the honor that befits it. But injustice has been done to knighthood in that avarice, extravagance, lust, pride and all the other vices have increased in it. And therefore,

son, every day, knighthood loses the ancient and honored lineage that befits it.

[10] Dear son, strength of hands, arms, shoulders, thighs, legs do not suit the knight so well as strength of soul, nor do the coat of mail, the lance and the sword pertain to them so well as do respect for law, truth, humility, boldness, a sense of shame and courtliness. And do you know why? Because strength of soul is more powerful and necessary than the virtues exterior to the knight, which are not of the humanity of the knight.[252]

[11] Son, goodness is appropriate to the knight so that he is not evil, and beauty so that he is not looked down upon, and wealth so that poverty does not lead him to evil or deception or treachery. To him belong agility so that he is neither lazy nor sluggish and wisdom so that he is not deceived. To the knight pertain all those things through which there is friendship between the prince and his people. Good knights make a good prince, and a good prince makes good knights. Through the goodness of the prince and the knights, the people are good. And through the opposite, there are wars, deaths, thefts and other evils through which the world is in such a troubled state.

[12] Know, son, that God entrusted the world to the guardianship of clerics and knights so that they can maintain it in peace, justice, wisdom and charity, because wisdom and charity are the opportunity through which God is known, loved and honored.

[13] Son, God commended knights in keeping to the prince, and He entrusted the princes to the knights, just as He commended the clerics to the keeping of the pope and the pope to the clerics. Therefore, behold, son, how God has ordained all this so well and see in what state the honor that befits knights lies.

[14] Weep, son, and lament the vices of knighthood. And do you know why? Because if knighthood maintained the lofty virtue and honor that pertain to it, the world would not be in such a troubled state and God would not be as unknown or as scantly loved and honored by His people as He is—that people whom He redeemed from infernal punishment through His bitter death and with His precious

---

252. The idea of "likeness" appears again here: the soul of the knight is a part of his human nature, while weapons and armor are "exterior" things, of a different nature than the knight's humanity. Therefore, the strength of the knight's soul is "more powerful [*virtuosior*] and necessary" to him than exterior things such as weapons.

blood so that there could be friendship, charity and gratitude between God and man.[253]

81. ON CLERICS

[1] A cleric is a man employed in praying to God on behalf of the people and in showing them the eternal path through the teachings of his words and by setting the example of a holy and upright life.

[2] Just as the origin of knighthood was to maintain justice, as we have already discussed in *The Book of the Order of Chivalry*, so, in the beginning, good and holy and devout men were chosen to pray to God for the people and to teach them good habits and good customs so that they can receive God's grace.[254]

[3] Clerics were granted benefices and tithes and first fruits to live on so that the divine office was not impeded by the need to earn temporal fruits.[255] Thus, clerics were established in parishes and in other places to say mass and to hear confessions and to preach to the people who work to create the fruits by which the clerics live.

[4] Just as a prince was assigned to knights, a prelate was assigned to clerics, that is, bishop and archbishop, cardinals and a pope, who should all live by the goods that are surplus to the simple clerics and who should keep them in order and under rule, according to their higher rank and office.[256]

[5] Clerics were granted virginity so that they would not have children to whom they would give away the wealth of the holy Church, which is entrusted to them so that the holy Church can be more merciful to the poor in Christ and so that it will be stronger and more feared because of it.

---

253. One possible argument against Llull's direct authorship of this chapter is that, unlike the 100 chapters of the *DP* proper, this chapter does not place the name of "God" (or a similar holy personage) as the final word of the chapter. This important detail seems to be one that Llull would have paid attention to. The French, as well as the Latin versions of this chapter all make "man" the final word (Llull 2005: 289 and 294).

254. The reference to *The Book of the Order of Chivalry* here and the direct comparison of the roles of clerics and knights seem to invite the insertion of a chapter on knighthood preceding it, whether by Llull or not. On this book, see Introduction, n. 8.

255. That is, if clerics have to work for a living, the divine office might be neglected.

256. See Ch. 27 and n. 73 for the concept of "ordination" and the "orders" of clerics.

[6] So high and excellent is the office of cleric that it was forbidden for any earthly prince to be above it in lordship. And for that reason, son, clerics have a lord who is the heavenly prince, that is, the prelate. The earthly prince was made subject to the prelate, to track down those who are condemned by the sentence of the prelate.

[7] This great honor, son, was granted to clerics to signify the honoring of God, for in this world there are no men so honored as clerics, as you can see in the sacrament of the altar and in other things.[257] Therefore, if you are obedient to and honor clerics, you will be an honorer of God.

[8] Just as cleric is the most honored office that exists in all the world, so, too, it is the most dangerous, for no men commit themselves so strongly to combat the devil and the vanity of this world as clerics do, and no men are as honored by God as clerics. And clerics promise to do more things to serve God than any other men.

[9] If honor and merit were greater in clerics than in other men and there were not also more danger in it, an opposition would exist between the merit and the honor and the justice of God. And because this is not the case, there are no men so harshly punished by God's justice as bad clerics are.

[10] Dear son, if you are a cleric, you must hold the patrimony that you receive from the holy Church apart so that it does not return to the earth from which it has come, so that it can be raised up to honor and exalt the holy Church and the Catholic faith, to signify honoring and praising and serving God.[258]

82. On Religion

[1] Religion is sovereign virtue in a man ordered in the contemplative rule and in the renunciation of the active life.[259] Know, son, that

---

257. "Sacrifice of the altar" refers to Communion, which only priests are allowed to perform (see Chs. 25, 27.4 and n. 73).

258. This may be an injunction against investing the wealth of the Church in financial ventures or, as mentioned in the paragraph on "chastity" above, might refer to clerics' passing on their wealth through inheritance.

259. "Religion" means here the organized monastic life. The word "order" refers concretely to the various monastic orders of Llull's days, such as Cistercians and Franciscans. A "religious," in this chapter, refers, then, to a member of one of the monastic orders in general. Llull briefly tells the story of the eremitic type of monasticism's de-

the origin of these religious men was in hermits who, out of the great love and fervor they felt for God, went away into the deserts and forests to worship and contemplate God.

[2] In the beginning, son, the hermitic life consisted of being alone in the mountains and living on herbs and wearing a hair shirt to mortify the flesh. But the number of hermits grew, and they joined together to have a rule and an order, and they chose a superior, that is, a prior and an abbot. And they built monasteries in unpopulated places to flee the world and to do penance and to offer hospitality to travelers.

[3] Sin and error multiplied in the world, son, and other religious came along to pray and to hear confessions and to teach theology and to confound sins and errors and to keep the peace among men. Religious like these live among us to cure our ills.[260]

[4] Poverty is chosen for religious persons so that they are not caught up in worldly possessions and so that their duties and studies are not impeded. Long and humble garments were chosen for them to signify humility and decency. They ask for alms to signify piety, charity.

[5] Meager food, fasts, afflictions, tears, weeping and contrition of the heart, prayer, devotion, obedience, conscience and other things like these, son, are the treasure and the wealth of religious. Therefore, son, if you desire to join the order of religion, it behooves you to enter into it with these riches and to persevere in them.

[6] Between God and man there is no higher rank than that of the religious. And do you know why? A blessed religious casts all things from his heart so that there is nothing there but God. Therefore, if the noblest heart that exists is that of a true religious, the most evil heart that exists is that of a false, hypocritical religious. And do you know why? Because he is more contrary to religion than any other person.

[7] If a true religious is a light and example to the peoples, an evil religious is a dark shadow of doubt over faith and is the beginning of

---

velopment into communal, cenobitic, monasticism. See Ch. 87 for Llull's promotion of the contemplative life as the highest "path" through life.

260. Here Llull describes the mendicant orders, such as the Franciscans and the Dominicans, a relatively recent phenomenon in his day.

error and infamy for the holy life. An evil religious is the most despicable man who exists.

[8] Religion is such a beloved thing that you abandon delights, parents, children, money, possessions, will, liberty to have religion.[261] And it is not men alone who leave these things behind for the sake of religion, for virgins and widows and other women who are in religion put themselves in cells and in monasteries from which they never again emerge so that they can adore and serve God.[262]

83. ON CONVERTING THOSE WHO ARE IN ERROR

[1] To convert is to return people who are in error to the path of truth so that they can be participants with the Catholics in the eternal path.[263] Know, son, that the work of conversion requires three things: power, wisdom and will, among which three things our Lord God Jesus Christ entrusted two to Saint Peter when He told him and begged him three times to feed His lambs.[264]

[2] If God had told Saint Peter in the person of the holy Church to convert those who are in error and had not given him power and wisdom, God's words would have been flawed. And if God constrained man's will by force to desire conversion, He would destroy free will,

---

261. In pursuit of similar goals, though outside of any official religious order, Llull abandoned his own family some three months after his "conversion to penance" (*VC* §9). In 1276, his wife Blanca Picany seeks an administrator for her household because Llull "has become so contemplative that he pays no attention to his temporal goods" (see Hillgarth 2001: 36-37; Document #12).

262. Llull is referring to the cloistering or "enclosure" of both men and women religious, who never leave the monastery or, in some cases, a narrow cell built onto the wall of churches into which they have entered after taking their monastic vows.

263. This is the heart of Llull's life and many of the ideas that drive his activities throughout his long life, from writing books on his Art to his missionary journeys to Tunis, are found in this chapter. At the time of his "conversion to penance," Llull made three resolves relating to the conversion of "those who are in error": 1) "to give up his life and soul for the sake of His love and honor; and to accomplish this by carrying out the task of converting...the Saracens who...surrounded the Christians on all sides"; 2) "to write a book, the best in the world, against the errors of unbelievers"; 3) to "incite" the pope, kings and princes "to institute...monasteries in which selected monks and others fit for the task would be brought together to learn the languages of the Saracens and other unbelievers" so that they could "be sent out to preach and demonstrate to the Saracens and other unbelievers the holy truth of the Catholic faith" (*VC* §5-§7).

264. John 21:15-17.

by whose destruction merit would be destroyed, and God would not be just. Therefore, to preserve free will and to charge the holy Church with guiding the lost, the Son of God sought to receive death in human flesh to save His people and to lift up the holy Church, in which God has so honored men.

[3] Dear son, the power to convert those who are in error rests in God's will. Because it is a good thing to convert a man who is in error, in accord with goodness, justice, mercy, piety, divine generosity, it follows that the divine will must wish it. And because He wishes it, God has given power to the pope and cardinals and other prelates and clergy in wealth and in peoples and in wise persons who have the knowledge required to convert those in error.

[4] Many Jews and Saracens who lack knowledge of the Catholic faith live under the rule of Christians. And Christians have the power to teach the faith to some of the infidels' children by force so that they can have that knowledge.[265] And through that knowledge, they can recognize that they are in error, through which recognition it is possible that they will convert and that they will convert others. Now, a prelate or prince who does not love this method because he fears that the Jews and the Saracens will flee to other lands loves the goods of this world more than the honor of God or the salvation of his neighbor.[266]

[5] Many a Jew would become a Christian if he had something with which he and his children and his wife could live. Thus, the person who does not wish to provide for them or to create a place where they can live acts contrary to the power that God has given him in giving him worldly goods.[267] Many a Saracen would become a Chris-

---

265. The idea of forcing Jews and Muslims living among Christians to listen to Christian evangelists was a part of the toolkit of conversion in this period. In 1299, Llull himself obtained a license from King James II of Aragón to preach in synagogues on Saturdays and Sundays and in mosques on Fridays and Sundays (Hillgarth 2001: 71-72, Doc. #35). Cf. Hames 2000: 104-114.

266. It was to the benefit of princes to keep Jews and Muslims as non-Christians (see the following note). Here Llull lists the major groups in need of conversion and the differing strategies necessary to convert each one: Jews, Saracens, idolaters and gentiles.

267. "Create a place where they can live" ("fa comú"). Presumably, the converted Jew would no longer be able to practice his trade among the Jews, or the Jews would no longer trade with the convert, so he might lose his livelihood. Too, the convert could no longer live in the Jewish quarter of the town, and it would be necessary to find a place for that person and his family to live among Christians. Llull's comments suggest

tian if he saw that those Saracens who become Christians were honored and were not despised by the people.[268] Therefore, the person who does not punish the dishonor that some do to baptized persons does not use the power that God has given him and does not wish for other Saracens to have knowledge of God.[269]

[6] You know well, son, that the pope has various messengers whom he can send to the lands where idolaters and gentiles live, and they can bring five hundred or a thousand or more of them from diverse lands and diverse nations, and can have them taught our language and our faith, and can show them good hospitality, and then can send them back to their own land so that their people can know our faith—of which they are now ignorant and in which they would believe if they knew about it—, for a man without faith, an idolater, is easy to convert.

[7] Many a holy religious, son, desires to die to honor God's Passion and for the salvation of his neighbor, and he would learn the language if there were someone to teach it to him, and he would go to preach the word of God if there were someone to send him. But there is no one who founds monasteries dedicated to learning various languages and there is no one who sends the friars.[270]

---

that Christians (and Christian rulers) were reluctant to provide living spaces for converts from Judaism. See Tartakoff (2011) for the "deep ambivalence" Aragonese rulers felt with regard to the conversion of Jews to Christianity. In *Felix,* Llull's alter-ego, the hermit Blaquerna, explains this situation in a story about a king "who rules over a city" and who receives large annual sums in tribute from the Jews. "And it came to pass that one very wealthy Jew became a Christian, along with his wife and children, and all of his belongings went to the king; and his wife, children, and he himself were so poor that they went from door to door begging, and were dying of hunger. The king's subjects wondered in great wonder at how he could accept money from usury [the source of the former Jew's wealth] and not give a man who had once been a Jew enough for him and his children to live on" (*SW* 2.711).

268. The mistreatment and mistrust on the part of "old" Christians of Jews and Muslims recently converted to Christianity will become a major source of conflict and social disintegration in Iberia over the following centuries. Llull, here, is an early voice identifying the problem of Christians who do not accept their "new" Christian brethren.

269. This seems to be directed at princes who should be punishing people who disrespect baptized former Muslims.

270. This statement has sometimes been used in attempts to date the composition of the *DP*, since Llull himself does not provide a date of composition, as he will do for works he writes after 1294 (see Santanach 2000: 31-33).

[8] There are many princes who would dedicate their income and their person and their people to spreading the Catholic faith if they had help from the holy Church in conquering the lands that it has lost, which the infidels hold to the Church's dishonor. And if 5.000 sous of income are paid to a single bishop, how much should be spent for the things just mentioned?[271]

[9] Would it not be easy to find a man who wanted to be bishop, even without the 1000 marks of income? Would there not be men who would agree to be bishops with even less income? And the person who waits for God to put it in his heart to bring about the above-mentioned things tempts the will of God, who clearly wished for him to do it, as the cross signifies.

[10] If all the religious who are prepared to preach were needed by the Christian peoples, there would be some excuse. But God so desires them to spread throughout the world that He has multiplied them so that there are enough for all purposes. And the friars who would become martyrs would preach to us more forcefully of faith and devotion by their example and their devotion than the friars who remain among us.

[11] Reason demonstrates that truth is stronger than lies. Therefore, if God is behind it, and saintly conduct of men and the sacrifice of sacred blood in the body of a man who dies to honor God, and if one does all one can through prayer and through alms and through penance, affliction and devotion, how could it be that, through long persistence and perseverance, one failed to cast the infidels from the error in which they live? And if this were impossible, it would follow that error and falseness have a greater power than the things just mentioned and that men carried out their duty in converting the world better than God. And that is not true.

---

271. Here Llull introduces the idea of a military crusade to the Holy Land, which is held by Muslims. Llull believes that secular rulers would willingly participate in conquering this territory if it had help from the Church. The Church clearly has the resources, since it can afford to pay a bishop 5000 sous, but, apparently, the will is lacking. It is difficult to establish any meaningful equivalent value of the "sou" and the "mark" in today's terms, but we can assume Llull wishes to indicate an extravagant sum. If we accept the valuation in *DCVB* that the "marc," which Llull mentions in the following paragraph, was "a silver coin that was worth 44 Barcelonian *sous*" in the 12th and 13th centuries, we can at least establish that by the 5000 *sous* mentioned here and the 1000 marks mentioned in the next paragraph Llull intends to refer to roughly equivalent amounts of money.

[12] We are not in the time of miracles, for devotion to converting the world was greater among the Apostles than it is now in the time in which we live. The infidels do not accept arguments based on authorities. Therefore, it is necessary to convert the infidels with the *Book of Demonstrations* and the *Art of Finding Truth*, which should be taught to them so that, using them, one can argue with them intellectually, so that they can know and love God.[272]

84. ON PRAYER[273]

[1] Prayer is a devout lifting up, a pious thought asking God for eternal bliss or for goods that are appropriate to this worldly life.

[2] Dear son, there are three types of prayer: the first type is when the soul remembers and understands and loves God and the reasons for which it adores God; the second type is when the mouth names and speaks what the soul remembers and understands and loves; the third is when man, by doing good works and thinking and loving good, makes a prayer to God.

[3] It is not a proper prayer to name God or to pray to Him while the heart is thinking about vanities, for the heart and the mouth must come together as one and at the same moment. Therefore, if you cannot keep your heart on what you are saying when you pray to God, make up new words and new thoughts for praying to God so that by the discovery of new words you can control your heart and bring it into concordance with the words that you are saying.[274]

---

272. Llull's point is that intellectual arguments are required because the three faiths do not follow the same authorities and, therefore, arguments from authority are useless (see n. 119). *The Art of Finding Truth*, written around 1274, survives only in Latin, with the standardized title *Ars compendiosa inveniendi veritatem*. This is the first elaboration of Llull's Art. It is also mentioned below in Chs. 85.2 and 91.19. *The Book of Demonstrations* (*Llibre de demostracions*) is among the first direct applications of the Art, attempting to show how it can be used to prove several essential truths of the Christian faith: God, the Trinity, the Incarnation. It was written in 1274-1276.

273. The chapter on prayer is one of the longest in the *DP*. Beyond stressing the importance of prayer itself, Llull also makes use of this chapter to review, near the end of the book, many of the catechetical materials from the first part of the book and to show how they can be used as a means of structuring one's prayers.

274. In the *Book of Contemplation*, Llull discuss the effect of "new words": "Any new, strange word is closer to the soul's desire for the things it doesn't have, than old words

[4] Son, in the morning when you get up, go to church to worship God and kneel down before the altar and make the sign of the cross in front of your face. With your corporeal eyes, look at the cross so that your soul can remember the holy Passion of our Lord Jesus Christ. Lift up the eyes of your soul and your hands to God and kiss the earth out of humility and to signify that you have come from it and that you will return beneath it. Salute the cross saying: "Adoramus te Christe et benediximus tibi, quia per sanctam crucem tuam redemisti mundum."[275] Say the *Paternoster* in memory of the Passion of Jesus Christ who said it on the night when He was delivered unto death. Salute the Queen of Heaven, Our Lady Saint Mary, with the *Ave Maria* and worship our Lord God in the angels and in the saints in glory.[276]

[5] When you have said these words on your knees in front of the altar, move to a different place if it is better suited to worship—for prayer is impeded by a crowd—and make your prayer in that place. First, worship God in the Fourteen Articles.[277] Then, worship God, adoring his goodness, greatness, eternity, power, wisdom, love, virtue, truth, glory, perfection, justice, generosity, mercy, humility, lordship, patience.[278]

[6] Ask God for faith, son, so that you can believe in Him even if you do not understand Him.[279] Ask Him to give you hope so that you can trust Him to take care of your needs. Ask God for charity so that you love Him and love yourself and your neighbor. Ask for justice so that you fear God's justice and sentence yourself to undergo suffering in this world for the love of God and to give satisfaction for your sins. Ask God for the light of wisdom so that He illuminates your soul

---

which the soul has used for those things in which it has not found satisfaction" (cited in Bonner 2007: 293, n. 99).

275. The "Adoramus te" prayer is in Latin in the Catalan text: "We adore you, Christ, and bless you, for by your holy cross you redeemed the world." I translate following the more common version of the prayer, which has "benedicimus" ("bless") rather than "benediximus" ("blessed"), found in the text.

276. See Chs. 8 and 6.

277. See Chs. 1-12.

278. This is only the second time that Llull gives the full list of all sixteen of the "uncreated virtues" (see Ch. 1 and n. 5).

279. Here, Llull recommends asking God for each of the three theological and four cardinal virtues in turn (cf. Chs. 52-58). He uses the specific virtue of fortitude to remind the reader, at the same time, of the seven vices (Chs. 60-66).

on His pathways and so that you can learn how to and desire to illuminate those who are in darkness. Ask God for fortitude against gluttony, lust, avarice, envy, sloth, pride, wrath. Ask Him for temperance in eating, drinking, speaking, dressing, spending, sleeping, waking.

[7] Know, son, that it is a much better thing beyond compare to ask God for the virtues just mentioned than to ask for health or life or money or honor or children or possessions or other things like these, for a person can fall under God's wrath through all these things and can go to infinite torments. And through the virtues, one goes to be blessed in heavenly glory, which lasts for all time.

[8] Dear son, pray for your father and your mother, for you received the being that you possess from them, which being you would not give in exchange for all the world. Pray for your wife and for your children, if you have any, for God grants great grace to a man when He gives him a wife, children to be his servants. Pray for your earthly lord, for God has given him to you to help and defend you and to punish you so that you do not lose God's glory.

[9] Son, make a general prayer—for that is most pleasing to God—and pray for the Holy Apostolic Father and for the cardinals and for the prelates and for the princes, for the religious, for all the Christian people, that God may give them grace to be defenders of the holy Catholic faith and to exalt it in order to honor God's holy Passion, that the Passion may be honored by the holy Church in the place where the Son of God was killed and lives, to honor the holy Church and all the Christian people.[280] Pray, son, for the Jews, Saracens, Tartars and for all the other infidels, that God may give them the light of grace so that they may be converted to the holy Catholic faith and that God, in his mercy, may give them procurators so that they can have preachers who teach them in the true path without fear of death.[281]

---

280. Here again Llull makes an argument to the pope, cardinals, prelates, princes, religious and all Christians to free the Holy Land from Muslim domination so that Christ's Passion can be celebrated by Catholics in the locality in which it took place.

281. The work of Llull's "procurators" can best be understood in this context as that of "representatives" or "delegates." As is evident here, the role of "procurador" was in many ways key to Llull's ideas of how the missionary project he envisioned should be carried out. In *Fèlix, or the Book of Wonders*, Llull describes "a man who had made himself procurator of the unbelievers so that they could find the path to salvation" (*SW* 2.758 and n. 5 for other works where this idea appears). In *Blaquerna*, Ch. 93, Llull describes how a cardinal had "his procurators and his officials go throughout the lands announc-

[10] In your prayers, do not forget the dead who are in Purgatory, who suffer grievous torments for the sins that they committed. Such sufferings are alleviated by the living in this world when they pray for them and when they give alms for the love of God.

[11] Keep a special saint—man or woman—in your prayers, son, for whom you have a special devotion, and pray to and honor him so that he may hold a place for you with God, for the saints in glory are so beloved by God that to multiply their glory they listen to those who pray to them and honor them in this world.

[12] Accuse yourself, son, and confess your sins and ask God in His mercy to pardon you, and thank God for having given you being and everything that you possess, and thank Him for not having made you deformed or an infidel or a rock or some other thing that is not as noble as the being that He has given you.

[13] If you suffer in serving God or because of your sins, give thanks to God, for great are the benefits that come through sufferings, for through trials suffered in patience, you are pleasing to God. And sufferings mortify the vanities of this world in the soul.

[14] You will never be able, son, to thank God for all the good that He has given you or for the Heaven that He wishes to give you. For that reason, turn to the Queen of all the world and to the saints in Paradise and pray to them that, in your stead, they give the thanks that you cannot.[282] For, to the degree that they are greater and nobler than you, they are better suited to give thanks for the goods that God has given you than you are.

[15] Do not be ashamed to pray to God, for God is an honored lord. And when in church, do not look at the other men or the women or listen to their words, for you will be disrupted by them in your prayers. Do not ask for the latest gossip, so that you do not cast God from your soul. Learn enough Latin so that you can understand the mass, for if you understand it, your prayer will be that much more pleasing to God.

[16] Do you know why you get bored by a long mass and a long sermon? Because you lack devotion and you do not know how to con-

---

ing the infernal punishments and the glories of Paradise and the death of this world, as is told in the *Doctrina pueril*, which a man wrote to his dear son."

282. The "Queen of all the world" is, of course, the Virgin Mary, often seen as a benevolent intercessor between God and humankind.

template God at length through the love in your heart and by lifting up your understanding to God and by remembering His words.

[17] Many a man has memory but does not know how to remember, and many a man has understanding but does not know how to understand, and many a man has will but does not know how to love. Therefore, son, if you knew how to remember and understand and love God's words, you would be calm in listening to them and you would be sad and upset when you stopped hearing them.

[18] If you are upset, son, or have some sorrow in your heart or have some troubles, if you wish to gladden, to console, to soothe your soul, give yourself over immediately to prayer, for prayer has such great power that it honors, consoles, soothes and gladdens every man who is suffering, upset, disconsolate, scorned. And do you know why? Because prayer is the connection between man and God.

[19] Son, fasts, afflictions, weeping, sighs, contrition, humble clothing and a frugal life are in accord with prayer. And do you know why? Because the things contrary to these obstruct prayer and cast God from human thought.

[20] Weep, son, in your prayer, for tears and words join together in prayer. And if you have a heart so hard that you cannot weep, there is a flaw in your love and in your contrition. Therefore, to mortify your sensual nature, which prevents you from weeping, imagine that someone is killing your father and mother or some friend you greatly love right before your eyes and that that person is asking you for help and that he is looking at you piteously and that you cannot help him. And when your corporeal nature begins to move, cast all things from your soul but God and remember His Passion, which He suffered for you, and remember the great sins that you have committed, for all these things will be a reason for you to cry.[283]

[21] If you cannot cry despite all these things, go up and do penance in the high mountains and flee the world and lead a harsh life and be alone and imagine the great infernal punishments that those in Hell suffer. And move your imagination over the different types of torments, for then you will cry.[284] And while you are in that place and

---

283. "When your corporeal nature begins to move," that is, when you begin to cry. Llull's method will allow for one to transfer sorrow for worldly concerns to those genuinely worthy of tears: Christ's Passion, our own sins. For the close connection between the emotions and the body, see n. 224.

284. See Ch. 99.

moment, weep and worship, son, the King of Heaven, for all the people in Hell would have eternal glory and would escape infinite suffering if they could weep for just one hour and adore our Lord God.

85. ON THE SOUL[285]

[1] The soul is a rational spiritual substance that gives form to the human body. Know, son, that Our Lord creates this soul from nothing. And He joins it with the engendered body in the womb of a pregnant woman, and the baby is made from the body and soul in the womb of the woman.

[2] Three powers are given to the soul: memory, understanding and will.[286] The soul does everything using these three powers. These powers work in four ways, as is explained in *The Art of Finding Truth*, for the soul does one thing in its powers when it apprehends its object remembering, understanding, loving; another when it apprehends remembering, understanding, hating; another when it apprehends forgetting, not understanding, loving or hating; another when it apprehends in a composite way using the three ways just mentioned.[287]

[3] There are five universal powers in every soul: vegetative, sensitive, imaginative, rational, motive. But in trees there is no sensitive soul, and in beasts there is no rational soul, and in the soul of man, all five powers are found. And so one says that the soul of man participates with all Creation.[288]

[4] The vegetative soul is the growth that plants and the body of a man or an animal make from their elemental nature. The sensitive soul is the power through which beasts and birds and men have five physical senses. The imaginative soul is the power with which one

---

285. For a graphic view of Llull's conception of the structure of the human soul, see Figure 2.

286. This understanding of the three powers of the human soul is generally attributed to Augustine. See *De Trinitate*, Books 9-10.

287. Here we glimpse the workings of the *ars combinatoria* that underlies Llull's Art. See n. 272 for the *Art of Finding Truth*. The best basic introduction to Llull's Art in English is Bonner 2007.

288. Figure 2 shows the hierarchy of "souls" that form the soul of man. In this schema, plants lack physical senses, while animals possess both the properties of the vegetative soul of plants (the capacity for growth, for example) and the physical senses.

imagines physical things. The rational soul is the essence that has the power to remember and to understand and to love. The motive soul is the power by which plants and beasts move toward what they desire and the soul of man moves toward what he loves.

[5] Know, son, that the soul takes everything that the five physical senses—sight, hearing, smell, taste, touch—present to it with the imagination and brings it together in common.[289] And the imagination offers this via the phantasy to the understanding, and then the understanding climbs higher to understand God and angels and intellectual things, which the imaginative cannot imagine.

[6] The phantasy is the chamber in the palate, above the forehead.[290] In the forehead, the imaginative brings together what it apprehends from physical things, and, from there, it enters into the phantasy with what it has apprehended and it illuminates that chamber so that the understanding can take what the imaginative presents to it. Therefore, when, through some happenstance, that process becomes disordered, a man becomes phantastical and has a distorted understanding and is mad.[291]

---

289. Although Llull does not mention it in full here, he is referring to a power of the sensitive soul known as the "common sense," the place where the sight of a dog, say, and the sound of barking could be brought together to create the full sensory "image" (that is what the imagination does) of a barking dog.

290. I have used the less common spelling of "fantasy" better to distinguish medieval understandings of this term from our own ideas of "fantasy" as a creative and, generally, positive mental activity. It is difficult to picture the anatomical placement of the "phantasy" as Llull describes it here according to modern notions of the locations of the palate and the forehead. Generally, the imagination or phantasy (some writers treated the terms as synonymous) were located in a "cell" ("cellula"; Llull's "chamber") in the brain located in the forebrain (what we would label the frontal lobe), behind the forehead. Compare Ch. 68, where Llull says the phantasy is "between the forehead and the back of the neck." For a thorough treatment of the "internal senses," which are those Llull is discussing here, see Wolfson (1935) and Harvey (1975). Siraisi (1990: 83) reproduces a sketch from a late 15th-century manuscript that, roughly, illustrates the location and sequence of sensation and cognition in a series of "cellulae," beginning with the "common sense" located at the base of the forehead between the eyes and moving backwards through imagination, "phantasia," cognition (the loose equivalent of Llull's "understanding") and memory.

291. Llull is speaking of a phantasy that has become corrupted through illness, perhaps, or injury ("accident") and offers its own distorted images as if they were the true sensory images presented by the imagination, with the result that the understanding becomes "gross" (I have translated Llull's "gros enteniment" as "distorted understanding," but we could also understand this as "imprecise" or "unrefined" understanding), unable to grasp the detailed distinctions in the reality around it.

[7] Know, son, that when you die, the rational soul—which is an immortal thing—remains. And by the power and the miracle of God, who wishes to reward the soul in Paradise or in Purgatory or in Hell according to its works, it remains with its three powers, called "virtues" above, by which virtues it can remember and understand physical things without the imagination and without the corporeal senses.[292]

[8] Dear son, many a man falls into doubt and error when he believes he imagines spiritual and intellectual things: these things cannot be imagined.[293] For just as eyes have one task and the ears another, the imaginative has the task of imagining that which is physical and the understanding has the task of understanding that which is physical as well as that which is spiritual. Therefore, since the understanding is higher in virtue than the imagination, it can understand what the imagination imagines. And it rises higher than the imagination, which cannot imagine that which is of an intellectual nature.

[9] Son, these matters about which I am speaking to you are extremely subtle for someone your age, but I wish to tell you about them so that you will want to understand them when you are old enough to do so.

[10] When the body of a man dies, son, do not think that the rational soul also dies. Rather, it goes to Paradise or to Purgatory or to Hell, according to the merits earned by its deeds. But the vegetative and sensitive and imaginative souls die with the death of the body. And do you know why? Because they are of the nature of the body, which is of a corruptible nature.

---

292. Since all our perceptions are linked to our physical senses, one might wonder how one can experience the pleasures of Heaven or the tortures of Hell after the death of the physical body. Here Llull explains that our pleasure or suffering in the afterlife can be experienced through two powers of the rational soul (memory and understanding) which remember and understand physical pain or pleasure.

293. Here Llull sets out one of the key principles of his view of the human soul: there is a stark separation between the powers we might think of as physical (all powers from the vegetative through the imaginative; see Figure 2)—and those considered "rational" or "intellectual": memory, understanding and will. Because of this clear division between the physical and the spiritual, it can (sometimes) be the cause of doubts and error to believe that one is perceiving spiritual things with the corporeal senses and the imagination.

[11] On the Judgment Day, when we will all rise again, each rational soul will recover its body, but there will be no need for the ordering of the powers of the soul then in the way that is necessary in this time in which we live, for from Judgment Day forward, man will neither eat nor drink nor lie with woman nor have a corruptible body. And do you know why? So that there can be eternal signification of the justice of God.

86. ON THE HUMAN BODY[294]

[1] The human body, son, is composed of the four elements and their composition is made from the matter that the man puts in the woman and from the matter that the woman has ready to receive it when she is impregnated.

[2] Because the four elements are corruptible within the body of man, the body itself is corruptible. Therefore, to sustain the body, man must eat and drink and sleep and wake and breathe in order to temper the concordance and the contrariety of the elements.[295]

[3] Dear son, the body has five senses: sight, hearing, smell, taste, touch.[296] Through these five senses, it participates with things outside it, without which it could not have sustenance, because natural heat constantly consumes the humidity of the body. Therefore, if humidity from exterior things did not enter the body through smell, taste, when the natural heat had consumed the humidity, the body would be dead.

[4] Dear son, a man can live without seeing, hearing, smelling, but without tasting, touching, breathing, no one can live. Therefore, let it be a general rule to you to be temperate in your eating and drinking and to smell healthy, fresh air. Smell odors that do not cor-

---

294. As the previous chapter focuses on the distinction between the rational soul and the physical powers below it, including the imagination, the common sense and the phantasy, this chapter begins at the lowest levels of the physical powers, the four elements, and moves up to the five physical senses.

295. For the reasons for the corruptibility of the elements in the human body, for the idea of tempering the balance of the elements in the body and for much of the explanation of the functioning of the senses that follows, see Ch. 77.

296. Later in his life, Llull will add a sixth sense to the traditional five: speech, which he names "affatus" (see Badia, Santanach & Soler 2016: 59-62).

rupt the humors in which the things from which the body takes life are mixed.

[5] Son, sight is in the eyes in a triangle. That is: the air is bright, and in the eyes with which one sees there is light, and the objects that one sees have light. For if light were not in these three things, one could not see, and when light is lacking in any one of these three things and the air is not purified by the light of the sun or fire to bear light, then one cannot see.

[6] Hearing is the sound that is made in air struck by a physical blow, which forms in your ears with the help of the water, which receives the imprint of the blow that was struck in the air. Now, when air and water are in disaccord in the brain and in the ears, the accord of the beaten air with the water whence sound is formed cannot take place to make hearing happen in your ears. And for that reason, men are deaf and do not hear. And because of the lack of hearing, they are mute and do not know how to speak, for children learn to speak and to move their tongues according to the voices that they hear.

[7] Smell is formed by heat and humidity. This heat and humidity come from fire and air, for fire and air have the nature of lifting the breath that descends and rises through your nose, pulling the air that participates with the body in odorative things, which are evaporative.[297] And your breath brings that matter to your nose, where you smell the odor, and, in that place, your humors take dryness from it for their mixings, according to how the odors agree with the disposition of the humors, and for that reason, pure air fortifies the humors, and corrupted air corrupts them.

[8] Taste is engendered by the humidity in the veins full of air that are below the tongue. And the mixture of the humidity of foods and the humidity that is in the veins begins in the back of the mouth, where the veins have their root. And then, son, taste comes to your throat according to the quality of the foods. But when the air that is in the veins of the tongue disagrees with the foods that you eat—say, because of an illness in the throat or because you are not accustomed to those foods—then foods that are sweet seem bitter to you.

---

297. "Odorative things" simply means "things able to be smelled" (GGL), which are, by their nature "evaporative," that is, they emit vapors. This is the "matter" that the breath brings to the nose, as described in the next sentence.

[9] Touch comes from the animality, that is, in the living flesh, where a person feels it when he is touched.[298] Now, water and earth are felt first, and fire and air afterwards. However, the senses are so nearly simultaneous in their perceptions that the imagination cannot imagine the first moment or the last between the sensation of earth and water and the sensation of fire and air. But, because fire and air are more deeply within the body than either earth or water, it is understood that one feels through earth and water before fire and air. And, again, because the more the body is of grosser matter, the more it is touchable, and the more it is touchable, the more sensitive it is, as long as it is animate.[299]

[10] Therefore, because in the spheres of the elements, according to natural desire, fire is above air and air is above water and water above earth, so, in compound elemental bodies, it is the opposite. For natural heat is more deeply inside the body than any of the other properties of the elements, and air more within than water or earth, and earth is closer to the outside of the body than water. And that is according to the greater or lesser simplicity of the elements, for the elements are closer within the body, in terms of their simplicity, in some parts of the body than in others.[300]

[11] Dear son, I could tell you many natural facts about the body, but I pass on quickly. Do you know why? Because I have a great deal to say about God.

87. On Life

[1] Corporeal life is an actualization by which the body comes to life, and spiritual life is to love God. Therefore, son, if you love the corporeal life, love health, for in health the soul and body come together. And by this joining, man lives. If you love the spiritual life, love and

---

298. The sensitive soul belongs to animals and man. Thus, the quality of "animality" is what enables the flesh, which pertains to animals and man, to sense, to feel when it is touched. See Figure 2.

299. "Grosser matter," in this case, means "earth" and "water."

300. Cf. Figure 2, which illustrates the construction of the elements within the human body with a series of concentric circles with fire in the center and earth in the outermost ring. As Llull notes, this is the opposite of the rest of the sublunary world, where earth is most central and is covered by water, above which is air and, then, the realm of fire. See Figure 3.

fear God, for by loving, fearing God, the soul lives in virtues and avoids vices and sins, which are the occasion of infernal death.

[2] Know, son, that three paths exist to signify the two types of lives: the lower path, the middle path and the sovereign path. The lowest path is a life of sin; the middle path is the active life; and the highest path is the contemplative life. Now, since the contemplative life is closer to God and further from sin than the active life, the contemplative life is nobler than the active life.

[3] On the lowest path, son, go the sinful men who love this worldly life in order to enjoy worldly delights. Now, these men are alive as far as the body is concerned, but with regard to their soul they die in sin and blame. And for that reason, son, do not go down the path that leads to eternal death.

[4] On the middle path are the men who lead the active life, that is, those men who possess the blessings of this world with the intention of doing good with them for the love of God. They have a wife and children and the delights of this world as is ordained. They thank God for these things and through them they avoid sinful acts. Such men possess this world and the other.

[5] In the contemplative life are the men who lead a harsh life and contemplate God with fasts, prayers, poverty, contrition, contempt for this world. These men, son, possess the other world more surely than do men who go down the middle path. And do you know why? Because they give up this world in exchange for the other and abandon the blessings of this world.

[6] Dear son, you are in a situation and at an age when you can go down whichever path you choose. Now, if the lowest path appeals to you, remember how briefly the life of this world lasts and how even young men are not immune to dying, and that man does not live while he sleeps or while he is angry, sad, fearful or has suffering and tribulations through illness or some other cause.[301]

[7] If you do the numbers, you will find that man sleeps as much or more than he wakes, and man is upset and suffers more of the time than he is happy and content. Therefore, since life in this lowest path

---

301. This is another passage in which Llull seems to devote more than rhetorical attention to the relationship between father and son, here even referring to the putative age of his "son" (see also Ch. 12.12, 53.3 and 88.6).

is so brief and the infernal death to which one goes on that path is so long, you will be a fool, son, if you choose the lowest path.

[8] Will you choose the middle path, son? If you do, choose an occupation that is as far away as possible from the lowest path, for in the middle path there are some occupations that are more noble and higher than others. And do you know why? Because they are closer to the contemplative life.

[9] If, son, you choose the contemplative path, choose and select the order that is furthest from the middle path, for just as in the active life there are some occupations that are closer than others to the lowest path, in the highest path, there are some orders that are further from the active life than others.[302]

[10] Dear son, within a single order, some duties are in better accord with the contemplative life than others. And do you know why? Because in the contemplative life there are some duties that are closer to the active life than others. Therefore, if you enter the religious life, if you can, take the duty that is the furthest from the active life.[303]

[11] If you choose the active life, do not read books that make the bottom path seem desirable and take up the great *Book of Contemplation*, through which the contemplative life is made desirable for contemplating our Lord God.[304]

---

302. Here again and in the following paragraph, Llull uses the term "religió" (see Ch. 82) to refer Christian monastic orders and the need to choose the specific order and, in the next paragraph, the specific responsibilities within that order that allow one to lead the most contemplative life. It seems that Llull did not fully follow his own advice in his life for, although later in his life he may have been interested in the Third Order of the Franciscans, a lay order, and therefore presumably one closest to the "active" life, for reasons unknown to us, he seems never to have formally become a member of that, or any other, order.

303. It is the job of abbot that is the most to be avoided if one wishes to fully immerse oneself in the contemplative life. In *Blaquerna*, Ch. 60, it is precisely for this reason that Blaquerna is unhappy with his election as abbot: it forces him to deal constantly with temporal matters and keeps him from spiritual ones.

304. *The Book of Contemplation* (*Llibre de contemplació*; written 1271-1274?) is Llull's first great work. It is a massive text, written first—Llull tells us—in Arabic and then translated into Catalan. No surviving copy of the Arabic original is known. Vast in scope, it consists of 365 chapters, one for each day of the year, plus an additional chapter for "leap year."

88. On Death

[1] Physical death is the separation of the body from the soul; spiritual death occurs in the soul that distances itself from God. Thus, son, there are two deaths: in physical death, the virtuous soul draws nearer to God and goes to Paradise when the body dies; spiritual death, which occurs in the sinful soul, condemns the body to suffer infernal fire eternally and it goes to be subjected to infinite sufferings.

[2] Meditate, son, on death so that you are not proud, for death disposes the body to great defilement in that it renders it powerless and puts it beneath the earth and makes it food for worms and makes it disgusting to see and touch and smell and returns it to dust and ashes.

[3] Fear death, son, so that you live serving God, and fear death because you do not know the hour when it will come for you, nor where nor why nor what you will die from. Because you know that you have to die and you have no idea of any of these things, death is greatly to be feared.

[4] Son, you die each day, for death draws nearer to you all the time. The dead people you see buried and rotting beneath the earth signify to you that just as they are, so shall you be. Just as they are forgotten and disobeyed by their children and by their family, so shall you be forgotten and disobeyed.

[5] Death will take all the goods that you possess away from you, and it will cause you to be despised and forgotten by the people. And as for the things that you own, there will come a time when men who do not know you or love you and will not speak about you will possess them. Nor, if you came back to life, would they give you a single piece of bread or a single cup of water.

[6] I wished for this death, so horrible and so dreadful, in my own father. And do you know why? So that I could possess his goods. And let this be an example for you and for your son, if you have one. So, son, will you desire the death of your soul so that your son can have your goods, for which, perchance, he will wish for your death?[305]

---

305. Here is another place in which Llull seems to speak more intimately of the father-son relationship than might be accounted for solely by his use of the literary, and biblical, trope of "dear son." See also Chs. 12.12, 53.3 and 87.6.

[7] The death of the body is a fearful thing, but a far more fearful thing is the death of the soul because you cannot flee the death of the body and you can escape the death of the soul. Now, why should something that you cannot escape be feared? Why should the death of the body, which happens so swiftly, be more fearful than the death of the soul, a death that lasts for all time?

[8] Desire to die to honor your Lord Jesus Christ, son, for He, who would not have died had He not wished to, wished to die out of love for you. Now, if it were possible that you would never die, still you should desire to die for the love of your God anyway; and if now, when you cannot escape death, you do not wish to die to honor God before the unbelievers who dishonor Him and do not believe in Him, how much less would you wish not to die if it were possible that you would never die!

[9] Dear son, which is better for you: to die once or to die forever in eternal fire? And which is better for you: to die a desirable death while honoring God or to die a hateful death, which kills a man against his will and without his earning any recognition or merit before God?

[10] Nothing in this world is as close to the other world as death. For without death you cannot pass over to it, nor can you go there by any means as honorable as through death, and by no other means can you be as similar to God Jesus Christ as through death. Since this is so, why do you fear to die for your God? And why do you not fear a death in which you do not receive recognition from God?

[11] Where, son, are all the emperors, kings, counts, barons, prelates who have passed from this life? And where is Alexander, who was lord of the whole world? Who is there who speaks about them or dedicates himself to honoring them?[306] And see, son, how the Apostles and the other martyrs who died for the love of God are honored, celebrated, remembered, prayed to.

[12] Be assured, son, that, in the times in which we live, one is better suited to die to honor God than to live and honor God. And do you know why? Because it is a better thing to die to honor God than

---

306. The reference is, of course, to Alexander the Great (356-323 BCE). Here Llull uses the topos of "ubi sunt?"—"where are they now?," "what has become of them?"—ubiquitous in medieval literature on the topic of death.

to live to honor God. And that which is better and nobler is the greater cause for which man exists.

[13] In darkness, son, are the eyes of our souls, and devotion has
grown cold, and charity is failing. For that reason, we do not wish to
die to honor God, nor do we fulfill the purpose for which we exist,
nor do we mortify our body so that our soul can live with God. And
because—in the times in which we live—we do not do the things for
which we were created, there is danger and fear that the world may
be judged to be in a parlous state by the justice of God.[307]

89. On Hypocrisy and Vainglory

[1] Hypocrisy is a semblance of virtue in which there is hidden vice.
And for that reason, son, hypocritical men make false representa-
tions and pretend to people that they are good, and they are evil and
full of vices and sins.

[2] Vainglory is a disordered heart moved to undeserved self-hon-
oring. And for that reason, son, men who are vainglorious do some
good things and some that have the semblance of good so that they
may be praised, honored by the peoples.

[3] In hypocrisy there are two paths: down one, it goes in company with vainglory; down the other, it goes in company with falseness.
Down the first, son, go those men who wear humble clothing and fast
and lead a harsh life and say humble and devout words and give the
appearance that they are good men. And they do all this so that they
can have honor and fame among the peoples.

[4] Down the same road go those men who are well-dressed, who
are well-horsed and who give and spend and fight in tournaments so
that people honor them and talk about them. Now, these men are
hypocrites in that they pretend to be good, and they are vile in their
hearts and in their intention.[308] They are vainglorious about their
deeds in that they give themselves glory and a good reputation based

---

307. Llull lived in a century in which millenarian thinking—the sense that the end
of the world was drawing near—was an important theme, inspired by figures such as
Joachim of Fiore (c. 1135-1202). This passage is one of the few times in which we
glimpse such ideas in Llull.

308. For the concept of intention and its relation to "the reason for which man
was created," see the important Ch. 92.

on something that is not enduring and is not the reason for which man was created, for he was not created to praise himself and not to be a praiser of God.

[5] Ah, son! How many alms and how much money, fabrics, beasts, arms and other things like these are given so that a person can have vainglory from them! And how easily and in what a brief time, son, the fame and happiness that those hypocritical and vainglorious men have along the roads down which they go pass away!

[6] Down the path where those men in whom hypocrisy and falseness join together, son, go many men who give the appearance of being good men so that they can deceive people. For with the semblance of good, you deceive a loyal man more quickly than with the semblance of evil.

[7] Since so many men go down this road and since it is so very difficult to protect oneself from a false, hypocritical man, ah! son, who is there who can protect himself from such men and who can be safe from them?

[8] There are some men who do good and do it in a hidden way so that people do not make fun of them. Now, insofar as they fear to suffer blame for giving a good example of doing good works, they have some root in hypocrisy and vainglory, by which they lose the merit that they would have if they did not love vainglory or hypocrisy. For, in the beginning, doing good secretly had no purpose other than assuring that one would not have vainglory from it.[309]

[9] Many a man speaks badly of his father or his brother or of some other man. And do you know why? So that people will praise him and leave off praising the person whose praise he envies. Many a man is a hypocrite and vainglorious and does not know that he is. And do you know why? Because he loves being honored so much that he does not recognize his own defects.

[10] If you wish to be the intimate of a vainglorious person, tell him something bad about someone else, for while you are telling him bad things about another person, he will begin to like you because he will think that you wish to say good things about him. And if you want

---

309. Llull imagines here a past time in which it was possible to do good secretly with the pure motivation of avoiding the vainglory that might arise from doing good works in public, but now things have gotten so turned around that people do good in secret to avoid being mocked for it. This is also a form of hypocrisy with vainglory.

to be despised, hated by a vainglorious man, reprimand him for his transgressions against his Lord God.

90. ON TEMPTATION

[1] Temptation is a test through which understanding is made certain. Temptation is the causation through which the end comes.[310] Now, if you wish to know about temptation, son, you must study it in three types: the first is angelical temptation, the second is diabolical temptation, and the third is the temptation of one man by another.

[2] Angelical temptation, son, is when the angel that God has given you advises you to do good works. And so that it can induce you to do some good deed, it advises you to do another, so that, through it, you can be led to do good. Thus, when you sit at the table and eat and drink with great desire, the angel in your conscience advises you to be temperate in your eating and drinking. And do you know why? So that you may be obedient and fight gluttony, which is a mortal sin, and have abstinence, continence, which are virtues.[311]

[3] Diabolical temptation, son, is when the devil, who is a malign angel, advises you to give alms or do some other good so that you have vainglory from it, which is a sin. Or he will advise you to commit some venial sin so that through it he can induce you to commit a mortal sin, and so on for the other things like these.[312]

[4] If you wish to know which temptation is angelical and which diabolical, understand, son, that angelical temptation gives suffering at the beginning and afflicts the body in its nature. And do you know why? Because the body has a nature that is readier to do evil than good. And since the body is more contrary to doing good, there is greater merit for the soul if it makes the body do good works.

---

310. The rather cryptic statement about the "end" may mean that temptation can lead to two outcomes: either we resist it or we succumb to it. Or it may suggest that based on our response, our own end, in either Heaven or Hell, comes.

311. Here the angel "tempts" one with being temperate in order to lead one to avoid the deadly sin of gluttony. This parallels the devil's tempting first with a venial sin in order to lead one to mortal sin outlined in the next paragraph.

312. For Llull's explanation of the difference between venial and mortal sins, see Ch. 92.

[5] After the body is conquered by the soul and, reluctantly, begins to do good, the soul, which is in better accord with doing good than doing evil, receives happiness and gratification from the good that it does. And it makes the body, which in the beginning was laggardly and lazy, diligent in those things in which the soul makes it labor so that it can do good works.

[6] Dear son, diabolical temptation is exactly the opposite, for in the beginning, it makes the body happy in starting to commit an evil deed and makes the soul—which is aware of the sin and the evil that it does when it accedes to the devil, who is its enemy—sad at the end.

[7] Human temptation, son, is when a beautiful woman paints her face and ornaments her clothing so that she can make people desire her and so that they talk about her beauty. Now, this temptation is engendered by vainglory and lust.

[8] One person tempts with the semblance of good so that he can do evil, or a man tempts another person with the semblance of evil so that he can discover patience, loyalty in him.[313] Thus, with dissimulation and with other things like these, some men tempt others, as is told in the *Book of Contemplation*.[314]

[9] There is a difference, son, between spiritual temptation and corporeal temptation, for spiritual temptation takes place in the soul and in its powers, that is, in memory, understanding, will, and corporeal temptation takes place in the body and in its five bodily senses.

[10] Dear son, great is the glory that men earn by fighting the temptation to do evil. But because man is weak and more ready to obey the devil and his own nature, which is corrupted by sin, and because so many men are conquered by temptation, I advise you, son, as much as you can, to flee diabolical temptations and the temptations of women and of evil men, by which one falls under the wrath of God.

---

313. Perhaps, you test a person by suggesting a disloyal act and, if the person refuses, you have discovered loyalty in that person.

314. On the *Book of Contemplation*, see n. 304. The discussion of temptation is found in Ch. 190.

91. ON HOW ONE SHOULD NURTURE ONE'S CHILD[315]

[1] Nurture is to accustom another person to habitual behaviors that bring him closer to natural conduct. For just as nature follows its course and does not stray from its path, so children accustom themselves to good or bad behavior at the beginning.

[2] Do you know, son, that there are two types of nurture? One pertains to the body, the other to the soul. The one that pertains to the body takes place in the five corporeal senses, which are sight, hearing, smell, taste, touch. Spiritual nurture takes place in the three properties of the soul, that is, in memory, understanding and will.

[3] Dear son, a man must hold his child very dear, and for that reason he should not be neglectful of his child so that he can observe and perceive which behaviors it accustoms itself to and inclines to, for by the nurture of the body, the child accustoms itself to the nurture of the soul, and by the nurture of the soul, it is accustomed to the nurture of the body.

[4] Temptation enters the soul through corporeal vision and for that reason a person should raise his child to see those things by which it does not grow accustomed to bad thoughts or to desiring beautiful clothes, whence pride and envy and squandering money are engendered, and so on for the other things like these.

[5] To accustom your child to hearing vanities, ugly words, romances, songs and instruments and other things that encourage lust is a venom and a poison in the memory, understanding and will of your child, through which venom and poison it wastes and squanders the goods that you leave it, and it imprisons its soul in eternal fire.[316] Therefore, to mortify that poison, words and books that speak of God

---

315. In *Blaquerna*, Ch. 2, "On Blaquerna's Birth and Upbringing," Llull portrays how much of the theory he outlines here is put into practice, almost point by point, by Blaquerna's parents, Evast and Aloma (Llull 2016: 92-95).

316. Here Llull shows that concern about the impact of entertainment media on children is not unique to the age of television, rock music, video games, smartphones and the internet. In his condemnation of romances (fictional stories) in particular, Llull is perhaps thinking of tales such as those of Tristan and Isolde or Piramus and Thisbe. *Blaquerna*, referred to in its colophon (and in some versions of the title) as a "romanç" (romance), may be seen, in fact, as a sort of counter-romance, an illustration of the proper form of entertainment. In this context, it is interesting to note that at the close of Ch. 100, Llull places *Blaquerna* as the next book to be taken up in his reading program for his "son."

and of contempt for this world are necessary before the venom and the poison increase into a habit.

[6] Lust is engendered by smelling amber and musk, and, through the corruption of the air, the body becomes ill. For that reason, a child should not be raised in an unhealthy place and you should not accustom it to odors that move it to vanities or to inappropriate thoughts.

[7] From the time the child is born until it has gained strength and natural heat, it should only be nourished with milk, for any other food is not good for it because the child's natural heat is not at its strength and cannot cook the food. And for that reason, children have ringworm and boils when you force food that nature cannot cook upon them.[317] And many children who would live if they did not eat or drink so much die because of abscesses.

[8] When the child is old enough to walk and run and play, you should feed it only what it needs, and you should not give it anything but bread in the morning or as a snack, if it asks for it. For if children eat roasted foods and fruits and the other things, they will not be able to eat when it is time to eat.[318] And when children eat delicate things beyond what their nature requires or the wealth of their father permits, many children get sick, and many men become poor.

[9] Wine that is too strong destroys natural heat and understanding, and it cuts short one's days. Wine that is too tempered causes a person to become drunk when he drinks wine at full strength.[319] And spicy sauces burn the humors and destroy the brain and natural heat. All these things and many others are harmful to children.

[10] When the child is overdressed, natural heat is destroyed, for children get hot with the exertions they make in playing, and their

---

317. We may think of the idea of "cooking" the food (known as "coction") as similar to our idea of "digestion." Infant digestions are not yet up to the task of digesting any food but milk. Other foods remain "uncooked" (undigested) and create harmful substances in the body which, because natural heat is not yet strong enough to cook them away (see in Ch. 78, where the ability of natural heat to rid the body of some waste products is discussed), can cause ringworm, boils, and other infections.

318. One of the few moments of parental conflict in *Blaquerna* is precisely over this point: Aloma gives her Blaquerna roast meat for breakfast and a *flaó* (a type of sweet or savory cheese pastry or pie) to take along to school in case he gets hungry later on. When Evast, the father, learns of this he "reproves Aloma greatly" (Ch. 2).

319. It was a general practice to temper wine with water. Here Llull argues for the need for temperance even in the tempering of wine.

pores open up, and natural heat escapes from them in vapor and sweat. And if you have put too many clothes on the child, there is no way for cold to close the pores, which cold would close the pores and natural heat would be preserved in the body. And the digestive power would be stronger because of this because of fewer clothes and the foods that children eat, through the activities that they do, would be digested more easily.[320]

[11] Rocking children in the cradle so that they won't cry is not a natural movement. Rather, it is contrary to the brain, which is shaken by rocking and does not achieve the aptitude it would otherwise attain. And for that reason, rocking hurts children more than tears and they end up crying more because you do not rock them than they would if you did not accustom them to rocking at all.

[12] Leaving the hair unshorn on a head full of boils trains bad humors to climb upward, and for that reason, hair on the head destroys the brain, and a person has bad breath and bad teeth and bad eyes and swollen lymph nodes and goiters and many other illnesses. For that reason, children whose heads are shorn are more healthy, and the bad humors are trained to go downward, where they do not do as much harm as they do in the upper parts of the body.[321]

[13] Know, son, that nature is wiser in nurturing children than is your mother, and what nature loses in children who are sons of rich men it gains in those children who are the sons of poor men. For that reason, open your eyes and see which children look healthier and more beautiful: the sons of rich men or the sons of poor men? And do you know why that happens? Because nature gives freely to the sons of poor people according to what they need and it cannot give

---

320. If one overdresses a child in order to protect them from getting cold, one ends up allowing too much natural heat to escape because it is natural for the body to maintain a proper temperature by opening pores to vent excess heat generated in the active life of children, and it is equally natural for these pores to close up again from contact with the cold outside the body when a proper level of natural heat has been attained in the body. Thus, trying to protect children from cold with excess clothing, ironically, makes them colder and makes them lose the natural heat that aids in digestion.

321. The importance of Llull's ideas of "up," "down," "ascent," "descent" as related to hierarchy of values in which "above" is always superior to "below" obtains in the parts of the body, too. If bad humors move upward they cause problems with the "higher" functions of the brain and of the face and neck. Shearing the head (somehow) serves to direct these bad humors downward toward the "bad" parts of the body.

what it would like to give to the sons of rich men. And do you know why? Because too many clothes and too much food prevent it.

[14] I have already said many words and I could say many more, son, about nurturing the body, but I would like to tell you now about the nurture that pertains to the soul. Know, son, that when your child has reached an appropriate age, you should show your child how to remember, understand and will. For just as the body wants to use its members when it has reached the appropriate time and the age to do so, the soul wants to use its powers when the child has reached the age in which it should use them.

[15] Rich men who do not make their sons or their daughters do anything and raise them for a life of leisure are not acting in a way that allows their children to learn to remember or to understand or to will, for idleness and forgetfulness and ignorance and not-willing accord with one another. And for that reason, son, the children of rich men are badly brought up, and they are lazy, weak, foolish and full of vice. And they waste the inheritance one leaves them, for they have no way to know how to protect and defend it from men who are full of wiles, false, treacherous and deceitful.

[16] The man who wishes to nurture his child well should not have a badly brought-up man in his house so that his son does not learn bad behaviors from him. And the lady that leaves her daughter at home when she goes out? It would be better that she take her along. Do you know why? So that the daughter will not believe the things she hears from the bad servant woman. And the man who entrusts his son to a badly brought-up man? It would be better to entrust his son to God and to chance.

[17] To accustom your child to remember and understand God and to go to church is to accustom the will to love God and its father and its mother. Memory that remembers and understanding that understands fear, shame engender a will that hates sins and loves virtues. For that reason, a child should grow and be raised with fear, shame, so that it loves good and hates evil.

[18] If the child is not taught to struggle, when it encounters difficulties, it will not have the patience or nobility of heart with which to overcome its difficulties. If the child is taught to say disparaging things when it hears positive things, it will feel envy, sloth, wrath, which are mortal sins. And if the child is kept and nurtured among vile men, it will flee good men.

[19] Do you want to raise your child well? Accustom its memory and its understanding to think on noble deeds so that its will loves the company of good men. Do you want to nurture the understanding of your son to be exalted, lofty in understanding? Teach him divine and natural science. Do you want him to have a lofty understanding for understanding subtly? Show him *The Art of Finding Truth* and *The Book of Definitions and Principles and Questions.*[322] Do you want your child to love God greatly? Make it remember and understand the vileness of this world and the goodness, greatness, eternity, power, wisdom, love and the other virtues of God.

92. On Rational Movement

[1] Rational movement is thought moved to think one thing after another; and rational movement is the soul's desire or hatred for being or not being.

[2] Dear son, just as you can move your body from one place to another, your soul can move your thoughts from one thing to another, loving one thing and hating another.[323]

[3] Within this movement I am discussing there are many diverse movements, for memory moves from remembering to forgetting and from forgetting to remembering, and the understanding is moved from understanding to not knowing, and from not knowing to understanding, and the will is moved from loving to hating and from hating to loving.

[4] In rational movement, son, there are two intentions: first and second. Now, if you know the nature and the property of these two intentions, you will know many things. And if you know how to keep them in the proper order in your soul, you will possess many virtues.

[5] The first intention is the final cause. The second is matter and form, and matter is the second intention in regard to form. And do you know why? Because form is closer to the final cause than matter.

---

322. For *The Art of Finding Truth,* see Chs. 83.12 and 85.2 and n. 287. For *The Book of Definitions and Principles and Questions (Llibre de definicions e de començaments e de qüestions),* see Ch. 73.3 and n. 189.

323. In Ch. 85.3-4, Llull has described "movement" as one of the "universal powers of the soul," together with the vegetative, the sensitive, the imaginative and the rational powers, which he also refers to as "souls" (see Figure 2).

[6] According to the way in which some degrees are nobler than others, God has wished that first intention be in accord with some degrees and second intention with others.

[7] There are leaves on a tree so that there can be fruit, and, because the fruit is worth more than the leaves, nature has first intention in the fruit and second in the leaves. Because man is a nobler thing than trees or beasts or the other things that are below man in nobility, God has wanted man to exist by first intention and the things that are not so noble by second intention.

[8] God is a nobler thing than man or any created thing, son, and for that reason, God wants man to have first intention in serving, loving, knowing Him, and other things by second intention. Therefore, if you have God by first intention, you must love Him more because He is good than because He has created you or so that He will give you glory.

[9] Do you know, son, what sin is? Sin is when you love the things you should love by first intention less than the things that you should love by second intention, and for that reason, men sin against God when they love God by second intention and themselves by first.

[10] The first movement, son, is when the soul moves its powers so suddenly that reason has no chance to agree rationally to the movement. And the second movement is when the soul agrees or disagrees rationally with the first movement. For this reason, a distinction has been made between a venial and a mortal sin, for the first movement does not take place with the use of free reason. But since reason has the freedom to agree or disagree with the first movement, the merit or the blame is in the second movement.[324]

[11] I could talk to you in many ways, son, about spiritual movement, but I have to talk to you about corporeal movement, which is of three types. The first is composed of three movements: the first movement is circular, that is, the movement of the heavens; the second is the movement fire and air make upwards; and the third is the movement water and earth make downwards.

[12] The second type of movement is of three types: the first is the movement from one place to another. The second is the movement the elements make in engendering things that grow, which move from lesser quantity to greater and from not being to being. The

---

324. See especially the discussion of free will in Ch. 67.

third movement is the movement the elements make in corrupting natural forms and returning them to non-being.

[13] The third type of movement, son, is in the five corporeal senses, for one movement is in seeing, another in hearing, another in smelling, another in tasting, another in touching, and for that reason there are five movements, each different from the others.

[14] Dear son, if you love knowledge and good works, this chapter should be especially dear to you among the other chapters of this book, for the soul is greatly illuminated when it knows how to have knowledge of the movements mentioned above with the intention of honoring and serving its glorious God.[325]

93. ON HABITS

[1] Habit is long perseverance in the same gratifying things. Because good habits are lovable and bad habits are hateable, and because every man has the freedom to choose good habits or bad, you will be a wise man, son, if you leave off bad behaviors and take up good habits.

[2] Good habits, son, are pleasing to the soul. And do you know why? Because peace exists between good habits and conscience. Therefore, bad behaviors and conscience are contrary to one other.

[3] Since the body is nature corrupted by sin, it is more in accord with bad habits than with good ones. And do you know why? So that the soul may have greater merit if it compels the body to accept good habits.

[4] Wise is the merchant who goes through diverse lands to earn money and bring merchandise to his own land in order to earn wealth. But you would be an even wiser merchant, son, if you went through diverse lands and chose the best customs that you found.[326]

---

325. It is important to note that this chapter with a rather dry-sounding title is the only chapter among the 100 chapters of the *DP* that Llull singles out quite explicitly as especially significant for his "son."

326. Llull was well aware that other cultures, including Islamicate cultures, might have customs superior to those of his own and that one should learn from them (cf. Ch. 79.3). Perhaps the most striking example of this is Llull's "Book of the Lover and the Beloved" ("Llibre d'amic e amat"), which is part of his "romance" *Blaquerna.* Llull says that his protagonist wrote this book "in the style" of the Muslim Sufi mystics, which he praises as granting its practitioners "deep devotion" (Llull 2009: 426-427).

[5] Do not love an old habit more than a new one for its age, and do not love a new one more than an old one for its novelty. And do you know why? So that you choose the better habit and reject the worse one.

[6] If bad habits were good solely because of their antiquity, the deeds of the devils, who have persevered so long in evil, would be good. And if the new habits were all bad, beginning to have faith would be bad.

[7] Make giving alms a habit, son, so that you accustom yourself to have hope in God.[327] Accustom yourself to prayer so that you desire heavenly glory and hold this worldly life in contempt. Be accustomed to finding your consolation in God so that you thank Him for the sufferings that He gives you for your sins, and for mine. So that you thank God for the goods that He gives you to possess through no effort of your own, accustom your heart to gratitude.

[8] Accustom your body to labor so that you are healthy and so that you are neither fat nor lazy. Accustom your soul to remember so that you do not forget and accustom your understanding to understand so that no one deceives you. And accustom your will to love so that you are pleasing to God.

[9] Practice obedience so that you are not proud and practice confession so that you do not forget your sins. Be temperate so that you are not a glutton. Be strong so that you are not conquered. Practice abstinence so that you often seek counsel.

[10] Accustom yourself, son, to contrition so that you become accustomed to weeping for your sins. If you want to have a bold and noble heart, accustom yourself to speaking before noblemen. If you want the company of good men, love their habits and hate what is hated by them.

[11] Have firmness in your heart so that you do not regret. Have measure in your hands so that you are not poor. Restrain your tongue so that you are not blamed. Listen so that you understand. Ask so that you learn. Give so that you find. Keep those things that are entrusted to you so that you are loyal. Mortify your will so that you are not suspicious. Remember death so that you are not covetous. Have truth in

---

327. The remainder of the chapter recalls the biblical book of Proverbs and the advice Christ gives in Matthew 6 and 7: a series of pithy instructions to guide his "son" through the social and spiritual worlds. See also Ch. 2.

your mouth so that you are not shamed. Love chastity so that you are not soiled. Have fear so that you have peace. Have daring so that you are not taken.

[12] Many are the good habits you can have, son, which will follow you wherever you go and will help you in your times of need and cannot be taken from you or stolen. They will be with you until death, and they will represent your soul to God.

94. ON THE FOUR ELEMENTS[328]

[1] Elements are the matter in which natural individuals are preserved, in whom are preserved the species desired by primordial matter.

[2] Dear son, there are four elements: fire and water and air, earth. Your body is composed and constructed from these four, as is everything that you eat or drink or touch or smell or hear, and everything that your eyes see beneath the moon, all of this comes from the four elements.

[3] Fire is above air and air is above water and water is above earth, and fire and air are light and water and earth are heavy. For that reason, fire and air move upward, and earth and water move downward.[329]

[4] Son, fire and water have power and action over air and earth, which are passive. Fire and water are contraries, and air and earth are contraries. And do you know why? Because fire is hot and water is cold, and air is wet and earth is dry.

---

328. Llull discusses the four elements—earth, air, fire and water—in several places in the *DP* (Chs. 77, 78, 86 and corresponding notes) and here devotes an entire chapter to them. This attention to the four elements is not surprising, since they are one of the foundations of his Art at this phase, known, in part because of this dependence, as the "quaternary phase" (Bonner 2007: 26-92). See also Yates (1954), who discusses Llull's "elementary exemplarism" and Pring-Mill (1962), whose work is the basis for Figure 1, which offers a graphic representation of many of the phenomena discussed in this chapter.

329. This hierarchy of the elements in based on imagining the sub-lunar world as a series of spheres or "realms" in which earth, land, is lowest, the sea is in a sphere above the land, air is above the sea, and a sphere of fire surrounds them all. As Llull observes in Ch. 86.10, the arrangement in the human body is the opposite: the "grosser elements" (earth and water) are closest to the exterior, and the more "subtle" elements (air and fire) are closer to the interior. See Figure 2.

[5] Fire, in its heat, is simple. Air, in its humidity, is simple. And water, in its coldness, is simple. And earth, in its dryness, is simple.

[6] Do you know, son, what "simple" means? A thing being in its own nature, without composition with another thing. And do you know what "composition" means? The joining of diverse things mixed into a single thing.[330]

[7] Composition happens in two ways: the first is when fire is dry by earth, and the air is hot by fire, and water is humid from air, and earth is cold by water. The other way is when all four elements are brought together in one elemental body, as in mine or yours or in other bodies in which the four elements are joined.[331]

[8] In the first composition, generation begins, and in the second, corruption. And do you know why? Because in the first, the elements are diverse and concordant two by two and, in the second, they are diverse, concordant and contrary two by two.

[9] Fire, heating the air, passes on to heat water and earth. And do you know why? Because air gives heated humidity to water, and water gives heated cold to earth, and water, in cooling earth, cools fire and air. And do you know why? Because water cools the dryness that fire receives from earth and the heat that air receives from the fire and the humidity that it receives from air.[332]

[10] Air, giving humidity to water, gives humidity to earth, which receives cold from water and gives dryness to fire. And for that reason, air gives back to fire the heat that it receives from it as soon as fire receives the dryness with the heat where there is humidity, by dryness mortified by humidity.

---

330. See Ch. 77, for the presentation of the difference between the elements in their simple state (second principle) and in their "compound" state (third principle).

331. When elements combine according to the sequence portrayed in Figure 1 and fire receives its dryness from earth in natural fashion, generation begins. See the explanation of the "proper" and "appropriated" qualities of the elements and the manner in which they combine in Ch. 77 and 78 and the notes there. When all four elements and their properties are combined in a single body, then it can come about that two elements will be contrary to one another, giving rise to corruption, as is explained in the following paragraphs. These concordances and oppositions are also illustrated in Figure 1.

332. This and the following paragraphs are perhaps best visualized by consulting Figure 1, in which one can follow the movement of properties from appropriated to proper around the circle of the elements. It is extremely important to note that, for Llull, the goal of all this discussion of the complex mixing and division of the elements is to signify the "resurrection and glorification in a resurrected body."

[11] With earth giving dryness to fire, it dries the humidity heated by fire and gives back to water the cold that it receives from it, drying the humidity that air gives to water.

[12] Through the four diverse and concordant and contrary operations discussed above, the elements bind themselves and come together, son, into one body and divide themselves into another. And because each element wants to be a simple body in itself, each element seeks a way to have its simplicity by itself, in itself, without being subject to the influence of the other elements. And by this, son, is signified resurrection and glorification in the resurrected body.

[13] From the four elements, son, derive four complexions: bile, blood, phlegm, black bile.[333] Bile is hot and dry and belongs to fire. Blood is hot and wet and belongs to air. Phlegm is cold and wet and belongs to water. Black bile is cold and dry and belongs to earth.

[14] Each of these elements is analyzed by physicians into four degrees. And do you know why? Because the humors are stronger in some things than in others. And for that reason, according to the degrees, the concordances of some elements with others are made to cure the sick.[334]

[15] Know, son, that the simple elements are invisible, although they are of a corporeal nature.[335] And thus they give the signification that God exists, although He is an invisible thing, for if what is corporeal exists, even though it is invisible, it follows clearly that there is an invisible thing that is not of corporeal nature, and is God.[336]

95. ON FATE AND FORTUNE

[1] Fate is the natural ordering of living things by divine providence. And fortune is something desired that arrives by chance, without de-

---

333. Llull uses the word "complexions" again here where we might expect "humors." I have again retained Llull's usage in the translation. See Ch. 78.6 and n. 229.

334. See Ch. 78.26-27 and n. 230 for a fuller discussion of the use of the degrees of the elements in the preparation of cures for illness.

335. See Ch. 77.3-6 for an explanation of the invisibility of the four simple elements.

336. The final argument of this chapter dedicated to the elements as corporeal things invisible in their simple form uses analogy to demonstrate the existence of God "as an invisible thing that is not of corporeal nature." The universe's most basic "elements" demonstrate its most important meaning: the existence of God.

liberate planning. Fortune is for something not consciously intended to happen.

[2] Dear son, God has ordained that the twelve signs and the seven planets have power over earthly things. Therefore, according to the nature and the celestial point under which a man is born, he is destined and fated in the stars concerning how long he will live and which occupation is best for him and in what land his affairs will be most successful.[337]

[3] Celestial bodies do not have power over the soul, but only over the body. And because the soul is the form of the body, the sovereignty that celestial bodies have over the body does not have power against the freedom of the soul. And for that reason, it often happens that what is fated to happen to a person according to the celestial bodies does not happen and, as accident, by the freedom of free will and discretion, the opposite of what has been fated for a man occurs.[338]

[4] Son, God is not contrary to His own power or to His own justice, mercy and for that reason, His power often makes the opposite of what is fated or cast in the stars for a man happen so that He may practice justice or mercy or grace on that man. For if the soul, which is created, can turn the body away from what is fated for it so that it can use its liberty, how much more, then, can God set the nature that the body has through celestial bodies aside so that He can employ His virtues on man.

[5] Trees and plants would follow the nature that celestial bodies give them according to what is ordained, but because man cuts trees and pulls up plants, man takes what has been ordained substantially in the stars away from earthly bodies in an accidental way.[339] There-

---

337. See Ch. 74.7-9 for a general discussion of astronomy and astrology. In the discussion of temperament in Ch. 78, Llull has discussed the way in which the configuration of the heavens at our birth determines our temperament.

338. Llull gives a specific example of what he means here by "accident" two paragraphs below.

339. The opposition between "substance" and "accident" that Llull invokes here is key to understanding his discussion here and in several other chapters (73, 75 and 85). Some Lullian definitions of these terms may be useful: "Substance is that *ens* that exists in itself for itself, without which no 'accident' can exist"; "Substance is that *ens* that naturally exists and acts for itself" (Bonner & Ripoll 2002, s.v. "substància"). "Accident is that thing that cannot exist on its own but in something else"; "Accident is that thing

fore, if man has this power contrary to the stars and fate over plants, how much more does God have this power over man!

[6] Sometimes fortune comes from nature, as when someone is born with six fingers on a hand or deformed and other things like these. By fortune, men find things that they do not expect to find, and by fortune, they get what they desire without doing anything to obtain it.

[7] Son, remember and understand these things and do not surrender yourself to the stars or to fate or to fortune. And understand God's power and use your reason in what you do, for men who trust in the stars show contempt for the power and justice and grace of God, and those who do what they do according to chance are the enemies of discretion and of reason, which is the light by which human understanding sees what man ought to do so that he is upright in his deeds and does not fall under the wrath of God.

96. ON THE ANTICHRIST[340]

[1] The Antichrist will be a man of flesh sent into this world in the semblance of Christ by the devil in Hell. For just as the heavenly Father sent His Son our Lord God Jesus Christ into the world to redeem the people who were lost, the devil—who is full of malice—will do everything in his power and will send the Antichrist as his messenger to destroy the people that Christ has redeemed.

[2] Dear son, the Antichrist will be born of woman and will be raised in Babylon. When he is of the age that Jesus Christ was when He began to preach, the Antichrist will preach for as long as Jesus Christ preached, and he will perform false miracles and will promise great gifts and will give whatever earthly benefits men ask him for so that they worship him and believe in him and deny our Lord Jesus Christ.

---

that has no existence in itself, but has it in 'substance'" (Bonner & Ripoll 2002, s.v. "accident"; translations mine).

340. The biblical bases for the idea of the Antichrist may be found in Matthew 24:24; Mark 13:22; 2 Thessalonians 2, 1 John 2:18-19 and 22; 1 John 4:2-3; 2 John 1:7; and Revelations 11, 13, 16, 19 and 20:7. Llull writes an entire treatise devoted to the Antichrist, *The Book against the Antichrist* (*Llibre contra Anticrist*; see Introduction) at about the same time as the *DP*. See Beattie 1997 on this text.

[3] He will make terrible threats and carry out great slaughters of those who do not believe in him or obey him, and he will adduce strong arguments and examples so that what he says appears to be true. Therefore, son, it will be necessary for men to prepare themselves with devotion and with charity so that they do not fear the threats of the Antichrist and have strong arguments and proofs to counter his.

[4] You can imagine, son, that many people will follow him and will believe him because of the things he will do. And if now, in the time in which we live, there are so many men already in error, without having what they desire and without witnessing false miracles and without being threatened with death or being preached to with strong demonstrations, how many more of these will there be in the time when the Antichrist comes!

[5] He will come to Jerusalem and preach against Jesus Christ to everyone in the square. And Elijah and Enoch will come and debate with him and will argue against his false arguments, and he will kill them in that square. And, with that, our Lord Jesus Christ will not put up with it any longer—the evil of that man—and He will kill him in front of all the people.

[6] Dear son, in the earthly paradise, the devil was contrary to the divine grace that God granted man, and for that reason, he led Adam and Eve to disobey God. It is appropriate, then, that, in the same place where our Lord Jesus Christ redeemed us, the Antichrist will die and lose his power in order to make manifest the power and the ordinations of God.

97. ON THE SEVEN AGES INTO WHICH THE WORLD IS DIVIDED[341]

[1] An age is a measured period of time and the length of life for living things.[342] Therefore, son, the First Age was from Adam to Noah,

---

341. For a discussion of Llull's views of time and history, see Romano & De la Cruz 2008: 432-436.

342. Llull clarifies at the beginning of this chapter that the word "age" in his title has two possible interpretations: an "age" as part of a periodization of history and "age" as in "what is your age?", "how old are you?" It is the first meaning, of course, that he discusses in this chapter.

and in that age, Cain killed his brother Abel, who were the first sons that Adam had.

[2] In that time, there were peoples who greatly loved the delights of this world and who did not know God and who lived for a long time. For that reason, God sent the flood so that the world could renew itself with other peoples who would be good.

[3] The Second Age was from Noah to Abraham. Noah was a holy man, and, because of the saintliness in which he lived, God told him to make a big ark, and to put his wife and his three sons and their wives in it, and to put one pair from each species of beast and bird there so that the world that died in the flood could be repopulated.

[4] When Noah and all these things were in the ark, God sent so much rain from the sky that the sea rose above the land and above the mountains and the whole world died, except for those who were in the ark.

[5] When Noah saw that the rain had stopped, he sent the crow to see if it could find any land, and the crow did not return. And then he sent the dove, who brought back an olive branch in its mouth as a sign that the sea had gone down and land was reappearing.

[6] Noah and those with him landed, and the world was populated from them, and the others died in the flood. And the nations grew and multiplied. Because they were afraid the flood might come back, they decided to build a tower in Babylon high enough that, if the flood returned, they could escape death in that tower. But before the tower was as tall as they had wanted to make it, God sent diverse languages to those who were building the tower so that they did not understand each other. For that reason, they could not build the tower as high as they had wanted. That was when the diversity of languages that now exists began.

[7] The Third Age, son, was from Abraham to Moses. Abraham knew God and had one son, whose name was Isaac, whose throat he intended to cut to make a sacrifice to God, to signify the sacrifice that Jesus Christ made of himself in dying for His people. But God sent a ram to Abraham to sacrifice, to signify that the humanity of Christ was hung upon the cross to redeem the human lineage, just as Isaac's death was redeemed by the ram.[343]

---

343. Here Llull gives a concrete example of biblical typology in which Abraham's willingness to sacrifice his son Isaac prefigures Christ's sacrifice on the cross. See n. 165.

[8] In that age, son, there were many prophets, the twelve tribes that were the people of Israel, and among them, there were many good men who loved God and who hoped for and desired the coming of our Lord God Jesus Christ.

[9] The Fourth Age was from Moses to David. Moses was a prophet and a holy man, and he spoke with God, who gave him the Old Law on Mount Sinai.[344] Moses was the person who brought the people of Israel out of the power of Pharaoh when, through God's power, he touched the sea with his rod and passed on foot with his people through the sea, which had opened up. Pharaoh and his people pursued Moses. And when Moses and his people had passed the sea, the sea closed, and Pharaoh and his people died.

[10] The Fifth Age, son, was from David to the Babylonian transmigration.[345] David was a very wise king. He played musical instruments to praise God, and he built the temple where God was worshiped, and he wrote the *Psalter* and did much good. In that age lived Solomon, who was his son, and he was a very wise man. And there was Absalom, who was David's son and the most beautiful man who ever lived. In that age, there were many Jewish kings who waged and won many battles against the infidels who wished to destroy the people of Israel.

[11] The Sixth Age was from the Babylonian transmigration until Jesus Christ, the Son of God. In that age, son, the Jews lost their own ruler, and they have never had one since. Nebuchadnezzar was a very powerful and proud king of the Gentiles, and he entered Jerusalem by force of arms and destroyed the Jews and their books. Because of the sin he had committed, God punished him for seven years, during which he believed he was an animal and, whatever he did, he did it like a beast.

[12] The Seventh Age is from Jesus Christ until the end of the world. In this age, son, our Lord God Jesus Christ was incarnated and crucified, and the Apostles lived. We are now in that age and will be until the end of the world.

---

344. On the Old Law, see Ch. 69 and Chs. 13-22 for the Ten Commandments.

345. The Babylonian transmigration is also known as the "Babylonian exile" or the "Babylonian captivity" (cf. Matthew 1:17). It refers to a series of attacks on Judah and deportations of Jews by Nebuchadnezzar, King of Babylon, in the early 7th and late 6th century BCE. Cf. following paragraph.

[13] The Eighth Age is after the end of the world, and this age will last for all time in the other world. In that age we will be resurrected and judged, and in that age the blessed will have glory without end, and the damned will have punishment for all time.

[14] Before that age comes to pass, God will send fifteen days in which the signs that signify the end of the world will be given, for the sea will rise up 40 cubits above the land and it will not spread over the land and will return to its place.[346] The fishes will cry out above the sea, and the beasts and the birds of the earth will huddle together and cry.

[15] Fire will burn the sea. Men will weep. A blood sweat will fall upon the earth. Castles and towers and all the buildings will fall. Rocks will split and fight each other. There will be an earthquake, and no one will be able to keep his feet, and the land will split open. Men will go weeping through the fields, and they will be so afraid that they will not be able to speak. Tombs will open up and the bones will come out. Stars will fall from the sky and will fly through the air. And those signs, son, will be so great and will terrify men so greatly, for then will be made manifest very clearly how great is the power of our Lord God.

98. ON ANGELS

[1] An angel is an invisible substance, incorporeal, who always sees God. God created the angels in the beginning, son, with matter and time and movement. And these angels stand before God in the imperial heaven where all the saints in glory are. This heaven does not move and is above the crystalline heaven, which is the heaven of light and brightness, and is immovable.[347] The crystalline heaven is above the heaven of the firmament in which the stars you see are, and which

---

346. It is important for Llull to specify that, although the sea will rise up 40 cubits higher than the land, it will not spread over the land, as had happened in the case of the flood: the human race is not destroyed by this event at the end of the world: they must be there to witness the power of God in Judgement.

347. Llull's "imperial heaven" is also known as the "empyrean heaven." See Figure 3 for the image of the heavens Llull describes here.

moves. This third heaven is above the seven heavens, which are the heavens of the seven planets that you see.[348]

[2] There is no heaven, son, above the imperial heaven. And just as the benign angels are in the highest heaven, the devils—who are malign angels fallen from the sovereign heaven—are in the infernal realm, which is the lowest place there is, which place is inside the heart of the earth, which is round, and around which rotates the firmament, the sun and the moon.[349] But because men are sinners, God allows the demons to go among us to tempt us and to carry off the souls of those who die in sin to Hell so that man can have the opportunity to fight against their false counsel.

[3] Every man, son, has a good angel who advises him to do good works and who helps him against the devil. And each man has a demon that advises him to do evil. For that reason, son, every man is obliged to obey his good angel and to honor it in some way each day, and to make a holy celebration for it once a year, every year.[350]

[4] The good angel—who never leaves a person wherever he goes—sees everything that a person does. Therefore, son, you do great dishonor to your good angel when you do not obey it, and when you obey the devil, who is its contrary. And it is a great villainy to commit lust and the other sins in front of an angel.

[5] Son, the good angels carry the souls of men who died in sanctity and good works into Paradise. And these angels pray to God and serve God, and each angel prays to God for the man God has entrusted to it.

[6] When you have eaten and drunk all you need, son, and you want to eat or drink more, and something is holding you back from

---

348. The seven planets in Llull's day were, in ascending order: the Moon, Mercury, Venus, the Sun, Mars, Jupiter, and Saturn.

349. The popular belief today that "medieval people thought the world was flat," supposedly until Columbus "proved" otherwise, is clearly shown here to be a modern myth.

Fallen angels are not specifically mentioned in the Bible except for the apocryphal Book of Enoch, but see 2 Peter 2:4.

350. Voragine (1993): Ch. 145, 2.207-211; Keck (1998): 161-165. Although the official Catholic Feast of the Guardian Angel was not established until long after Llull's day, Llull may be referring to the Feast of St Michael and All Angels, held on September 29 and often considered a Holy Day of Obligation (a day when Catholic Christians were supposed to attend Mass). Voragine, in the passage just cited, directly associates the guardian angel with the feast of St Michael.

eating more, it is your good angel advising you not to eat or drink any more. And do you know why? So that you have temperance, abstinence, continence, fortitude, which are virtues.[351] And it advises you in the same way when you want to commit lust or when you want to make disparaging remarks about someone.

[7] When you are lying in bed and you hear the bell that sounds to tell you to go to mass to pray to God, the good angel advises you to get up and go give thanks to God, who created you and has given you the morning and the bed where you have lain at night. And the bad spirit advises you to sleep so that you do not give thanks to God.

[8] When the poor man, thin, poorly dressed, stands in front of you and asks "for the love of God," the bad angel advises you not to give him alms. And do you know why? So that you act with avarice and do not trust in God's generosity. But the good angel advises you to give so that you have charity and trust in the wealth of God.

[9] It happens many times, son, that angels take the form of a man or of some other thing in the air. And demons do the same thing. And do you know why? So that they can lead men wherever they wish. Therefore, if the angels transfigure into forms that are not their own so that they can lead men to good works, how greatly, then, are men to be blamed when they are disobedient to them!

[10] Love and honor your angel, son, for it will cost you nothing of your own and you can lose nothing by it. But in everything in which you obey the demon, you will lose, in yourself and in all your goods, and, in the end, if you obey him, he will cause you to fall under the wrath of God.

99. ON HELL

[1] Hell is in the middle place within the heart of the Earth that is sealed and enclosed and in which there is punishment for all time. These punishments happen in four places. One is in the Hell where the damned who can never come out are. Another is the Hell that is called Purgatory, in which one does penance because one has not

---

351. Llull explains why people submit to the temptation to overeat in Ch. 60. He has described this same process of "angelical temptation," here called "advice" rather than temptation, in Ch. 90.

satisfied one's penance in this world. The third Hell is the place where the prophets prior to the Incarnation of the Son of God went, and this Hell is called Abrahe.[352] The fourth Hell is the one where the infants who died before they could be baptized go.

[2] Dear son, just as it is a good thing to think on the glory of Paradise so that you love God, so, too, it is a good thing to think on the infernal torments so that you fear God, who can give these torments to whomever He wishes. Thus, so that you will fear God, I will show you some different ways in which you should meditate on the infernal punishments.

[3] Think, son, and imagine a great multitude of people who are on the banks of the sea, and imagine that the sea is all aboil and full of burning fire, and that huge fishes come out of the sea, and that they pull one man after another into the sea. If you hold this thought, you can imagine how great will be the cries and shouts—and the fear—of those men, who will not be able to defend themselves from these fishes, which will be infernal dragons from which they cannot escape.

[4] When you are sitting by the fire, and you see the pot of fava beans or chickpeas boiling, and some beans climb to the top and others sink below, think, son, that the fishes of the sea would rise and sink in the same way if the water in the sea were boiling as fiercely as the water in the pot on the fire. Whence, you can imagine the pain of those men who will be in boiling water like the fish in the sea. And that water will boil much more fiercely than the pot of beans.

[5] Dear son, when you see the creeks and great torrents where water rushes and tumbles down rocks, picture how many are the sinners and the infidels who fall each day without ceasing into the mouth of the infernal dragon. Whence, you can imagine how great your fear would be if you were on a high bank and fell into the mouth of a dragon full of flaming fire—and the dragon had big sharp teeth.

[6] Can you see, son, some embers on top of the others in a big fire and some coals on top of the others? The people condemned to

---

352. Llull is referring here to the concept of the "sinus Abrahae" or the "Bosom of Abraham," the place of comfort where righteous people who died before Christ made salvation possible went to await Christ's opening of Hell. It is mentioned in the New Testament in the parable of Lazarus (Luke 16:19-31). See also Ch. 9, in which Llull recounts the appearance of Christ to free the prophets from Hell.

Hell, son, will be like this, one on top of the other for all time. And the body of each one will be as full of burning fire, within and without, as are the great embers that you see in the fire.

[7] Son, so that you fear the infernal fire, which lasts for all time, go to the furnace where they make glass or to the oven where they bake bread and consider how much you would ask for in exchange for being in that fire for a single hour. Now, if in exchange for all the world—if someone was giving it to you—, you would not be in that fire for a single hour, how much more should you fear that, in exchange for a worldly pleasure that swiftly passes, you would be in the infernal fire, which lasts for all time!

[8] When you watch lead or gold or silver being melted, imagine that there is a great pit full of melted lead or gold. If you were standing at the mouth of that pit, you would be afraid if someone bound your hands and your feet and put you in a sack and tied a great stone around your neck and threw you into the pit. And so, be afraid, son, of the pit that is full of melted gold and silver where men who have lost God's glory in exchange for gold or silver will be.[353]

[9] When you see ice in water, and in the middle of that ice there is a rock or piece of wood or some other thing, consider, son, how the sinners, who, because of the heat of lust, have lost the heavenly kingdom, will be completely naked inside great mountains of ice and snow, in Hell.

[10] When you go outside the walls of the city, and you come across dead animals that people have thrown into the moat, and you see packs of dogs, big and small, who gnaw the ears or the eyes or the face or the arms or the legs of these animals and who go into their belly and gnaw their bones and eat their heart and their entrails, that is the time, son, when you should think about the damned in Hell, who will lie scattered in the fields and will see demons in the shape of dogs and lions and serpents who will bite the heads and arms and members of those men. And they will not be able to die, nor will they be able to escape that punishment.

---

353. Here and in the following paragraph Llull touches on the idea that specific torments will be assigned in Hell that reflect the nature of the sins committed during life (an idea that will be much expanded upon by Dante): being thrown into a pit of molten gold for those who pursued wealth; being frozen naked in mountains of ice for those who sinned in the heat of lust. Llull has introduced this idea in Ch. 65.4.

[11] When you are at the slaughterhouse, and you see how butchers cut the throats of rams with their huge knives and kill oxen with mallets and skin them with very sharp knives and then cut and chop them up with big knives, think, son, how great is the infernal suffering of those men whom the demons torment in Hell and who cannot die.

[12] If you go hunting, and you see the dogs fall upon a hare or rabbit and kill and break and tear and flay it from every side and it has no help nor can it defend itself, you will glimpse how the demons, who are so many and so evil, swarm upon the souls of sinners to torment them and to give them unimaginable pain.

[13] If you were a king and you were in a great desert all alone, and you had nothing to eat or drink, and you were about to die of great hunger and great thirst, you would trade your entire kingdom for a piece of bread or a cup of water. If you are prepared to exchange your whole kingdom for that, then take care that, for a single mortal sin, you do not have eternal hunger and thirst in Hell, without being able to have a crust of bread or a drop of water.

[14] Go to the sea and guess how many drops of water there are in it, and look at the sand and estimate how many grains of sand there are in the sea, and raise your eyes to the sky and count the stars, and think how many grains of millet would fit into the space between the sky and the earth. Know, son, that a sinner will be more years in infernal torments, beyond compare, than is the number of these things.

[15] Understand, son, what great suffering the soul of the man in Hell endures, for his memory will remember that he will have pain forever, and his understanding will understand that he has lost glory without end, and his will will hate the memory that remembers infinite pain and the understanding that understands the glory that it has lost. Whence, for that reason, each of these powers will have pain from the others and in itself.

[16] Do you know, son, what the sailors who go to sea do when they encounter bad weather? They cast crates containing gold and silver into the sea and they throw away the merchandise they are carrying. And do you know why? So that they can escape death. Whence, so that you can escape and flee infernal torments, cast all things from your heart, and hold nothing else there but our Lord God or what is pleasing to God.

100. ON PARADISE

[1] Paradise is seeing God and being with God in glory. Therefore, if my eyes cannot see the entire sea and my hands, son, cannot write all the glory of Paradise for you, since it is true that the glory of Paradise is far greater beyond compare than all the sea, nor is all the world as great as the glory that the saints in Paradise have in our Lord God, [2] I do not wish to tell you or write everything that I could tell you, son, in order to signify the glory of Paradise because we have to think about other things, and this book would seem too long to you. But I will tell you briefly some few words about heavenly glory.

[3] Dear son, in Paradise, God shows Himself in His unity and Trinity and essence to the memory, understanding and will of the soul. And this manifestation is so great that the memory and understanding and will attain all their fulfillment, which fulfillment they could not have if they possessed the whole world—or a thousand thousands of worlds—without the manifestation just mentioned.

[4] If you enter Paradise, son, your corporeal eyes will see the body of our Lord God Jesus Christ and your spiritual eyes will see His soul, and your understanding will see a nature like your own possessing deity.

[5] In front of our Lord Jesus Christ, son, you will see Our Lady Saint Mary, and you will see the procession and the ranks of all the angels, archangels, martyrs, prophets, virgins, confessors, abbots, and you will hear them all praise and bless our Lord God with songs of very great sweetness as long as God will be in heaven or His glory shall endure, that is, eternally, without end.

[6] When the memory will remember, and the understanding will understand that the glory will last forever and that it will have no end, who can tell the glory that the will will have or signify it to you? Son, to love all God and to possess all God, and to want always to exist and to exist always, and to love all the glory of the saints in Paradise and to have glory in all their glory, and to remember and understand this glory...can you think how great is the glory among the saints in glory who have all the glory just mentioned?[354]

---

354. What happens to the memory, understanding and will of souls in Paradise is directly contrasted to what happens to those same powers in souls condemned to Hell (see preceding chapter, next to last paragraph).

[7] Dear son, if you enter Paradise, you will have a glorified body that will never die and will be wherever you wish it to be and will pass through whatever place you wish it to pass. The moment you want to be in a place, you will be there. You will be brighter than the sun. You will feel no hunger, thirst, heat, cold, pain or any suffering, and you will be in this bliss—and in far greater—all the time.

[8] Dear son, consider this glory that I am speaking to you about often so that you may attain it and remember the brief span of this worldly vanity, by which many men lose heavenly glory. In your ponderings, make a comparison between the blessings of this world and the glory of the other world and understand what a wise exchange one makes if, with a single coin, one knows how to possess a treasure greater than all the blessings of this world.

[9] When you sit at the chessboard, make this calculation: compare the first square to all the blessings of this world, and, in the second, put all blessings that would be in two worlds like this one, and, in the third square, put the blessings of four worlds, and so on, multiplying the blessings by all the squares on the board. And when the squares on the board are not enough, make more squares from the stars in the sky and from the drops of water in the sea and from the grains of sand and from all the points that would fit between the sky and the earth. And when all that is not sufficient to equal the number, take all the men that have been and are and will be in the past, present and future.[355] And if you can do that, still, for all that, it will not be enough for you to make a comparison of the glory of all the worlds just mentioned with the glory of Paradise, for all the glory mentioned above will be finite, and heavenly glory will never ever end.

[10] Where, son, is glory that is like the glory that is loved by infinite will, eternal, all-powerful, all-wise, all-just, all-perfect, that is, the will of the God of Glory? And what glory is like the glory that the saints possess, in that they are loved by the human natures of Jesus Christ and Our Lady Saint Mary, who are better creatures than all the other created things?

---

355. The earliest French and Occitan manuscripts have "take all the moments that have been..." (perhaps through a reading "momens" where our text has "homens" [men]). This is another interesting reading, given the emphasis on past, present and future, that is, on time, in this second part of the phrase.

[11] The more I speak to you, son, of heavenly glory, the more I recognize my own inability to recount and to signify the glory of Paradise. For that reason, I must leave this topic and we will speak about *The Book of Evast and Blaquerna.*[356]

[12] But I wanted to tell you enough so that you can think how blessed will be those who enter into such glory and who will take action so that the infidels abandon their error and are not in eternal fire and have the glory mentioned above through the grace of our Lord God.[357]

The book of *Doctrina Pueril* is finished, with the grace and help of our Lord God, which book we place and entrust to the protection and blessing of Our Lady Saint Mary, Glorious Virgin, and of her Son, our Lord Jesus Christ.

---

356. Llull offers, as the next step in his program of education for his "son," a discussion of a work of literary fiction, in this case, Llull's own "romance" *Blaquerna.* This work, written between 1276 and 1283 (see n. 1), recounts the fictional life of Blaquerna, the son of devout middle-class parents who rejects matrimony and climbs through the various levels of the religious life from monk to abbot to bishop to pope, and, finally, to hermit.

357. Llull does not fail, as his final thought in the *DP*, to refer once again to one of his primary concerns throughout this book and throughout his life: the obligation of Christians to engage in the conversion of non-believers to the Christian faith.

Bibliography

PRINCIPAL MANUSCRIPTS OF THE *DOCTRINA PUERIL* USED IN THE EDITION TRANSLATED HERE

1. Catalan Manuscripts

A   Munich, Staatsbibliothek, Cod. Hisp. 61 (14c.-15c.). This manuscript, which likely comes from the Lullian school of Barcelona, contains various works by Llull. It serves as the base manuscript for Llull 1972, and Llull 2005 beginning with Ch. 97.7.

B   Barcelona, Biblioteca de Catalunya, ms. 3187 (14c.). The version of the *Doctrina pueril* that it includes is mutilated after Ch. 97.7. It appears that in 1616 it was sent to Rome for the Causa Pia lul·liana, and that in the 19th century it was part of the Torres Amat collection of the Biblioteca del Seminari de Barcelona, from which it disappeared before 1936. The collector Frederic Marès left it to the Biblioteca de Catalunya in 1986. It is the base manuscript for Llull 1906 and Llull 2005.

M   Palma, Biblioteca Pública, ms. 1024 (beg. 17c.). It is a *Codex descriptus* of the incomplete ms. *B*.

2. Latin Manuscript (used for the Chapter on Knights)

L³   Lyon, Bibliothèque Municipale, Fonds Général, Ms. 258 (beg. 15c.). A miscellaneous volume of predominantly Lullian content. At the end of the *Doctrina pueril* we find this colophon: "Hunc librum dictauit dominus Raymundus lulii de maiorica miles factum anno domini .M.° ccc. XIII" (f. 271).

MODERN EDITIONS OF THE *DOCTRINA PUERIL*

Obres de Ramon Llull, I: *Doctrina pueril. Libre del orde de cavalleria. Libre de clerecia. Art de confessió,* ed. Mateu Obrador, Palma, Comissió Editora Lul·liana, 1906. Facsimile ed.: Palma, Miquel Font, 1986.

Ramon Llull, *Libre de doctrina pueril*, ed. Mateu Obrador, Barcelona, Gustau Gili, 1907.

Ramon Llull, *Doctrina pueril*, ed. Gret Schib, Barcelona, Barcino, 1972 (Els Nostres Clàssics A, 104).

Ramon Llull, *Doctrina pueril*, ed. Joan Santanach i Suñol, Barcelona - Palma de Mallorca, Patronat Ramon Llull, 2005 (Nova Edició de les Obres de Ramon Llull, 7).

EDITIONS OF MEDIEVAL TRANSLATIONS OF THE *DOCTRINA PUERIL*

Raymond Lulle, *Doctrine d'enfant. Version médiévale du ms. fr. 22933 de la B.N. de Paris*, ed. Armand Llinarès, Paris, Librairie C. Klincksieck, 1969 (Bibliothèque Française et Romane, Série B: Éditions Critiques de Textes, 7).

La versione occitanica della "Doctrina pueril" di Ramon Llull, ed. Maria Carla Marinoni, Milano, Edizioni Universitarie di Lettere, Economia e Diritto, 1997.

Raimundi Lulli Opera Latina, Tomus XXXIII, 7-9. Annis 1274-1276 composita, ed. Jaume Medina, Turnhout, Brepols, 2009 (Corpus Christianorum, Continuatio Mediaevalis, 215), pp. 9-561.

WORKS CITED

AQUINAS, Thomas, *Summa theologica*. In English at: http://newadvent.org/summa/3001.htm#article8; in Latin at: http://www.corpusthomisticum.org/sth3001.html.

AVICENNA (1930 [1973]), *Treatise on the Canon of Medicine of Avicenna*, trans. Oskar Cameron Gruner, New York, AMS Press.

BADIA, Lola (1992), "Poesia i Art al *Llibre del gentil* de Ramon Llull", in *Teoria i pràctica de la literatura en Ramon Llull*, Barcelona, Quaderns Crema (Assaig, 10), pp. 19-29.

BADIA, Lola (2004), "La Ciència a l'obra de Ramon Llull", in *La Ciència en la Història dels Països Catalans*, I. *Dels àrabs al Renaixement*, ed. Joan Vernet and Ramon Parés, Barcelona-València, Institut d'Estudis Catalans - Universitat de València, 2004, pp. 403-442. Consulted at: http://www.narpan.net/documents/ciencia_llull_lola.htm and cited by section numbers there.

BADIA, Lola (2009), "Literature as an *ancilla Artis*: The Transformation of Science into Literature According to Robert Pring-Mill and Ramon Llull", *Hispanic Research Journal* 10, 1, pp. 18-28.

BADIA, Lola, Joan SANTANACH, and Albert SOLER (2009a), "Le rôle de l'occitan dans la production et la diffusion des œuvres de Raymond Lulle (1274-1289)", in *La voix occitane. Actes du VIIIe Congrès de l'Association Internationale d'Études Occitanes. Bordeaux, 12-17 octobre 2005*, ed. Guy Latry, Bordeaux, Presses Universitaires de Bordeaux, pp. 369-408.

BADIA, Lola, Joan SANTANACH, and Albert SOLER (2009b), "Per la lingua di Ramon Llull: un'indagine intorno ai manoscritti in volgare di prima generazione", *Medioevo Romanzo* 33, 1, pp. 49-72.

BADIA, Lola, Joan SANTANACH, and Albert SOLER (2010), "Els manuscrits lul·lians de primera generació als inicis de la *scripta* libràtia catalana", in *Translatar i transferir: la transmissió dels textos i el saber (1200-1500). Primer col·loqui internacional del Grup Narpan "Cultura i literatura a la baixa edat mitjana" (22 i 23 de novembre de 2007)*, ed. Anna Alberni, Lola Badia, and Lluís Cabré, Santa Coloma de Queralt, Obrador Edèndum, pp. 61-90.

BADIA, Lola, Joan SANTANACH, and Albert SOLER (2016), *Ramon Llull (1232-1316) as a Vernacular Writer. Communicating a New Kind of Knowledge*, Woodbridge, Tamesis.

BATLLORI, Miquel (2004), *Il Lullismo in Italia. Tentativo di sintesi*, ed. Francesco Santi and Michela Pereira, Rome, Pontificio Ateneo Antonianum, Centro Italiano di Lullismo. (Italian translation of Miquel Batllori [1993], *Ramon Llull i el lul·lisme*, Valencia, Tres i Quatre, pp. 221-335.)

BEATTIE, Pamela (1997), "Eschatology and Llull's *Llibre contra Anticrist*", *Studia Lulliana* 37, pp. 3-24.

BONLLAVI, Joan (1521), "Epistola proemial", in Ramon Llull, *Blanquerna*, València, Impremta de Johan Jofre. Facsimile ed.: introduced by Joan Santanach, Barcelona, Edicions de la Universitat de Barcelona, 2016.

BONNER, Anthony (2007), *The Art and Logic of Ramon Llull: A User's Guide*, Leiden-Boston, Brill (Studien und Texte zur Geistesgeschichte des Mittelalters, 95).

BONNER, Anthony (2008), "The Interreligious Disputation, Ramon Llull's Ingenious Solution", *Quaderns de la Mediterrània: Ramon*

Llull and Islam, the Beginning of Dialogue / Ramon Llull y el islam, el inicio del diálogo 9, pp. 149-155.

BONNER, Anthony, and Maria Isabel RIPOLL PERELLÓ (2002), *Diccionari de definicions lul·lianes / Dictionary of Lullian Definitions*, Barcelona - Palma de Mallorca, Universitat de Barcelona - Universitat de les Illes Balears.

BOSER, César (1895), "Le remaniement provençal de la *Somme le roi* et ses dérivés", *Romania* 24, pp. 56-85.

BRAYER, Edith (1968), "La littérature religieuse (Liturgie et Bible), I. Catalogue des textes liturgiques et des petits genres religieux", with the collaboration of Walter Mettmann, *GRLM* 6, 1, pp. 1-21.

BRUNDAGE, James A. (1995), *Medieval Canon Law*, London - New York, Longman.

CARRERAS ARTAU, Tomás, and Joaquín CARRERAS ARTAU (1939-1943), *Historia de la filosofía española. Filosofía cristiana de los siglos XIII al XV*, 2 vols., Madrid, Real Academia de Ciencias Exactas, Físicas y Naturales. There is a facsimile ed., with preliminary studies by Pere Lluís Font, Jaume Mensa, Jaume de Puig, and Josep M. Ruiz Simon, Barcelona-Girona, Institut d'Estudis Catalans - Diputació de Girona, 2001.

CCC: United States Catholic Conference (1997), *Catechism of the Catholic Church: With Modifications from the Editio Typica*, New York, Doubleday.

CASAGRANDE, Carla, and Silvana VECCHIO (2000), *I sette vizi capitali. Storia dei peccati nel Medioevo*, Torino, Einaudi.

COHEN, Jeremy (1982), *The Friars and the Jews: The Evolution of Medieval Anti-Judaism*, Ithaca, Cornell University Press.

DANDO, Marcel (1964), "Deux traductions provençales partielles du *Libre de Doctrina pueril*, de Raymond Lulle, associées à des remaniements de la *Somme le Roi*", *Romania* 85, pp. 17-48.

DCVB: Alcover, Antoni Maria, and Francesc de B. Moll (1968-1969), *Diccionari català-valencià-balear*, 2nd ed., 10 vols., Palma de Mallorca, Editorial Moll.

DECLC: Coromines, Joan, Joseph Gulsoy, Max Cahner, Carles Duarte, and Angel Satué (1980-1991), *Diccionari Etimològic i Complementari de la Llengua Catalana*, 9 vols., Barcelona, Curial Edicions Catalanes.

DE LA CRUZ PALMA, Óscar (2002), "La información sobre Mahoma en la *Doctrina pueril* de Ramon Llull", *Taula. Quaderns de pensament* 37, pp. 37-49.

Domínguez Reboiras, Fernando (1987), "Introducción", in Ramon Llull, *Raimundi Lulli Opera Latina, Tomus XV, 201-207, Summa Sermonum in Civitate Maioricensi annis MCCCXII-MCCCXIII composita*, Turnhout, Brepols (Corpus Christianorum, Continuatio Mediaevalis, 76), pp. IX-CXV.

Domínguez Reboiras, Fernando, and Jordi Gayà (2008), "Life", in Fidora & Rubio 2008: pp. 3-124.

Dondaine, Antoine (1948), "Guillaume Peyraut, vie et oeuvres", *Archivum Fratrum Praedicatorum* 18, pp. 162-236.

EI2: Bearman, P., et al., ed. (1955-2005), *The Encyclopaedia of Islam (Second Edition)*, Leiden, Brill.

EI3: Fleet, Kate, et al., ed. (2007-), *Encyclopedia of Islam Three*, Leiden, Brill.

Eiximenis, Francesc (2008), *Francesc Eiximenis: An Anthology*, intro. Xavier Renedo and David Guixeras, trans. Robert D. Hughes, Barcelona-Woodbridge, Barcino-Tamesis (Serie B: Textos, 50).

Fidora, Alexander (2011), "Ramon Llull's *Doctrina pueril*: Approaching Religion from a Historical Point of View", *Quaderns de la Mediterrània* 16, pp. 145-151.

Fidora, Alexander, and Josep E. Rubio, ed. (2008), *Raimundus Lullus: An Introduction to His Life, Works and Thought*, trans. Robert D. Hughes, Anna A. Akasoy, and Magnus Ryan, Turnhout, Brepols (=Raimundi Lulli Opera Latina, Supplementum Lullianum 2, Corpus Christianorum, Continuatio Mediaevalis, 214).

Franklin-Brown, Mary (2012), *Reading the World. Encyclopedic Writing in the Scholastic Age*, Chicago, University of Chicago Press.

Gayà Estelrich, Jordi (1980), "Sobre algunes estructures literàries del 'Libre de Meravelles'", *Randa* 10, pp. 63-69.

Gayà Estelrich, Jordi (1995), "Introducción general", in Ramon Llull, *Raimundi Lulli Opera Latina, Tomus XX, 106-113, In Monte Pessulano et Ianuae Annis MCCCIII-MCCCIV Composita*, ed. Jordi Gayà Estelrich, Turnhout, Brepols (Corpus Christianorum, Continuatio Mediaevalis, 113), pp. IX-LXXVIII.

GGL: Colom, Mateu (1982-1985), *Glossari general lul·lià*, 5 vols., Palma de Mallorca, Editorial Moll. Online version (2016): *Nou glossari general lul·lià*, Barcelona: http://nggl.ub.edu/presentacio.

González Muñoz, Fernando (2004), "Liber Nycholay. La leyenda de Mahoma y el Cardenal Nicolás", *Al-Qantara* 25, pp. 5-43.

HAMES, Harvey J. (2000), *The Art of Conversion: Christianity and Kabbalah in the Thirteenth Century*, Leiden, Brill.

HARVEY, E. Ruth (1975), *The Inward Wits: Psychological Theory in the Middle Ages and the Renaissance*, London, The Warburg Institute (Warburg Institute Surveys, 6).

HEIDARZADEH, Tofigh (2009), *A History of Physical Theories of Comets. From Aristotle to Whipple*, New York, Springer (Archimedes, 19).

HILLGARTH, Jocelyn N. (1971), *Ramon Lull and Lullism in Fourteenth-Century France*, Oxford, Clarendon Press.

HILLGARTH, Jocelyn N. (2001), *Diplomatari lul·lià: documents relatius a Ramon Llull i a la seva família*, Barcelona, Universitat de Barcelona (Col·lecció Blaquerna, 1).

ISIDORE OF SEVILLE (1982-1983), *Etimologías*, 2 vols., ed. José Oroz Reta, Madrid, Edición Católica (Biblioteca de Autores Cristianos, 433-434).

JACKSON, Peter (2008), "The Mongols and Europe", in *The New Cambridge Medieval History*, Part VI. *The Northern and Eastern Frontiers*, ed. David Abulafia, Cambridge, Cambridge University Press, pp. 701-719.

JOHNSTON, Mark D. (1987), *The Spiritual Logic of Ramon Llull*, Oxford, Clarendon Press.

JOHNSTON, Mark D. (1996), *The Evangelical Rhetoric of Ramon Llull: Lay Learning and Piety in the Christian West Around 1300*, Oxford, Oxford University Press.

KECK, David (1998), *Angels & Angelology in the Middle Ages*, New York, Oxford University Press.

KIELY, Edmond R. (1947), *Surveying Instruments: Their History and Classroom Use*, New York, Bureau of Publications, Teachers College, Columbia University.

LANGLOIS, Charles-Victor (1928), *La vie en France au Moyen âge du XIIe au milieu du XIVe siècle*, IV. *La vie spirituelle: enseignements, méditations & controverses d'après des écrits en français à l'usage des laïcs*, Paris, Hachette.

LEVY, Emil (1909), *Petit dictionnaire provençal-français*, Heidelberg, Carl Winter's Universitätsbuchhandlung.

LEWIS, Michael J.T. (2001), *Surveying Instruments of Greece and Rome*, Cambridge, Cambridge University Press.

LLULL, Ramon (n.d.a), *The Tree of Science*. Consulted at: http://lullianarts.narpan.net/TreeOfScience/TreeOfScience-1.pdf and http://lullianarts.narpan.net/TreeOfScience/TreeOfScience2. pdf.

LLULL, Ramon (n.d.b), *The Desired Philosophy Tree*, trans. Steven Abbott and Yanis Dambergs. Consulted at: http://lullianarts.narpan. net/downloads.htm#T.

LLULL, Ramon (1914), *Obres de Ramon Llull*, IX. *Libre de Blanquerna*, ed. Salvador Galmés and Miquel Ferrà, Palma de Mallorca, Comissió Editora Lul·liana. Facsimile ed.: Palma, Miquel Font, 2002.

LLULL, Ramon (1926), *Blanquerna: a Thirteenth-Century Romance*, trans. E. Allison Peers, London, Jarrolds.

LLULL, Ramon (1980), "Vita coetanea", in Ramon Llull, *Raimundi Lulli opera latina, Tomus VIII, 178-189, Parisiis anno MCCCXI composita*, ed. Hermogenes Harada, Turnhout, Brepols (Corpus Christianorum, Continuatio Mediaevalis, 34), pp. 259-309.

LLULL, Ramon (1987), *Blanquerna*, ed. Robert Irwin, trans. E. Allison Peers, London, Dedalus.

LLULL, Ramon (1988), *Llibre de l'orde de cavalleria*, ed. Albert Soler, Barcelona, Barcino (Els Nostres Clàssics A, 127).

LLULL, Ramon (1993a), *Doctor Illuminatus. A Ramon Llull Reader*, ed. and trans. Anthony Bonner and Eve Bonner, Princeton, Princeton University Press.

LLULL, Ramon (1993b), *Llibre del gentil e dels tres savis*, ed. Anthony Bonner, Palma de Mallorca, Patronat Ramon Llull (NEORL, 2).

LLULL, Ramon (1994), *Ramon Llull's New Rhetoric: Text and Translation of Llull's Rethorica Nova*, ed. and trans. Mark D. Johnston, Davis, Hermagoras Press.

LLULL, Ramon (1995), *The Book of the Lover and the Beloved. Lo libre de amich e amat. Librum amici et amati*, ed. Mark D. Johnston, Warminster, Aris & Phillips Ltd.

LLULL, Ramon (1996), *Llibre dels articles de la fe. Llibre què deu hom creure de Déu. Llibre contra Anticrist*, ed. Antoni Joan Pons i Pons, Jordi Gayà Estelrich, and Gret Schib Torra, Palma de Mallorca, Patronat Ramon Llull (NEORL, 3).

LLULL, Ramon (2005), *Doctrina pueril*, ed. Joan Santanach i Suñol, Palma de Mallorca, Patronat Ramon Llull (NEORL, 7).

LLULL, Ramon (2009), *Romanç d'Evast e Blaquerna*, ed. Albert Soler and Joan Santanach, Palma de Mallorca, Patronat Ramon Llull (NEORL, 8).

LLULL, Ramon (2010), *Ramon Llull: A Contemporary Life*, ed. and trans. Anthony Bonner, Barcelona-Woodbridge, Barcino-Tamesis (Serie B: Textos, 53).

LLULL, Ramon (2011-2014), *Llibre de meravelles*, ed. Lola Badia (dir.), Xavier Bonillo, Eugènia Gisbert, Anna Fernàndez Clot, and Montserrat Lluch, Palma de Mallorca, Patronat Ramon Llull (NEORL, 10 and 13).

LLULL, Ramon (2013a), *Llibre d'intenció*, ed. Maria Isabel Ripoll Perelló, Palma de Mallorca, Patronat Ramon Llull (NEORL, 12).

LLULL, Ramon (2013b), *The Book of the Order of Chivalry*, trans. Noel Fallows, Woodbridge, Boydell Press.

LLULL, Ramon (2015), *The Book of the Order of Chivalry / Llibre de l'Ordre de Cavalleria / Libro de la Orden de Caballería*, translated into English and Spanish and introduced by Antonio Cortijo-Ocaña, Amsterdam, John Benjamins.

LLULL, Ramon (2016), *Romance of Evast and Blaquerna*, intro. Joan Santanach and Albert Soler, trans. and notes Robert D. Hughes, Barcelona-Woodbridge, Barcino-Tamesis (Serie B: Textos, 60).

MADRE, Alois (1973), *Die theologische Polemik gegen Raimundus Lullus. Eine Untersuchung zu den Elenchi auctorum de Raimundo male sentientium*, Münster, Aschendorff (Beiträge zur Geschichte der Philosophie und Theologie des Mittelalters, Neue Folge, vol. 11).

MANSI, Joannes Dominicus (1961), *Sacrorum conciliorum, nova et amplissima collectio*, vol. 24, Graz, Akademische Druck- und Verlagsanstalt.

McVAUGH, Michael R. (1993), *Medicine before the Plague: Practitioners and Their Patients in the Crown of Aragon, 1285-1345*, Cambridge, Cambridge University Press.

MILLÀS-VALLICROSA, J. (1931), *Assaig d'història de les idees físiques i matemàtiques a la Catalunya medieval*, Barcelona, Estudis Universitaris Catalans.

MILLS, David, ed. (1992), *The Chester Mystery Cycle: A New Edition with Modernised Spelling*, East Lansing, Colleagues Press (Medieval Texts and Studies, 9).

MUMMEY, Kevin, and Kathryn REYERSON (2011), "Whose City Is This? Hucksters, Domestic Servants, Wet-Nurses, Prostitutes, and Slaves in Late Medieval Western Mediterranean Urban Society", *History Compass* 9, 12, pp. 910-922.

NEWHAUSER, Richard (1993), *The Treatise on Vices and Virtues in Latin and the Vernacular*, Brepols, Turnhout.

OE: Llull, Ramon (1957-1960), *Obres essencials*, 2 vols., Barcelona, Selecta (Biblioteca Perenne).

OED: *Oxford English Dictionary* (2016), Oxford, Oxford University Press. Consulted at: http://www.oed.com/.

OS: Llull, Ramon (1989), *Obres selectes de Ramon Llull (1232-1316)*, 2 vols., ed. and intro. Antoni Bonner, Palma de Mallorca, Editorial Moll.

PERARNAU, Josep (1990), "El *Llibre contra Anticrist* de Ramon Llull. Edició i estudi del text", *Arxiu de Textos Catalans Antics* 9, pp. 7-181.

PINGREE, David (2009), *Eastern Astrolabes*, Chicago, Adler Planetarium.

POLO, Marco (2016), *The Description of the World*, ed. and trans. Sharon Kinoshita, Indianapolis-Cambridge, Hackett Publishing Company, Inc.

PRING-MILL, Robert D.F. (1955-1956), "The Trinitarian World Picture of Ramon Lull", *Romanistisches Jahrbuch* 7, pp. 229-256.

PRING-MILL, Robert D.F. (1962), *El microcosmos lul·lià*, Oxford, The Dolphin Book Co. Ltd.

ROGGEMA, Barbara (2009), *The Legend of Sergius Baḥīrā: Eastern Christian Apologetics and Apocalyptic in Response to Islam*, Leiden-Boston, Brill.

ROMANO, Marta M. M., and Óscar DE LA CRUZ (2008), "The Human Realm", in Fidora & Rubio 2008: pp. 363-459.

ROSA, Luigi La (1991), *Storia della catechesi medievale*, Esur, Messina.

ROWELL, S.C. (2008), "The Central European Kingdoms", in *The New Cambridge Medieval History*, Part VI. *The Northern and Eastern Frontiers*, ed. David Abulafia, Cambridge, Cambridge University Press, pp. 754-778.

RUBIO, Josep Enric (2008), "The Natural Realm", in Fidora & Rubio 2008: pp. 311-362.

RUBIÓ I BALAGUER, Jordi (1985), *Ramon Llull i el Lul·lisme*, Abadia de Montserrat, Publicacions de l'Abadia de Montserrat.

RUIZ SIMON, Josep M. (1999), *L'Art de Ramon Llull i la teoria escolàstica de la ciència*, Barcelona, Quaderns Crema.

SANTANACH, Joan (2000), "Perduts, amagats, retrobats. Història de dos manuscrits de la *Doctrina pueril*", *Els Marges* 68, pp. 106-117.

SANTANACH, Joan (2002), "'Cové que hom fassa apendre a son fill los .XIIII. articles': la *Doctrina pueril* com a tractat catequètic", in *Li-*

teratura i Cultura a la Corona d'Aragó (s. XIII-XV). Actes del III Col·loqui "Problemes i Mètodes de Literatura Catalana Antiga", Universitat de Girona, 5-8 de juliol del 2000, ed. Lola Badia, Miriam Cabré, and Sadurní Martí, Barcelona, Publicacions de l'Abadia de Montserrat (Textos i Estudis de Cultura Catalana, 85), pp. 419-430.

SANTANACH, Joan (2005), "Manuscrits, còpies i traduccions. Ramon Llull i la transmissió de la Doctrina pueril", in Actes de les I Jornades Internacionals Lul·lianes "Ramon Llull al segle XXI" (Palma, 1, 2 i 3 d'abril de 2004), ed. Maria Isabel Ripoll Perelló, Palma de Mallorca, Universitat de Barcelona (Col·lecció Blaquerna, 5), pp. 297-324.

SANTANACH, Joan (2008a), "Literatura i apologètica en Ramon Llull, o de messies i profetes al Llibre del gentil e dels tres savis", in El rei Jaume I. Fets, actes, paraules, ed. Germà Colón Domènech and Tomàs Martínez Romero, Barcelona, Fundació Germà Colón Domènech (Col·lecció Germà Colón d'Estudis Filològics, 4), pp. 185-201.

SANTANACH, Joan (2008b), "On the Book of the Gentile and the Doctrinal Coherence of Ramon Llull", Quaderns de la Mediterrània: Ramon Llull and Islam, the Beginning of Dialogue / Ramon Llull y el islam, el inicio del diálogo 9, pp. 165-168.

SANTANACH, Joan (2011), "Les traduccions llatines de la Doctrina pueril de Ramon Llull", Studia Lulliana 51, 106, pp. 99-123.

SIRAISI, Nancy G. (1990), Medieval & Early Renaissance Medicine: An Introduction to Knowledge and Practice, Chicago, University of Chicago Press.

SOLER, Albert (1998), "Espiritualitat i cultura: els laics i l'accés al saber a final del segle XIII a la Corona d'Aragó", Studia Lulliana 38, pp. 3-26.

SOLER, Albert (1999), "Il papa angelico nel Blaquerna di Ramon Llull", Studi Medievali 3, 40, pp. 857-877.

SOLER, Albert (2010), "Els manuscrits lul·lians de primera generació", Estudis Romànics 32, pp. 179-214.

SW: Selected Works of Ramon Llull (1232-1316) (1985), 2 vols., ed. and intro. Anthony Bonner, Princeton, Princeton University Press.

SZPIECH, Ryan (2012), Conversion and Narrative: Reading and Religious Authority in Medieval Polemic, Philadelphia, University of Pennsylvania Press.

TARTAKOFF, Paola (2011), "Christian Kings and Jewish Conversion in the Medieval Crown of Aragon", Journal of Medieval Iberian Studies 3, 1, pp. 27-39.

VEGA, Amador (2003), *Ramon Llull and the Secret of Life*, trans. James W. Heisig, New York, Crossroad Publishing Company.

VORAGINE, Jacobus de (1977), *Vides de sants rosselloneses. Text català del segle XIII*, 3 vols., ed. Charlotte S. Maneikis Kniazzeh and E.J. Neugaard, preface Joan Coromines, Barcelona, Rafael Dalmau (Publicacions de la Fundació Salvador Vives Casajuana, 48, 51 and 53).

VORAGINE, Jacobus de (1993), *The Golden Legend. Readings on the Saints*, 2 vols., trans. William Granger Ryan, Princeton, Princeton University Press.

VORAGINE, Jacobus de (1995), *Die altokzitanische Version B der "Legenda aurea" (Ms. Paris, Bibl. Nat., n. acq. fr. 6504)*, ed. Monika Tausend, Tübingen, M. Niemeyer (Beihefte zur Zeitschrift für Romanische Philologie, 262).

VOSE, Robin (2009), *Dominicans, Muslims and Jews in the Medieval Crown of Aragon*, Cambridge, Cambridge University Press.

WEBSTER, Roderick, and Marjorie WEBSTER (1998), *Western Astrolabes*, Chicago, Adler Planetarium.

WITTLIN, Curt (1983), "Les traduccions catalanes de la 'Somme le Roi' ('De vicis i virtuts') de fra Llorenç", *Boletín de la Sociedad Castellonense de Cultura* 59, 3, pp. 395-433.

WOLFSON, Harry Austryn (1935), "The Internal Senses in Latin, Arabic, and Hebrew Philosophic Texts", *The Harvard Theological Review* 28, 2, pp. 69-133.

YATES, Frances A. (1954), "The Art of Ramon Lull: An Approach to It through Lull's Theory of the Elements", *Journal of the Warburg and Courtauld Institutes* 17, 1/2, pp. 115-173.